About Island Press

Island Press is the only nonprofit organization in the United States whose principal purpose is the publication of books on environmental issues and natural resource management. We provide solutions-oriented information to professionals, public officials, business and community leaders, and concerned citizens who are shaping responses to environmental problems.

In 1994, Island Press celebrated its tenth anniversary as the leading provider of timely and practical books that take a multidisciplinary approach to critical environmental concerns. Our growing list of titles reflects our commitment to bringing the best of an expanding body of literature to the environmental community throughout North America and the world.

Support for Island Press is provided by Apple Computer, Inc., The Bullitt Foundation, The Geraldine R. Dodge Foundation, The Energy Foundation, The Ford Foundation, The W. Alton Jones Foundation, The Lyndhurst Foundation, The John D. and Catherine T. MacArthur Foundation, The Andrew W. Mellon Foundation, The Joyce Mertz-Gilmore Foundation, The National Fish and Wildlife Foundation, The Pew Charitable Trusts, The Pew Global Stewardship Initiative, The Rockefeller Philanthropic Collaborative, Inc., and individual donors.

WHY
DO WE
RECYCLE?

WHY

DO WE

RECYCLE?

Markets, Values, and Public Policy

Frank Ackerman

ISLAND PRESS

Washington, D.C. • Covelo, California

Library of Congress Cataloging-in-Publication Data

Ackerman, Frank.
    Why do we recycle: markets, values, and public policy / by Frank Ackerman.
        p.   cm.
    Includes bibliographical references and index.
    ISBN 1-55963-504-5 (cloth). — ISBN 1-55963-505-3 (pbk.)
        1. Refuse and refuse disposal—Costs. 2. Recycling (waste, etc.—Economic aspects. 3. Environmental policy. I. Title.
    HD4482.A27   1997
    338.4'33637282—dc20   96-32777
                                                                    CIP

Printed on recycled, acid-free paper ♺

Manufactured in the United States of America

10 9 8 7 6 5 4 3 2 1

to Robin and Janet

CONTENTS

ACKNOWLEDGMENTS

Much of the research described in this book was done at Tellus Institute, where I had the opportunity to work with an extremely dedicated and talented group of people. Literally dozens of past and present staff members participated in our solid waste research; my apologies, and thanks, to those I have failed to mention. Lori Segall is the principal author of the study described in Chapter 8, and John Stutz is the principal author of the research behind parts of Chapter 9; both of them had a hand in many other areas as well. Irene Peters, Brian Zuckerman, and Paul Ligon each worked closely with me over a period of years on several different studies discussed in this book. Sidney Atwood, Monica Becker, Marc Breslow, Mark Briebart, Roger Geller, Gretchen McClain, Charles Munitz, Mark Rossi, Todd Schatzki, Karen Shapiro, and Anne Weaver, among others, played important roles in various stages of the work described here. Long ago, John Schall launched me, and everyone at Tellus, into the field of solid waste, and laid out the initial stages of our research agenda. He and Michael Simpson ensured that we were constantly in touch with recycling practitioners in the field.

The support of sponsors such as EPA's Office of Solid Waste, the California Integrated Waste Management Board, and numerous other agencies made our work possible. Clare Lindsay at EPA is responsible for the questions asked in several parts of this book, though I of course am solely responsible for the answers. Several Tellus studies described here received financial support from EPA, but, as the prefaces to the original studies make clear, none of them represent the opinions, policy, or recommendations of EPA (or other sponsoring agencies, for that matter).

I wrote this book in my new position at the Global Development And Environment Institute (GDAE) at Tufts University. I would like to thank GDAE codirectors Neva Goodwin and William Moomaw, and Jonathan Harris, David Kiron, Kevin Gallagher, and others, for providing a congenial and intellectually stimulating atmosphere in which to work. They will undoubtedly recognize the extent to which this book has been influenced by our study of consumer behavior, in the GDAE program on Frontier Issues in Economic Thought, which I am now directing. The results of our work on consumption have been published in Goodwin, Ackerman, and Kiron, editors, *The Consumer Society* (Island Press, 1997). That book, like this one, was made possible by the hard work of Todd Baldwin, Stacye White, and others at Island Press.

Patricia Dillon of the Gordon Institute (in another corner of Tufts University) kindly shared with me her research materials on recycling in Germany. James Finn, formerly of the Aseptic Packaging Council, provided copies of his copious files on the drink box debate. Two historians gave me the opportunity to read their work in progress, and helped me to expand and improve my discussion of the history of recycling. Susan Strasser's *Waste and Want: Disposal, Recycling, and American Consumer Culture* (Metropolitan Books, New York, 1998), and Benjamin Miller's *Fat of the Land: New York's Waste* (W.W. Norton, New York, 1996) will both be essential reading for those who are interested in trashy books.

Numerous friends and colleagues made helpful comments on earlier drafts. Special thanks are due to Kevin Gallagher, Clare Lindsay, Arthur MacEwan, Bruce Nordman, Gordon Robertson, Susan Strasser, and Neil Talbot, who read and commented on the entire manuscript. Valuable feedback on particular chapters, or on the discussion paper that was the predecessor to the first three chapters, came from Peter Anderson, Bruce Biewald, Samuel Bowles, Maarten deKadt, George Garland, Neva Goodwin, Barbara Goldoftas, Dinah Koehler, Douglas Koplow, David Kotz, Ben Miller, Jeff Morris, and Irene Peters. Becky Sarah offered a combination of editorial suggestions, encouragement, and support throughout the process of writing. My daughters Robin and Janet were very much on my mind as I wrote, particularly in my discussion of our connection to and responsibility to the future.

Introduction

 ────────────────────────────────────

There was a time when the reasons for recycling were obvious. During the 1980s and the beginning of the 1990s, it was widely believed that a "landfill crisis" was imminent. Recycling was therefore considered critical to avoid the huge expense and environmental burden of additional landfill construction. One result, about which much will be said in this book, was that recycling programs spread across the country with astonishing speed. A less obvious result, which explains the existence of this book, is that state agencies, the Environmental Protection Agency (EPA), and concerned industry groups began to sponsor research on numerous aspects of waste management and recycling.

I spent seven years (from 1988 to 1995) studying recycling and related issues at the Tellus Institute, a nonprofit research and consulting group in Boston. In the crisis atmosphere of those years, the magnitude and pace of the research effort were overwhelming: at its peak we had twenty staff members studying issues related to solid waste. Little of our work has ever been published, except in detailed technical reports to clients. Business pressures typically discourage consultants from taking the time to publicize their results, and we were no exception.

Curiously, we rarely even took time to reflect on the fact that our voluminous hard work was not pointing to any simple solutions to the landfill crisis. We found that well-run recycling programs save money in some but not all communities (see Chapter 4); many policy proposals

1

designed to provide market incentives for waste reduction and recycling had little or no effect (see Chapter 2); and for some products, the least environmentally harmful packaging might be completely nonrecyclable—and hence, in most places, destined to be landfilled (see Chapter 5).

As it gradually became clear that most of the United States was not facing an immediate landfill crisis, the research funding dried up and the pace and scope of our work diminished. In the absence of a crisis to be solved, a free-market critique began to be heard: perhaps recycling was an expensive mistake, and economic efficiency dictated a return to old-fashioned garbage disposal. One response from recycling advocates was to claim, on the basis of intricate calculations, that recycling is almost always profitable. I wish that I could be persuaded of this view, but unfortunately I do not think that the facts support it.

In the absence of a crisis, it is also easier to make sense of the pattern of our results. The thesis of this book is that while recycling is not always profitable in the short term, it is nonetheless a valid response to a long-term environmental problem, which cannot be reduced to narrowly economic terms. The identification of broader environmental objectives does not mean, however, that recycling programs are detached from the economy, or can afford to ignore questions of cost-effectiveness and efficiency. Recycling is increasingly integrated into the system of supply of industrial raw materials, a fact that creates problems as well as opportunities. It is important to keep trying to improve the bottom-line results of recycling programs—and at least equally important to remember that the original motivation and ultimate measures of success for recycling will not be found on a balance sheet.

There is an odd disconnection between theory and practice when it comes to recycling. On a practical level, it is increasingly the case that everyone does it; on a theoretical level, neither environmental advocates nor their critics talk much about it. The disconnection can be found on the shelves in bookstores. Recycling is a favorite topic of books full of "household hints to help save the planet"; nothing, it seems, is better suited for do-it-yourself environmental improvement than household waste. But books analyzing the fate of the earth and the state of the environmental movement have almost nothing to say about recycling and solid waste. While recycling is by far the most common practical step that people take to help the environment, the hopes and fears of environmentalists are focused elsewhere. In part, this is as it should be: other problems, much more difficult to address at the household level, are clearly more urgent than recovery of materials from trash.

At the same time, the disconnect between environmental debate and daily life lends an air of abstraction to the debate. Thus one of my goals is to examine the relationship between recycling and broader issues of environmental policy. Can the familiar activity of recycling illuminate the way we think about the environment, or vice versa? This leads to questions about the role of the market in environmental policy. Reliance on the market has become increasingly popular, and the design of market-based incentives for environmental objectives is one of the intellectual fashions of the decade. Recycling, however, has a life of its own that does not depend on the market, and we will see in Chapter 2 that simple arguments for market incentives in this area are problematic. Reflection on the reasons for recycling reveals the existence of widely held, if often implicit, beliefs that are difficult to reconcile with a market-based analysis. In the most general terms, my goal is to explore the conflict between the imperatives of the market and the principles that are revealed by recycling, as they affect our environmental future.

This book, then, can be read in part as the presentation of a series of little-known research findings, which I hope to persuade you are fascinating and important. In part it is about the connection between recycling and other environmental issues. And in part, as any contemporary discussion of environmental policy must be, it is about the roles of and the limitations on the market.

This is not another book of household hints about recycling. Nor is it about how to start or improve a community recycling program. Books on the latter subject quickly become out of date; the interested reader will do better to consult the monthly magazines that cover the field of recycling. Publications such as *BioCycle, Resource Recycling,* and *Waste Age* provide ongoing tutorials in recycling program operation, along with all manner of news and gossip from the world of recycling, and ads for wonderfully implausible machinery for your sorting, baling, and grinding needs. Just as news and analysis about recycling is surprisingly separate from other environmental issues, the organizations and people advocating recycling are often distinct from the broader environmental movement. An impressionistic description of one of the many recycling conferences (which are publicized in the same magazines) opens Chapter 3.

Like all authors, I harbor the secret fantasy that inexplicably vast numbers of people will want to read my book. In my more realistic moments, I hope that it will be useful to three somewhat distinct groups. For recycling professionals and advocates, who think about the issue all the time, the book needs little introduction. For students in environmental studies or environmental economics courses, it may provide a connection between familiar activities and new theoretical concepts. For the general reader interested in rational debate about public policy—a species that is in hiding for the moment, but hopefully not yet on the endangered list—it may suggest a new perspective on the market and the environment.

For the sake of readers of any variety, a brief overview of the chapter topics is in order. This book consists of ten chapters, grouped into three major sections: Chapters 1–4 present the debates about recycling and its economic and environmental costs and benefits; Chapters 5–7 focus on research and policy concerning packaging; and Chapters 8–10 discuss aspects of waste reduction and materials policy for the future.

Recycling enjoys widespread, often passionate support (see Chapter 1), though it has its free-market critics as well. While contemporary programs are new, recycling in general has a long and complex history. There are multiple economic and environmental benefits to recycling; the discovery that most communities do not face a landfill crisis only means that one category of benefits, the reduction in disposal requirements, is of limited immediate value. The continuing debate over the merits of recycling concerns the magnitude and importance of the other environmental benefits it provides.

The use of market incentives to promote recycling is increasingly popular, and could potentially reconcile the rival perspectives of recycling advocates and their market-oriented critics. However, as shown in Chapter 2, market incentives have been less effective than is commonly believed or hoped. One leading incentive proposal, unit pricing (charging by the bag or can) for garbage collection, has been badly oversold; in fact, it achieves measurable but quite modest results. Other potentially appealing options, such as elimination of subsidies for virgin material production, or collection of a disposal fee when products are sold, face similar limitations.

It may be impossible, even in principle, to reconcile the environmental and market perspectives on recycling. Chapter 3 explores three reasons for this irreconcilability. First, technology choices that are crucial to recycling and the environment may be subject to increasing returns, undermining the technical arguments for the market. Second, beliefs and decisions about responsibilities to future generations cannot be evaluated within a market framework. Finally, many goals and objectives are inherently "priceless," and would be misrepresented or corrupted by the process of assigning monetary valuations to them.

Nonetheless, recycling programs must inevitably concern themselves with immediate, monetary costs and benefits. Much can be done to make recycling more cost-effective. Chapter 4 demonstrates the central role played by truck-related collection costs, and the importance of minimizing these costs. It also illustrates the extreme variability of the revenues received by recycling programs, which continually frustrates attempts at predicting the bottom-line economic results.

One of the largest of the Tellus Institute studies, referred to above, was a three-year effort to compare the life cycle environmental impacts of all major packaging materials. Presentation of its surprising results and their implications for packaging policy are found in Chapter 5. With the exception of one problem material, the study shows that the best packages for the environment are generally the lightest-weight ones. When weight reduction conflicts with recyclability of packaging, the former is often more environmentally beneficial, a finding that leads to seemingly paradoxical conclusions.

The most dramatic recent changes in packaging policy and recycling have occurred in Europe, primarily in Germany, rather than in the United States. Chapter 6 reviews the progress of the German "green dot" recycling system, which has received little attention in the United States since its controversial beginnings in 1993. The German experience is important, not only because it quickly achieved very high recycling rates, but also because it has inspired similar (though not identical) systems in other countries, and sparked a widespread discussion of the concept of producer responsibility for waste.

Producers are held responsible for solid waste in the United States in one important instance. Beverage container deposit legislation, the "bottle bill" for short, requires bottlers of beer and soft drinks to charge deposits when they sell containers, and refund the deposits when the containers are returned to them. Nine states have adopted bottle bills, while California has a related but modified system. Our study of the issue, described in Chapter 7, concludes that the California system has economic advantages over the standard bottle bill approach, and identifies some of the unpriced benefits, such as litter reduction, that motivate support for bottle bills. The one clear advantage of a standard bottle bill over our approach is that it would facilitate use of refillable bottles—but in the United States, unlike Europe, refillable bottles have all but vanished.

Organic debris, traditionally the largest and most easily "recycled" type of household material, has taken on a new and almost frivolous form with the rise of yard waste. The potential for organic waste reduction and composting is analyzed in Chapter 8. The cheapest approaches to organic waste management are those that do not require additional truck collection, such as "grasscycling" (leaving grass clippings on the lawn) and home composting. Organic waste, including paper, is also important because in landfills it gives rise to methane, a greenhouse gas. Any strategy that keeps organic wastes out of landfills will help reduce climate change impacts.

Although waste prevention is sometimes more beneficial than recycling, it is much easier to design a recycling program. Is there a systematic, cost-effective way to promote waste prevention? A very similar problem has been addressed much more extensively in the field of energy conservation. Chapter 9 presents the analogy between waste prevention and energy conservation. Many electric utilities have turned to "demand side management"—promotion of energy efficiency in their customers' homes and businesses—as an alternative to building new power plants. While it goes against the current movement toward deregulation, an extension of the framework of utility regulation to waste management might create similar opportunities for systematic waste prevention.

Chapter 10 concludes the discussion by considering the long-run implications of material use and recycling. Freedom to use and discard cheap materials is a large part of what makes us feel affluent. Changes in both technology and behavior affecting material use will ultimately be required for a sustainable future. Is sustainability compatible with affluence? Technologically, sustainability eventually will require increasing reliance on renewable biomass materials. Behaviorally, sustainability requires increasing material conservation; what will motivate conservation? The market-based answer is that scarcity will eventually result in rising prices, making it worth everyone's while to conserve and recycle. But this would mean the loss of many of the "benefits" of affluence and the return to a relationship between wages and material prices that characterizes developing countries (or the nineteenth-century United States). The contemporary commitment to recycling hints at other motivations for conservation, which will, in the long run, be indispensable.

To enter the story that is being told here, start by asking yourself the question posed in the title. Why do *you* recycle? If you answer that it saves space in your local landfill, or saves money by reducing the amount of garbage to be collected, you are in good company. Many people offer those answers—and they are not always wrong. But neither are they always right. And right or wrong, the hope of saving money and landfill space cannot explain the passion and the extent of recycling today. To understand recycling, you will have to look beyond your trash can. That's what this book is about.

CHAPTER 1

Beyond the Trash Can

 ———————————————————————————

Let me begin with a confession.

I worked for ten years at Tellus Institute, a nonprofit environmental research group in Boston. Not only did we study recycling for most of those years, we also had our own in-house paper recycling program. We had plenty of paper to recycle: in the course of our research we were constantly receiving, reviewing, and creating documents; at the end of any project, if not before, most of the accumulated papers had to be removed in order to make room for the next project. Like most of the staff, I kept a recycling bin close to my desk. According to the company that picked up our recycling, we recovered at least 3 tons, about 50 trees' worth, of paper annually.

For many years our recycling program only accepted white office paper. Fax paper, colored paper, glossy advertising, and other types of paper still had to be thrown out. From time to time we received elaborate reports with colored-paper inserts or chapter dividers between the white-paper text sections. When I was done with such reports, I usually removed the staples or tore apart the binding, separated and discarded the colored pages, and recycled the remaining white paper. But one day, rushing to meet a deadline on an important project I was managing, I tossed an entire small publication, printed on mixed colors of paper, into the trash.

Minutes later, as luck would have it, a friend of mine who was working on the same project came into my office. It was a familiar, comfortable situation; she and I had often worked together on similar tasks. As we settled down to attack the problem of the day, she smiled at me—but only for a moment. Almost immediately, she spotted the publication I had just thrown out, scowled and pulled it out of my trash can. "I thought you BELIEVED in recycling," she said sadly, as she began ripping out the colored pages so that the remaining white pages could be recovered.

Recycling As Religion

Like my co-worker and me, millions of people do believe in recycling, and act on that belief on a regular basis. "In the first week in November 1992, more adults took part in recycling than voted," says Jerry Powell, editor of *Resource Recycling* magazine. Recycling, according to Powell, is "more popular than democracy."[1]

Both the extent of recycling and the speed of its expansion are remarkable. Curbside collection, in which a truck picks up newspapers, containers, and other materials from households, is fast becoming standard in urban and suburban areas. By 1994 there were more than 7200 curbside collection programs in the United States, serving more than 40 % of the population; virtually all of these programs were less than six years old. Hundreds of new curbside programs are still being initiated every year.[2] As extensive as it is, though, curbside collection is not the only form of recycling. Additional materials are recovered through countless drop-off centers, commercial and office programs, and other channels. All this activity has had noticeable effects on the solid waste stream that flows out of homes and businesses. One study estimated that 21% of all municipal solid waste was recycled or composted in 1992, up from 10 % just seven years earlier.[3]

Why do we recycle? Rarely is there a monetary reward. In most towns, no one pays you to put out your recyclables at the curb. Our office recycling program did not pay us for the documents we saved from the trash can. The increasingly common recycling boxes in public places rely on social pressure rather than financial incentives. Recycling is an impressively pure form of altruism, a widespread commitment to the greater good. It is especially worth noting today, in an era of cutbacks and conservatism, that large numbers of people do behave altruistically on a regular basis.

Who is it that recycles? A handful of survey researchers have studied participation in recycling, with mixed results. Not surprisingly, they have found that altruistic motivations for recycling are important in all social groups; other findings in this literature are less conclusive. Some have reported that recycling is more common among women, whites, and high-income, high-education households, while other, conflicting studies have found that the rate of recycling is about the same for all demographic and socioeconomic groups.[4] A recent analysis of neighborhoods within four Boston-area communities found that recycling rates depend on the percentage of the adult population that has graduated from college, and on the amount that each town spends on public education about recycling. Income, race, and other factors had no separate effect.[5] But such demographic research reveals only part of the story of recycling.

For municipal planners and managers, recycling is necessarily a matter for detailed calculations. For the participants, it is more often seen as part of a bigger picture. We recycle because we consider it worthwhile to conserve landfill space, or save energy and materials. In short, we recycle because we believe it is the right thing to do, because it is good for the environment.

In one sense, altruistic public behavior seems out of step with the 1990s, an era when individualistic, selfish voices have increasingly shaped the contemporary discussion of economic policy. But the misstep may be the interpretation of recycling as solely an economic policy. In another sense, the commitment to recycling echoes the tenor of the times, as moralism and professions of faith have become more and more prominent in social and political debate. If "family values" are now acknowledged to be a vague but powerful force in public life, why not recognize a similar role for ecological values?[6]

Suppose, then, that we view recycling as akin to a religious practice, an organized expression of widely held ecological values. The language and symbolism of recycling support this view. Any church needs ritual observances, and curbside recycling provides the opportunity for the weekly offering and collection. After collection there is the modern miracle of transubstantiation, as old packages and papers come to life again. In states that have deposits on beverage containers, it is common to speak of the process of redemption.

The image of recycling as religion pervades the news media. "Boston has been slow among cities and towns," said the *Boston Globe*, "to get religion on curbside recycling, but starting this morning the administration is pursuing its new trash program with all the zeal of a convert." A *Wall Street Journal* article, entitled "Curbside Recycling Comforts the Soul, But Benefits Are Scant," observed that recycling "makes people feel good. For many, a little trash sorting has become a form of penance to acknowledge that the values of our high-consumption society don't always nurture the soul."[7]

Those who do get religion, the true believers, often display intense commitment to a higher objective, even at the cost of considerable personal effort. My friend who insisted on correcting my momentary lapse in office recycling is far from the most extreme. I know someone who drives back and forth across the Bay Area in California to find recycling centers that accept small quantities of hard-to-recycle household goods. The damage she does to the environment by driving so far almost certainly exceeds the good she does by recycling a little more.

I've heard more than one story of domestic conflict, in households that already recycle all the big, easy things, about the urgency of reusing or recycling a few additional items. Should you throw out used plastic sandwich bags or wash and dry them for reuse? (My advice: of course it is desirable to reuse containers and packaging whenever it is feasible; rigid sandwich-sized plastic containers may be easier to reuse than bags. However, if discarding a few sandwich bags is your greatest transgression, it is time to direct your environmental efforts to problems bigger than yourself.) Often, when people hear that I am studying recycling, they ask my permission to throw out one or another marginally reusable or recyclable product. I am not alone, it seems, in wanting to confess my sins in this area.

Recycling as religion arises from shared values; it provides public rituals that reaffirm those values; the faithful organize aspects of their lives around it, even at noticeable cost and inconvenience to themselves. But the ecological values that form the basis for this behavior are complex and multi-faceted. What accounts for the emphasis on recycling in particular? Despite studying it professionally for several years, I find it hard to argue that waste management is our most urgent environmental problem. At most, it is one among many issues that clamor for our attention. Other problems pose more serious threats to our well-being than the disposal of solid waste.

What distinguishes recycling is not its importance, but rather the ease with which individuals can participate, and the visibility of actions taken to promote the common good. You may care passionately about the threat of global warming or the destruction of the rain forests—but you can't have an immediate effect on these problems that is perceptible to yourself or others. The rain forest salvation truck doesn't make weekly pickups, let alone the clean air truck. When a 1990 Gallup poll asked people what they had done in connection with environmental problems, 80 to 85% answered that they or their households had participated in various aspects of recycling; no other significant steps had been taken by a majority of respondents.[8] Like the drunk looking for his wallet under the lamppost, we may focus on recycling because it is where the immediate tasks are best illuminated.

Faith in the Free Market

Recycling is also illuminated from another direction, casting a very different shadow. A second great system of secular belief, faith in the free market, offers a contrasting vision of recycling and the environment. The "anti-recyclers," as they have been called, look at recycling from a purely economic point of view.[9] They claim that the government should not set recycling targets or subsidize local recycling programs. Just get the prices right, allow unfettered competition, and the market will achieve the most efficient level of recycling, as with everything else.

The anti-recycling argument briefly seemed to have been undercut by the 1995 surge in prices for recycled materials, which greatly increased the profitability of recycling (see Chapter 4). However, by early 1996 prices were declining from the 1995 peaks, although they may not fall all the way back to the 1992–1993 lows. When prices fall, they drag down the profits of many recycling programs—and therefore, the anti-recyclers will likely return in force. Thus it is worth looking at their critique in some detail.

The basic point of the anti-recycling position is that the decision to recycle is just a business proposition, a matter of economic calculation like any other. For example, Christopher Boerner and Kenneth Chilton, economists at Washington University in St. Louis, argue that "markets—even those for recycled products—work best when relatively free of government intervention. . . . Local governments should take a hard-nosed approach to recycling by continuing to collect those materials [on which they make a profit] . . . and by abandoning other, uneconomical curbside programs."[10]

Business journalism repeatedly emphasizes this point. In the *Wall Street Journal* article mentioned earlier, Jeff Bailey argues that recycling is usually uneconomic, quoting municipal officials, waste management industry executives, and consultants, on the additional costs imposed by recycling (as of late 1994, when prices were just beginning to rise). The landfill shortage that motivated many recycling programs, says Bailey, was always imaginary; there is enough landfill capacity for at least 16 years of disposal, and it is easy to create more when it is needed.

Bailey also debunks the legend of the *Mobro 4000,* the garbage barge from Long Island that was turned away from one port after another in

1987. At the time, the voyage of the *Mobro* was widely interpreted as evidence that there would soon be no place left to put our garbage, confirming the worst fears of a landfill shortage and emphasizing the need for recycling. The revisionist history, supported by other sources as well as Bailey, attributes the *Mobro*'s troubles to an unsuccessful deal between a Long Island Mafia boss (now in jail for conspiring to murder other trash haulers) and an inexperienced barge owner. The *Mobro* arrived in several southern states, and later in Caribbean ports, before signing firm agreements with any local landfills, leading to suspicion that it carried hazardous waste. Other garbage shipments to the same destinations, with signed disposal agreements in hand before they departed, continued during and after the *Mobro*'s journey.[11]

One of the most thoughtful critiques of recycling in the business press comes from Frances Cairncross, environment editor of *The Economist*. Surveying both European and American evidence, she also finds that landfilling is cheap and recycling is expensive, in part for lack of markets for recycled materials: "Voters appear to love recycling. It seems to meet some deep human need to atone for modern materialism. Unfortunately, people do not seem to feel quite the same craving to buy products made of recycled materials."[12]

Traditional disposal is so cheap, and accounts for so little of household expenditure, says Cairncross, that no plausible policy of economic incentives will lead people to throw out much less. Landfilling would remain a bargain even with a generous price increase to reflect its environmental costs. Cairncross recommends a reduced emphasis on recycling, to be replaced by negotiation with rural communities or foreign countries that are willing to provide increased disposal capacity.

This survey of the critics would not be complete without a look at the underground classic of the anti-recycling movement, Judd Alexander's intriguing but idiosyncratic treatise, *In Defense of Garbage*.[13] Alexander, a former executive at American Can Company and James River Corporation (a paper company), challenges many aspects of modern recycling beliefs and practices.

Alexander argues that little of value is lost in our trash cans. Less than 1% of all nonrenewable resources used in the United States ends up as municipal waste, a pittance in comparison to the huge quantities of fuels and construction materials that the nation consumes. Paper, the leading renewable resource in the trash, is largely produced from managed tree farms grown for that purpose, not from natural forests. The individual products commonly identified as symbols of wastefulness, says Alexander, represent insignificant waste management burdens, and bring substantial savings and convenience to their users.

Drawing on his experience in industry, Alexander is at his best in describing the benefits of new packaging technologies. Specialized, multi-layer plastic packages developed for lettuce, cheese, meat, and other foods have dramatically reduced spoilage, food waste, and shipping costs. Such packages are virtually certain to be nonrecyclable. It is unlikely, he says, that packaging will be redesigned for ease of recycling or disposal, since packaging materials cost much more (sometimes hundreds of times more) to produce than to discard. In fact, the cost of production, not the comparatively minor cost of disposal, has driven the ongoing reduction in packaging weight.

Although the anti-recyclers make many important arguments about the economics of the issue, one senses that they (with the occasional exception, such as Cairncross) are fundamentally unsympathetic to the environmental objectives of recycling advocates. The critique of recycling turns a bit irritable, if not outright cranky, at times. Thus Alexander, for instance, finds aspects of contemporary recycling policy to be not only expensive, but also inequitable: "If 5¢ is an appropriate deposit for a beer can weighing a shade over half an ounce, then $9.19 would be the right deposit for a six-and-a-half pound Sunday newspaper."[14] However, beverage container deposits were introduced in part as litter prevention measures—and few people are so intoxicated by the Sunday paper that they toss it out the car window.

An unusually prominent and vehement anti-recycling broadside appeared just before this book went to press. A *New York Times Magazine* article, "Recycling is Garbage," by John Tierney, mocks and distorts the environmental arguments for recycling at some length.[15] Citing the anti-environmental views of several neoconservative "think tanks" as his principal sources, Tierney concludes that environmental enthusiasm for recycling is entirely misplaced. Not content with simply reporting the real costs of recycling, he also embarks on a financial fantasy designed to show that the expense of recycling is absurdly large.

First, Tierney calculates the cost of paying everyone $12 per hour for time spent in household recycling. Then he adds $4 a week for rental of a square foot of floor space in everyone's kitchen to store the recycling containers. These fictitious costs are 14 times as large as the real costs of New York City's recycling program, allowing him to claim that recycling a ton of material "really" costs as much as buying a one-ton used car.

If this is a good idea for recycling, surely it should be applied in other areas of life. We all could bill the IRS for time spent keeping records and filling out forms, and for rental of file drawers used in these activities. But that way lies madness, or at least the dissolution of civil society. Life is not a business, and participation in society is not a reimbursable business expense.

In the Beginning

The debate over the merits of recycling is, like most municipal recycling programs, relatively new. Yet although recycling as we know it today is a recent invention, the activity of reprocessing, reshaping, and reusing materials has occurred throughout human history. A historian has described the centuries before industrialization in England as "a golden age of recycling," when used clothing, building materials, metals, and other materials were constantly being recovered and remade into newer goods. Paper, in preindustrial England, was made entirely from recycled fabrics such as rags.[16]

Paper continued to have almost 100 % recycled content until well into the nineteenth century. The U.S. paper industry was originally centered in western Massachusetts, close to the abundant sources of rags in the urban Northeast. But by mid-century, expansion of the industry had led to a chronic shortage of rags, and to desperate searches for additional sources of cloth. At one point, rag dealers imported Egyptian mummies solely for their wrappings. The ultimate solution, the technology that allowed efficient production of paper from wood, was developed in Germany in the 1840s and introduced in America in the 1860s. By the 1880s the paper industry had almost abandoned Massachusetts, moving west to be closer to its new sources of raw material.[17]

Nineteenth-century American households, out of necessity, were continually engaged in remaking and reusing old material objects, including clothing, furniture, kitchenware, tools, and more. Many goods, when they were no longer useful to the household itself, could be sold or bartered to itinerant peddlers. The peddlers bought rags, metal, rubber, glass, and other materials, all of which were resold to industry for recycling.[18]

It is hard to imagine, therefore, that much of value remained in nineteenth-century trash. Yet there was evidently enough to support an additional form of recycling, perhaps the first method of recycling that was an integral part of the waste management process. Scavengers picked over urban garbage dumps, looking for rags and anything else of value; the scavenged materials were then sold to junk dealers. A Winslow Homer etching from 1859 shows scavengers hard at work in Boston's Back Bay—today a fashionable address, but then, literally, a dump. Scavengers were sometimes politely referred to as *chiffoniers,* i.e., collectors of "chiffon" (a French word that meant ornamental trifles, as well as a type of silk). A more earthy description arose from the practice of ocean dumping of garbage by New York City and other coastal communities. There the scavengers, who rode on the garbage barges, or scows, and sorted through the refuse up to the last moment, were called "scow trimmers."[19]

Although landfill scavenging lives on today in many cities of the developing world, the practice died out in the United States in the early years of the twentieth century. Several factors contributed to its demise. The decrease in the use of rags by the paper industry shrank one of the most lucrative markets for scavengers—and for peddlers and junk dealers, whose businesses also declined. Changes in waste management practices, including widespread experiments with incineration and "reduction" (stewing garbage in large vats in order to render grease and other useful by-products; see Chapter 8), reduced the opportunities for scavenging. Progressive Era reformers favored professionalism and public control over waste management, and opposed scavenging as a dirty and unsanitary practice. Class, racial, and ethnic prejudice toward the scavengers was unfortunately interwoven with the sensible concern for public health and hygiene.[20]

Older modes of recycling have diminished in importance, but never entirely vanished. Today's scrap yards, the modern descendants of early junk dealers, are quite efficient at recycling junked cars and other metal waste; they recover much more steel than the local recycling programs that collect cans. Household repair and reuse are far from completely disappearing, even if most of us cannot match our great-grandparents' accomplishments in this regard. Used furniture and major appliances almost never end up at landfills; instead, they seem to circulate in a vast, informal network of yard or garage sales, donations, and a new form of curbside scavenging that occurs late at night or early in the morning before the garbage truck arrives.[21]

The hallmark of these traditional styles of recycling is that they are motivated primarily by economic considerations. Scrap dealers who crush abandoned cars and resell the metal, like college students who salvage furniture that their neighbors have abandoned, may or may not believe that they are helping the environment; regardless of their beliefs, they are helping themselves. The same is true for businesses that generate and recycle large quantities of particular wastes. Many supermarkets, for example, have long found it profitable to recycle their cardboard cartons. In contrast, what is new in contemporary municipal recycling is not only the organization of formal programs to promote it, but also the primacy of altruistic or ecologically concerned motivations: in almost all cases, modern recycling offers no personal economic benefit for participation.

Seen in this light, modern recycling may have begun during World War II, as households were exhorted to save paper, cardboard, metals, rubber, and other materials to contribute to the war effort. By the end of the war, more than one-third of all paper and paperboard products were being recovered, along with large quantities of other materials. Patriotism, rather than environmental concern or monetary reward, was the motivation, though modest payments were made to voluntary and nonprofit organizations that organized collection drives. Junk dealers who survived through the 1930s now did a booming business assembling the collected materials and selling them to the war industries; some of these junk dealers went on to prosper in the scrap metal industry after the war. Since wartime recycling responded to moral incentives rather than to the market, there was no guarantee that the amounts collected would match the amounts that industry could use or would pay for. There may have been a recycled paper glut as early as 1942, although it was rarely discussed for fear of undermining the collection of other, more clearly valuable materials.[22]

Recycling: The Next Generation

After the war, recycling vanished for some time, reappearing only in the 1960s. (The trajectory of recycling is curiously parallel to the participation of women in the paid labor force; perhaps both required extraordinary disruptions of mid-century "business as usual," brought about once by war and again by turbulent social change.) There was no mystery to the return of recycling; it was part of the unfolding environmental awareness of the times. The impetus to recycle included not only a general urge to take action and reduce wastefulness, but also more specific reactions to the spread of litter, and to the threat of pollution from landfills.

The 1960s were the period when no-deposit beverage containers first made their presence felt in the marketplace, and all too often along the roadside as well. While Lady Bird Johnson campaigned from the White House for highway beautification, others concluded that recycling of beverage containers was the answer. At the same time, awareness of the hazards of chemical pollution was spreading rapidly, particularly after the publication of Rachel Carson's *Silent Spring* in 1962. The almost unregulated landfills of the day frequently leaked dangerous pollutants into the soil and groundwater. As communities began to resist proposals for new landfills, recycling seemed to offer an environmentally attractive way to reduce the need for disposal.

Thousands of grassroots recycling centers were set up in the late 1960s and early 1970s, primarily collecting newspapers, glass bottles, and aluminum cans. Some of the first municipal recycling programs appeared at the same time, often collecting only newspaper; by 1974 more than 100 communities had some form of recycling collection. A mid-1970s slump in the demand for recycled paper, however, brought many of these early efforts to an end. Only aluminum can recycling continued to thrive throughout the 1970s, collecting one-fourth of all cans by 1975.[23]

At about the same time, federal policymakers began to address the problems of solid waste and recycling. The Solid Waste Disposal Act of 1965 initiated research and development on waste disposal, and offered technical and financial assistance to state and local disposal programs. The Resource Recovery Act of 1970 broadened the focus to include recycling and waste-to-energy (incineration), proposing the development of a national policy on material requirements, use, recovery, and disposal. These federal laws also drew states into the business of solid waste planning, since waste management plans were prerequisites for receiving federal aid.[24]

Waste management received more attention in Washington after the creation of the Environmental Protection Agency (EPA) in 1970. In 1976 the Resource Conservation and Recovery Act (RCRA) gave EPA broad authority over landfills and incinerators; among many other provisions, RCRA established national environmental standards for landfills, which were made stricter by amendments passed in 1984. Enforcement of these standards raises the cost of landfilling, making alternatives such as recycling more economically attractive. However, any stirrings of environmental activism in the federal government were brought to a halt in 1981; crisis-oriented efforts to clean up hazardous wastes were virtually the only EPA activities that moved forward during the Reagan administration. Initiatives in recycling and waste management in the 1980s came from grassroots groups and from state and local governments.

In the late 1970s and early 1980s, the search for alternatives to landfilling led to a brief but intense fascination with incineration. The idea of burning garbage has been episodically popular; previous waves of incinerator construction peaked in the 1890s and 1930s. The rise and fall of the latest wave is chronicled in *War on Waste*, by Louis Blumberg and Robert Gottlieb (Island Press, 1989). More than garbage disposal was involved: after the "energy crisis" became a household word in 1973–1974, the newest models of incinerators seemed doubly attractive, generating steam or electricity as they got rid of waste. Indeed, the industry prefers to call the new facilities waste-to-energy plants, to distinguish them from older incinerators that made no use of the energy that was released. The Public Utilities Regulatory Policies Act (PURPA), passed in 1978, required electric utilities to buy the power produced by waste-to-energy plants and other independent generators on very favorable terms, boosting the prospects for incineration.

Yet the more that people saw of the new incinerators, the less they liked them. Just as with another quick fix to the energy crisis, nuclear power plants, one environmental problem after another appeared, each problem leading to installation of additional, expensive pollution controls. While debate continued about whether pollution hazards had been sufficiently reduced, there was no doubt that the cost increases made incinerators far more expensive than anticipated—and in particular, far more costly than even the newest, most carefully controlled landfills. Like nuclear plants, incinerators have a disturbing waste disposal problem of their own: the ash that comes out of an incinerator is much more toxic than the garbage that goes in, and must be buried in an expensive, specialized landfill. Unlike nuclear power plants, the amount of energy obtainable from waste-to-energy facilities is quite small. Rough calculations we did at Tellus Institute showed that even the unlikely strategy of burning all of a state's garbage might generate less than 2% of the state's electricity needs.

Community groups opposed to incineration sprang up across the country. The results of widespread opposition again echoed the experience with nuclear power. Orders for new incinerators reached a peak in 1985, and then declined rapidly; by 1987 cancellations exceeded new orders.[25] The huge waste-to-energy plant proposed for Los Angeles, the case study described in detail in *War on Waste*, was among the casualties of 1987. Today about 10% of all municipal solid waste is incinerated. Most states in the Northeast, along with Florida, Minnesota, Hawaii, and Alaska, have above-average rates of incineration, while most other states have little or none. Nationwide, the number of operating incinerators peaked in 1991, and is now gradually shrinking.[26]

Even as acceptance of incineration faded away in the late 1980s, concern about waste disposal continued to grow. And in 1987 the voyage of the *Mobro* seemed to dramatize (inaccurately, as it turns out) the urgency of the problem. A public opinion poll found that from 1983 to 1988, about two-thirds of the population believed that the government was doing too little to solve waste disposal problems; another poll found that the proportion of people who said that their own community faced a "very serious" problem of waste disposal rose from 24% in 1988 to 49% in 1990.[27] As a result, there was a renewed push for bigger and better recycling.

While the recyclers of the late 1960s and early 1970s had often concentrated on one or a few materials, the new generation of recycling programs targeted a broader range of wastes. The first facilities designed to process mixed recyclables were established in the early 1980s;

by 1994 there were more than 1200 self-described "material recovery facilities," or MRFs (rhymes with "surfs"), engaged in sorting, baling, and marketing the materials collected by local recycling programs. In the absence of federal initiative, states took the lead in setting standards for recycling. By 1994, comprehensive recycling and waste reduction laws had been adopted in 40 states and the District of Columbia; 44 had legislated or announced goals for reduction and recycling, ranging from 20 to 70 %.[28]

Yet a funny thing happened on the way to the landfill crisis. As the anti-recyclers observed, most places never ran out of disposal capacity. In part this is due to a simple error, now widely recognized. Data on landfills is sparse, and many early accounts merely compared the numbers of landfills closing and opening each year, without considering their size. In fact, huge numbers of small landfills are closing, while small numbers of huge ones are opening, resulting in increases in disposal capacity in some states.

The trend toward larger landfills has been accelerated by environmental regulations, which make it prohibitively expensive to build small facilities; pollution control and compliance costs are not proportional to the size of a landfill.[29] Community resistance to siting new facilities also discourages construction of numerous small landfills. While it is difficult to obtain approval for landfills in many areas, it is not always proportionally harder to obtain approval for bigger ones. Other factors that helped avert a landfill crisis include the success of recycling and composting in diverting waste away from disposal, and the economic recession of the early 1990s, which reduced the amount of waste generated by businesses.

If Recycling Is the Answer, What Is the Question?

The years of the most rapid growth in recycling, in the early 1990s, were also the years in which the most popular justification for recycling vanished. In all but the most densely populated parts of the country, there was no immediate landfill crisis. Recycling of many household wastes was often a little more expensive than sending them to a landfill. On the other hand, large and growing numbers of people acted as if they thought that recycling was worthwhile. At this point, the paths of recycling advocates and anti-recyclers clearly diverge. Should economists try to persuade people that enthusiasm for recycling is a mistake, that it is time to go home and learn to love garbage disposal? Or should we look beyond the trash can, for a more complex picture of the motivations for continued recycling, even in the absence of a crisis?

The issues related to garbage and recycling have become part of contemporary culture, and even appear in recent fiction. In the novel *Closing Time,* Joseph Heller's sequel to *Catch-22,* the aging and somewhat hypochondriacal John Yossarian attempts to convince his doctors that, despite the lack of visible evidence, he is actually desperately ill. Yossarian's mind wanders freely from personal to social ills, among which garbage is quite prominent: "Another oil tanker had broken up. There was radiation. Garbage. Pesticides, toxic waste, and free enterprise." Later, Yossarian yearns to persuade another doctor that the universe is unreliable and depressing, since "there were holes in the ozone, they were running out of room for the disposal of garbage, burn the garbage and you contaminate the air, they were running out of air."[30]

Taken literally, Yossarian's seemingly global grievances reveal the local origins of the book. The novel is set (to the extent that it occurs in any recognizable locale) in New York City; Joseph Heller lives on Long Island. These are among the areas where the landfill crisis remains most acute, and where incineration, as an alternative to landfilling, has been most actively and controversially promoted. In a story written from, or about, another part of the country, Yossarian would have a different list of complaints.

On a deeper level, Yossarian's plight is an appropriate image even for non–New Yorkers. He is sure that something is wrong, and that garbage is somehow involved. He is unsure whether it is an individual physical malady or a social or environmental malaise. He is desperately and unsuccessfully seeking the advice of experts in diagnosing the problem. Outside the hospital, Milo Minderbinder, the endlessly entrepreneurial quartermaster of *Catch-22,* is still prospering in the marketplace by knowing the price of everything and the value of nothing. Although Yossarian goes to work for Minderbinder's vast enterprise, he is never quite satisfied, always looking for something more mysterious and meaningful in life.

It is a metaphor suited to solid waste, and to much more. The impetus to recycling can be seen in terms Yossarian would understand: something is wrong; garbage is involved; experts have failed in their attempts to diagnose the problem; cooperation with the forces of the market is inescapable, but cannot be the whole of the story. What is needed is another, better diagnosis. In the absence of a landfill crisis or immediate profits from recovered materials, what problems is recycling trying to solve?

Recycling enjoys such broad and diffuse support that there is nothing like a standard source describing the benefits it is supposed to achieve. The closest thing to a national policy statement is the EPA's 1989 document, *The Solid Waste Dilemma: An Agenda for Action.* Written at the height of concern over the landfill crisis, *Agenda for Action* repeatedly emphasizes the difficulty of siting new landfills, and the need to conserve landfill space. Other reasons for recycling, although mentioned, appear secondary in importance.[31]

But according to the Institute for Local Self-Reliance, a Washington-based nonprofit group that supports local recycling efforts, "The recycling movement was not a reaction to the landfill crisis, for there was none in the late 1960s when the movement began. Rather, they reacted to the level of waste in our economy and the pollution and suffering these habits cause worldwide."[32] A recent guide to recycling cites several environmental benefits, including conservation of raw materials, energy, and water in manufacturing; reduction of harmful emissions from materials extraction and manufacturing industries; reduction of litter and ocean dumping; avoidance of landfill or incinerator emissions; and reduced need for disposal capacity.[33]

A typology of environmental reasons for recycling might begin with a distinction between benefits that arise in the waste management process, and those that arise in extractive and manufacturing industries. It may be helpful to think of two sets of three categories each. Waste management benefits attributable to recycling include

(1) reduction in the need for disposal capacity,

(2) lowered emissions from landfills and incinerators, and

(3) reduction in litter and improper disposal.

Benefits resulting from use of recycled materials in industry include

(4) reductions in energy use and related emissions,

(5) reduction in extraction and manufacturing process impacts and emissions, and

(6) the long-term value of conservation of raw materials.

Much of this book is an attempt to spell out and evaluate these benefits, and to identify the policies that promote them. Only a few introductory words will be said here.

The critique of the landfill crisis argues that the first of the six types of benefits, reduction in the need for disposal capacity, is not in itself an adequate justification for recycling. Even so, it would be a mistake to dismiss the problem of disposal capacity too quickly. It is an important issue in selected areas where landfill space is limited, such as the urban Northeast, or Florida (where geological conditions are uniquely unsuitable for landfilling). Moreover, disposal capacity can become locally scarce in an area that refuses to build new facilities. Many people remain passionately opposed to siting new landfills in their communities. Rather than bemoaning this NIMBY ("not in my back yard") syndrome, policymakers could take community opposition as evidence of the high implicit value placed on avoiding landfills. The higher that valuation, the more worthwhile it is to recycle.

Opposition to new disposal facilities is based in part on fears of air and water pollution, bringing up the second category of benefits. The more we recycle, the less stuff there is to ooze out of landfills, or waft out of incinerators. This problem was more important in the past: new landfills and incinerators, meeting current pollution control standards, have much lower pollutant emissions than their predecessors. The most serious landfill pollution problems reflect either past dumping of hazardous industrial wastes into municipal landfills (a practice that is now prohibited, but has given rise to several Superfund sites), and/or leaks from old landfills built without liners, leachate collection systems, and other now-standard controls. But new technology has not eliminated pollution from waste disposal: it is still reasonable to worry that, in time, even the best-designed new landfill may develop leaks. In addition, decomposition of paper and other organic matter in landfills produces methane, which contributes to the greenhouse effect. Landfills account for 4% of greenhouse gas emissions in the United States, the most important nonenergy contribution to climate change potential.[34] Methane control systems, required on new landfills, will gradually reduce but not completely eliminate this problem.

Turning to the third category of benefits, litter and illegal disposal are only rarely the focus of research or public policy. However, they are issues which many people seem to take seriously. Deposit legislation, in effect in ten U.S. states, most of Canada, and many European countries, is in part an attempt to minimize beverage container litter. Questions of litter and illegal disposal are taken up in Chapters 2 and 7.

By many standards, the environmental impacts of material production outweigh those of waste disposal. Extraction and manufacturing of a ton of material requires far more energy, and gives rise to far greater air and water emissions, than does the ultimate disposal of that same material. Production of secondary (recycled) material generally has lower impacts than production of the same amount of virgin material. In the extreme, in the case of aluminum, secondary production requires only about 5% as much energy as virgin production, and gives rise to correspondingly reduced air and water emissions from power plants. No other common recycling process saves quite that much, but all achieve some savings. Thus the greatest environmental benefits of recycling may be found in production rather than in disposal—that is, in the fourth and fifth categories of benefits introduced above. The issues of production impacts are discussed in Chapter 5.

Of course, none of this tells us how to value the environmental benefits of recycling. Are there reasons to value energy savings at more than the current price of energy, or does the market already tell us how much energy conservation is worth? Where recycling lowers toxic emissions from mining and manufacturing, how important is that reduction in toxicity? The problem of valuation of nonmonetary gains becomes even more important in the final area of environmental benefits from recycling, namely the conservation of natural resources as a step toward long-term sustainability. What is an environmentally sustainable future worth to us? And how great a contribution to long-term sustainability is made by a little more recycling today? These ultimate questions are the subject of Chapter 10.

In all of the categories of benefits, the advantage of recycling is that it leads to less stuff: less waste in disposal, or less virgin material use in production. Thus an even better way to obtain the same environmental benefits is to simply use less material in the first place. This idea, sometimes called "source reduction," or, less cryptically, "waste prevention," has become increasingly popular in recycling circles in the 1990s. The rhetoric of waste management has advocated waste prevention for years; only recently has there been movement beyond rhetoric, toward measurement and analysis. Reducing the amount of material used to deliver a product or service often does more for the environment than switching to recycled material; in those cases where "reduction or recycling" is an either-or choice, the results can appear counterintuitive for recycling advocates. Important examples of opportunities for waste prevention appear in Chapters 5 and 8, and the issues raised there are examined further in Chapters 9 and 10.

The discussion of the various categories of environmental benefits has taken us a long way from the anti-recycling critique, which called for exclusive reliance on the logic of the marketplace. One way to describe the debate over recycling would be to say that the environmental benefits are of great importance to recycling advocates, but are minimized or ignored by the anti-recyclers. A possible route to a reconciliation of these opposing views would be the use of market incentives, such as adjustments in prices and taxes, to achieve the environmental goals of recycling and waste prevention. This question is the subject of the next two chapters. As fashionable as market incentives for environmental policy have become, their performance to date in the areas of solid waste and recycling has been uninspiring, as will be seen in Chapter 2. Theoretical explanations for this practical failure—that is, reasons why some environmental goals cannot be reached through the market—are presented in Chapter 3.

Notes

1. As quoted in "Recycling: Is it Worth the Effort?," *Consumer Reports,* February 1994.

2. Robert Steuteville, "The State of Garbage in America: Part I," *BioCycle,* April 1995, and "Part II," May 1995. The 1994 figure was an increase of about 600 over 1993. *BioCycle*'s first annual "State of Garbage in America" report found about 1000 curbside recycling collection programs in operation in 1988.

3. Franklin Associates, *The Role of Recycling in Integrated Solid Waste Management to the Year 2000* (Stamford, Connecticut: Keep America Beautiful, Inc., 1994), Summary p. 6.

4. See Joanne Vining, Nancy Linn, and Rabel J. Burdge, "Why Recycle? A Comparison of Recycling Motivations in Four Communities," *Environmental Management,* Vol. 16, No. 6 (1992), and the literature cited there.

5. Paul Ligon, John Stutz, and Brian Zuckerman, "Increasing Participation Rates in Local Curbside Recycling Programs" (Boston: Tellus Institute, 1995). The study compared collection data from individual truck routes to the corresponding census tract information.

6. For an attempt to identify environmental values that are shared throughout our society, see Willett Kempton, James S. Boster, and Jennifer A. Hartley, *Environmental Values in American Culture* (Cambridge: MIT Press, 1995).

7. "Boston Recycles, At Last," *Boston Globe* editorial, November 14, 1994; Jeff Bailey, "Curbside Recycling Comforts the Soul, But Benefits Are Scant," *Wall Street Journal,* January 19, 1995.

8. Riley E. Dunlap and Rik Scarce, "Poll Trends: Environmental Problems and Protection," *Public Opinion Quarterly,* Vol. 55 (1991), 651–672, tables 44–46. The only other steps that a majority said they had taken were talking with friends about pollution, "trying not to litter," and several variants on buying environmentally benign products or avoiding harmful ones, in some cases merely buying the right product "whenever possible."

9. Jerry Powell, "The Anti-Recyclers: Who Are They?," and "The Anti-Recyclers: What's Their Message?," *Resource Recycling,* September 1992.

10. Christopher Boerner and Kenneth Chilton, "False Economy: The Folly of Demand-Side Recycling," *Environment ,* Vol. 36, No. 1, January/February 1994.

11. See William Rathje and Cullen Murphy, *Rubbish! The Archaeology of Garbage* (New York: HarperCollins, 1992), p. 241. The definitively researched account of the *Mobro*'s journey can be found in Benjamin Miller, *The Fat of the Land: New York's Waste* (New York: W.W. Norton, 1996).

12. Frances Cairncross, *Green, Inc.: A Guide to Business and the Environment* (Washington, D.C.: Island Press, 1995), p. 157.

13. Judd Alexander, *In Defense of Garbage* (Westport, Connecticut: Praeger, 1993).

14. Alexander, *In Defense of Garbage,* p. 47.

15. John Tierney, "Recycling is Garbage," *New York Times Magazine,* June 30, 1996. For my response, see Frank Ackerman, "Trashing Recycling: The New Face

of Anti-environmentalism," *Dollars & Sense*, November–December 1996. Numerous replies to Tierney have appeared in the recycling community; a particularly detailed one, from the Environmental Defense Fund, is available on-line at http://www.edf.org/issues/NYTrecycle.html.

16. Donald Woodward, " 'Swords into Ploughshares': Recycling in Pre-Industrial England," *Economic History Review*, second series, Vol. 38 (1985), 175–191.

17. Judith McGaw, *Most Wonderful Machine: Mechanization and Social Change in Berkshire Paper Making, 1801–1885* (Princeton: Princeton University Press, 1987), Chapter 7.

18. Susan Strasser, *Waste and Want: Disposal, Recycling, and American Consumer Culture* (New York: Metropolitan Books, 1998).

19. Martin Melosi, *Garbage in the Cities: Refuse, Reform, and the Environment, 1880–1980* (College Station, Texas: Texas A&M University Press, 1981), and Miller, *Fat of the Land*. The Winslow Homer etching is reproduced in Rathje and Murphy, *Rubbish!*, p. 194.

20. Melosi, *Garbage in the Cities*, and Louis Blumberg and Robert Gottlieb, *War on Waste: Can America Win its Battle With Garbage?* (Washington, D.C.: Island Press, 1989), Chapter 7.

21. Rathje and Murphy, *Rubbish!*, pp. 188–191.

22. Randy Woods and Charles Peterson, "World War II and the Birth of Modern Recycling," *Recycling Times*, May 2, 1995; Blumberg and Gottlieb, *War on Waste*, p. 198; Rathje and Murphy, *Rubbish!*, pp. 195–196.

23. Blumberg and Gottlieb, *War on Waste*, pp. 199–200; Rathje and Murphy, *Rubbish!*, p. 196.

24. Martin Melosi, "Down in the Dumps: Is There a Garbage Crisis in America?," *Journal of Policy History*, Vol. 5 (1993), pp. 100–127.

25. Brenda Platt, Christine Doherty, Anne Claire Broughton, and David Morris, *Beyond 40 Percent: Record-Setting Recycling and Composting Programs* (Washington, D.C.: Island Press, 1991), p. 4.

26. Steuteville, "State of Garbage in America."

27. Dunlap and Scarce, "Poll Trends," Tables 11 and 21.

28. Steuteville, "State of Garbage in America."

29. There are good reasons to expect bigger landfills to have lower costs per ton in general. See Frank Ackerman and Monica Becker, "Economies of Scale in Landfill Costs," *Journal of Resource Management and Technology*, December 1990.

30. Joseph Heller, *Closing Time* (New York: Simon & Schuster, 1994), pp. 20, 28.

31. *The Solid Waste Dilemma: An Agenda for Action* (Washington, D.C.: Environmental Protection Agency, 1989), e.g., pp. 12, 14, and 18.

32. Platt et al., *Beyond 40 Percent*, p. 4.

33. Jennifer Carless, *Taking Out the Trash: A No-Nonsense Guide to Recycling* (Washington, D.C.: Island Press, 1992), pp. 4–7.

34. *Inventory of U.S. Greenhouse Gas Emissions and Sinks: 1990–1993* (Washington, D.C.: EPA, 1994), Table ES-1, p. ES-3.

CHAPTER 2

Getting the Prices Wrong

 ————————————————————————————

How much difference does a decade make? Imagine an environmental-
ist who became understandably despairing at the government's opposition to her cause in the mid-1980s, and, as in the story of Rip Van Win-
kle or various sentimentally silly movies, went to sleep for a decade.
Upon awakening she would see countless changes, for better and for
worse. Some important types of air and water pollution would be lower
than she remembered, and going down. On the other hand, she might
notice that old-growth forests in the West, and tropical rain forests,
were also going down. Both Congress and the White House changed
hands while she slept; on balance, the news from Washington might
strike her as at best a modest improvement. There would be many more
details to catch up on, which she could download from the World Wide
Web—once she got used to the idea that personal computers now came
with hard disks and modems.

She would certainly be astonished at how far and how fast recycling
had spread; it would undoubtedly strike her as the environmental success story of the decade she missed. Nothing in her past would have prepared her for the transformation of a scattered volunteer effort into a
nationwide institution. Likewise, if she ventured into the world of environmental theory and policy debates, she would be equally astonished
at how completely a new idea had taken over. Advocacy of market in-

centives for environmental protection is now almost as popular in theory as recycling is in practice.

A decade ago, environmental protection meant telling polluters what they had to stop doing: banning the worst substances and practices, setting strict limits on milder hazards, requiring certain investments in pollution control and prevention, and so on. To policymakers today, that sounds as dated as disco music. There is no need to set emission limits or require particular pollution control devices at each industrial facility; just get the prices, taxes, fees, or other incentives right, the new tune goes, and the market will achieve environmental progress more efficiently and painlessly on its own. The promise of market incentives is frequently counterpoised to the bad old days of "command and control" regulation, an epithet with a sinister Stalinist sound to it. In fact, with the demise of communism (which also happened during our observer's nap; she really should have stayed awake) she could almost conclude that command and control regulation had taken its place as the leading enemy of the free market.

No short summary could begin to describe the literature on market incentives for environmental protection. The high-profile "Project 88" study, with influential government and academic sponsors, raised the issue forcefully in policy circles beginning in 1988. The EPA's 1989 solid waste policy statement, *Agenda for Action,* strongly endorsed market incentives for waste reduction and recycling. Resources For the Future, a Washington, D.C.–based environmental research institute, has produced numerous theoretical and applied studies of the economics of market incentives. *Costing the Earth,* by Frances Cairncross, is a readable account of the potential for market incentives in many areas. Paul Hawken, in *The Ecology of Commerce,* relies heavily on environmental taxes as a solution to the many problems he describes.[1] Virtually any recent academic writing about environmental economics will also sing the praises of market incentives, in more technical language.

With everyone marching so merrily in the same direction, there must be a need for someone to rain on the parade. Our research at Tellus Institute led to rather skeptical conclusions about the effects of some market incentives. I directed two major studies of proposed incentives for recycling for the state of California, and found that neither proposal would have much effect on recycling rates. (Both are described below, one for the first time outside of specialized technical reports.) While market incentives may be a major innovation in theory, they accomplish surprisingly little in practice when it comes to recycling.

This chapter takes a brief look at the theory of market incentives, and then examines the evidence concerning three major categories of incentives for waste prevention and recycling: unit pricing (e.g., per-bag charges) for garbage collection; elimination of existing subsidies for the use of virgin materials; and advance disposal fees, charged at the time of sale on products that will eventually generate waste.

Means, Ends, and Markets

Arguments for market incentives for environmental protection can be made on either of two levels; market mechanisms can be viewed either as the means or as the ends of public policy. On the one hand, it is sometimes said that the market is the most efficient means to reach a predetermined environmental objective. On the other hand, a more theoretical perspective favored by economists claims that the efficiency of the market, adjusted to incorporate environmental values, is itself the objective.

The contrast between the two views can be illustrated with an example. Advocates of market incentives might assert that a polluted river is best cleaned up by a system of effluent taxes on sources of water pollution, rather than by mandating specific emission levels or control devices. This might be simply a pragmatic conclusion about methods of achieving water quality standards, which can be tested by examining the pros and cons of different clean-up techniques. The water quality standards may have been established through public debate, and need not have any particular grounding in economic theory or calculation.

Alternatively, economists often argue that the market is uniquely efficient in allocating resources. If effluent taxes establish the right price on water pollution, market competition should allocate the optimal amount of resources to cleaning up the river, as it does to everything else. In this case, there is no role for public debate in setting water quality standards; the point is that the market outcome *is* the standard. So long as the prices are set correctly, it is impossible to improve on the allocation of resources achieved by the market.

The first of these two interpretations is easy to understand and, in principle at least, easy to test. However, it is a relatively mundane, pragmatic point, and hardly explains the passion with which market incentives are advocated today. The second interpretation is more ambitious, attempting to bring a wide range of environmental problems within the framework of economic theory. This synthesis has a dual appeal, allowing economists to show that they are addressing the problems of the environment, while allowing environmentalists to share in the respectability and rigor of economics. Since this more ambitious approach is also more opaque to noneconomists, a bit of explanation is in order.

In the simplified model of economic life that is found in textbooks, an unregulated competitive market leads to optimal use of all resources. Volumes have been written debating the reasonableness and applicability of this model to the real world; selected topics from those debates will appear in subsequent chapters. For now, one aspect of the simple model is important, namely its failure to consider pollution. Economic theory assumes a principle of noninterference between people: nothing that I do in the course of my business affects your economic welfare, except through our market transactions. This principle of noninterference is violated if my town, located upstream from you, runs a business that pollutes the river and forces your town to spend money on water purification (or makes you sick). In such cases, the unregulated market does not lead to the best allocation of resources.

The theoretical solution to this problem was developed by the economist Arthur Pigou in 1920. The impact of my town's pollution on your town's water supply is called an "externality," since it is a real cost of operation that is external to our business; we have forced someone downstream to bear that portion of our costs. Pigou's solution was to suggest that a tax should be levied on the effluent from the polluting business, equal to the value of the damages it causes to others. Such a tax "internalizes" the former externality; the downstream costs are now correctly reflected in the accounts of the upstream business. The tax can be used to compensate the downstream communities—and it provides an ongoing incentive for the polluters to find ways to reduce their pollution. If externalities are internalized in this manner, Pigou demonstrated, the resource allocation achieved by the market is once again optimal.

This is the basis for the more complex, theoretical argument for market incentives. To achieve the hoped-for efficiency and optimality of the market economy, it is necessary to identify and evaluate all important externalities, and internalize them, usually through taxes on the polluters. Such slogans as "getting the prices right" or "making the polluters pay" embody the essence of the argument. Market incentives for environmental protection are needed, as a matter of theory, to make the market live up to its promise of optimal resource allocation.

The distinction between the two arguments can be seen in the case of recycling. The pragmatic argument is that since we have decided to have recycling, taxes and fees structured to encourage it are more efficient than regulations mandating participation or other approaches. This may or may not be the case; little has been done to compare the administrative and other burdens of new incentive schemes with the costs of other routes to recycling.

The theoretical argument is that because of externalities, there is currently too much waste disposal and too little recycling. As a waste management strategy, landfilling is unfairly cheap; as a source of raw materials, virgin production receives unwarranted subsidies. Internalizing the externalities would raise the costs of these activities, making recycling of waste and the use of secondary raw materials look comparatively more attractive. Getting the prices right would lead to the "right" level of recycling, higher than current levels.

This argument, we will see below, is problematic: although considerable effort is required to correctly internalize the externalities, the effect on the level of recycling is likely to be very small. To the extent that new incentives have influenced recycling, it is often as a result of getting the prices wrong. This is particularly apparent in the case of the most popular market incentive for recycling, involving the price of garbage collection.

Unit Pricing for Garbage Collection

Most urban and suburban U.S. households receive fixed-price garbage collection services, regardless of the quantity of waste they discard. In small towns and rural areas, unlimited dumping rights at a local landfill or transfer station are often available for a fixed fee. The cost of garbage collection is often included in municipal property taxes or fees, especially in older urban areas. Newer suburban communities sometimes require households to contract with private collection services, but fixed monthly fees are common for private services as well. Municipal provision of unlimited garbage collection may reflect its origins as an urgent public health measure in the filthy, crowded cities of the late nineteenth century.[2]

Recently, as attention has shifted from the problems of sanitation to those of waste reduction and recycling, widespread interest has emerged in the practice of charging households by the bag or can for the waste they discard. This approach is sometimes referred to in the solid waste literature as unit pricing, variable collection rates, or volume based rates. Unit pricing for garbage collection appears to be one of the points on which recycling advocates and anti-recyclers can most easily agree. The theoretical argument for market incentives is often raised in this connection: if households can discard more waste at zero additional cost, they will throw out too much stuff. But if households have to pay for additional garbage collection and disposal, they will reduce their use of this service to a more efficient, optimal level.

Before the 1980s, unit pricing for garbage collection was apparently confined to a few West Coast communities. The current wave of interest began with Seattle's well-publicized introduction of unit pricing in 1981, and rose to nationwide importance in the late 1980s. Today more than 2000 communities have instituted unit pricing for garbage collection, and the number continues to grow.

As unit pricing programs have spread across the country, economists studying them have not been far behind. Although the tone of the studies is optimistic about the potential for price incentives, the empirical results provide grounds for pessimism. The problem is that people just do not respond very much to moderate prices for garbage collection. The initial introduction of unit pricing causes a modest reduction in waste disposal; small price changes thereafter have almost no additional effect, while big price increases might lead to unacceptable levels of illegal dumping.

Turning to the gory statistical details, studies of unit pricing often report two key measures. One is the initial reduction in waste achieved by the introduction of per-bag garbage charges; the other is the additional reduction in waste that will result from a price increase, after unit pricing is already in effect. The later impacts are usually expressed in terms of the "price elasticity"—the percentage change in the quantity of waste caused by a 1% increase in price. (Since price increases generally cause reductions in demand, price elasticities are negative numbers.) An elasticity of –0.2 means that a price increase of 1% causes a 0.2% reduction in garbage collection; an elasticity of –1 means that a 1% price increase causes a 1% reduction. A price elasticity close to zero means that prices have little effect on behavior, while a larger elasticity means that behavior is more dramatically influenced by prices.

It is important to distinguish between the effects of unit pricing with and without curbside recycling. In the absence of curbside recycling, the effects are particularly small. The most elaborate study of unit pricing to date was carried out by Robin Jenkins.[3] She analyzed data for nine communities, five with unit pricing and four without, from periods in the 1980s before any of the communities had instituted curbside recycling. She found that instituting a $1.00 fee per 32 gallon trash bag (a common fee level) would reduce waste generation by 15%. For communities which have unit pricing, Jenkins estimated a price elasticity of –0.12, consistent with most of the earlier studies she cited. An extension of Jenkins' model to a larger set of communities, in a World Resources Institute (WRI) study she coauthored, found an even smaller effect: in the absence of curbside recycling, introduction of a $1.00 fee per bag would reduce waste generation by only 12 % in the WRI data set.[4]

Thus in the absence of curbside recycling, unit pricing is remarkable not for how much it accomplishes, but for how little. Instituting unit pricing, at the rate of $1.00 per bag of trash collected, apparently causes a one-time reduction in waste generation of 12 % to 15 % by weight. Unit pricing achieves a much greater reduction in volume, since people "stomp" on their trash to save on collection fees; this is of little value for waste management, since garbage trucks would compact the waste in any case. Once unit pricing is established, the price elasticity of waste generation may be as small as –0.12.

A price elasticity of –0.12 is very small; it implies that an 8 % price increase causes only a 1 % drop in garbage disposal. Most consumer purchases have much larger price elasticities. By way of comparison, price elasticity estimates range from –0.2 to –0.7 for residential energy use, and may be as great as –0.6 to –0.7 for cigarette purchases.[5] Even when paid for by the bag, residential waste collection is one of the least price-sensitive purchases made by households.

Recent discussion has emphasized the benefits achieved by combining unit pricing with curbside recycling. But notice that the theoretical grounds have now shifted. When a community charges by the bag for garbage collection but provides free recycling, it is not getting the prices right for waste management as a whole. Recycling, too, has a cost in most cases. Unless the revenues plus the environmental benefits from recycling exactly offset its costs, free curbside recycling consists of getting the prices wrong by design. This does not mean that free curbside recycling is the wrong thing to do; it does mean, however, that it needs a different theoretical justification.

What is achieved by unit pricing in combination with curbside recycling? A study of recycling in an upstate New York county found that the presence or absence of unit pricing had little effect on community recycling rates. Some studies of unit pricing in communities with curbside recycling have found price elasticities of –0.22 to –0.26, higher than those found for unit pricing without recycling, but still lower than elasticities for most other goods and services.[6] The WRI/Jenkins model estimates that introducing a $1.00 per bag fee in a community with curbside recycling reduces waste disposal by 20 %.

Other studies have sometimes found even larger reductions. For example, a review of 21 small, affluent communities reported an average

40 % reduction in waste when unit pricing was introduced. Increases in recycling and composting accounted for half of the reduction in waste disposal on average, though with wide and often inexplicable variation between communities. However, the reductions in waste achieved in these 21 towns cannot be entirely attributed to the introduction of unit pricing. Curbside recycling began at the same time as unit pricing in seven communities, and may have barely preceded unit pricing in some of the others.[7] Thus the estimate of 40 % waste reduction combines the effects of introducing unit pricing per se with the effects of simultaneously starting or expanding a recycling program in many of the communities.

Two Choices or Three?

An unusually detailed study that should give pause to advocates of unit pricing was performed by Don Fullerton and Thomas Kinnaman.[8] In 1992, Charlottesville, Virginia, introduced a fee of 80¢ per bag for garbage collection, six months after beginning curbside recycling. Fullerton and Kinnaman weighed the garbage set out at the curb by 75 households both before and after the introduction of unit pricing. They found an initial 14 % reduction in the weight of garbage, and estimated the price elasticity for garbage collection at –0.08; that is, they found even less response to price incentives than the WRI/Jenkins study did.

The most important finding from the Charlottesville study is the evidence of substantial illegal disposal. By combining garbage weight measurements and survey responses from the 75 households, Fullerton and Kinnaman argue persuasively that at least 28 % of the reduction in garbage collection achieved by unit pricing occurred though illegal disposal. It should be noted that the sample households were drawn from nonstudent neighborhoods of a university community, and had significantly higher income and educational levels, on average, than the city as a whole. The study could not distinguish whether illegal dumping by these households consisted of unauthorized use of university or commercial dumpsters, or use of illegal dumpsites outside of town.

The same authors also offer a unique theoretical perspective on pricing for waste collection, drawing out the implications of their empirical study.[9] If households had only two choices, recycling or proper waste disposal, Fullerton and Kinnaman would agree with the common assumption that a fee should be placed on garbage collection, since recycling is environmentally preferable. However, they point out that there are three choices, of which improper disposal is clearly the least desirable. Simply increasing the fees for proper garbage disposal provides an incentive for improper disposal as well as recycling.

Economic theory implies that in order to get the prices right for all three choices, the largest per-unit charge should be placed on improper disposal, and the smallest on recycling. Improper disposal, though, is done surreptitiously, and cannot be taxed directly. Fullerton and Kinnaman demonstrate that the same result, market incentives that discourage improper disposal, could be achieved by taxing all goods when they are sold, and then refunding the tax when the goods are either recycled or disposed of properly. Far from charging for garbage collection, this suggests a rationale for rewarding proper garbage disposal, at least to the extent of refunding the disposal tax.

While most studies of unit pricing briefly mention the danger of increased illegal dumping, the work of Fullerton and Kinnaman is the first to provide a detailed analysis of the problem. It suggests the ultimate limitation to the use of unit pricing as an incentive for recycling: the higher the fee, the greater the incentive for improper disposal. The WRI/Jenkins study finds that the right price for garbage collection, including an estimate of the value of landfill externalities, averages $1.83 per bag in densely populated communities. Fullerton and Kinnaman speculate that fees of that magnitude in big cities might be more effective incentives for illegal dumping than for recycling or waste reduction.

There are limits, therefore, to the level of fees that can be charged, and to the waste reduction and recycling that unit pricing can achieve. Moreover, unit pricing can only be justified by the pragmatic argument for market incentives—if it works better than anything else available, do it. (On the other hand, if its administrative costs outweigh its modest gains, don't do it.) There is little basis for the grander theoretical claim that unit pricing is achieving an optimal allocation of resources.

Virgin Material Subsidies and Taxes

While unit pricing seeks to influence household disposal decisions, other incentives aim to affect producer choices among materials. Existing tax codes, laws, and regulations often favor virgin materials over recycled ones, resulting in an unfair competitive advantage. Eliminating all preferences for virgin materials would create a "level playing field," improving the competitive position of secondary materials in the marketplace. Internalizing the externalities associated with virgin material production, either by subsidizing secondary materials or by taxing virgin ones, would go even further, tilting the playing field in favor of recycling.

Changes in virgin material subsidies and taxes are politically difficult to implement, and the discussion has remained largely theoretical. Still, there have been several studies of the magnitude of existing virgin material subsidies and their effects on recycling. These studies have generally found that, while virgin material subsidies pass the Dirksen significance test ("A billion here, a billion there, soon you're talking real money," as the late Senator Everett Dirksen once said), they are not important barriers to recycling.

The EPA's *Agenda for Action,* among its many recommendations, called for an assessment of existing obstacles to recycling. One result was a study, *Federal Disincentives: A Study of Federal Tax Subsidies and Other Programs Affecting Virgin Industries and Recycling,* performed in 1989 but only released in 1994 after extensive review and revision.[10] The study notes that the 1986 federal tax reform eliminated many provisions that had favored extractive industries; tax advantages for virgin materials presented a more serious obstacle to recycling before that date.

Examining the laws and regulations in effect in 1989, the study found that energy subsidies were the most important federal disincentive, while other federal tax provisions and regulations were too small to affect recycling markets. In the case of the paper industry, total federal subsidies to virgin production amounted to no more than 2.6% of the industry's cost of materials, with energy subsidies accounting for more than half of that amount. Energy subsidies are potential barriers to recycling because extraction and processing of virgin raw materials almost always uses more energy than recycling and processing of secondary materials. Thus if subsidies for energy use were removed, virgin materials would become more expensive relative to their recycled counterparts, improving the market position of recycling.

Two studies have tried to measure federal energy subsidies. The Department of Energy's Energy Information Administration identifies subsidies worth $5 to $13 billion a year, while the Alliance to Save Energy, an energy conservation advocacy group, obtains estimates of $23 to $40 billion (in 1992 dollars).[11] Energy subsidies in the tens of billions of dollars are large enough to warrant public debate; they are not insignificant when compared with the budget and tax cuts that are the subject of ongoing controversy in Washington. But subsidies of this magnitude do not, in most cases, create a noticeable advantage for virgin over secondary material production.

An article by Douglas Koplow, examining energy subsidies to the aluminum industry, appears to make the opposite point, finding a significant effect on aluminum prices.[12] In fact, his analysis of aluminum is the exception that proves the rule. Aluminum production is extremely energy-intensive, requiring three to six times as much energy per ton as the production of steel, paper, or plastics. The cost of electricity represents 25 to 30 % of the cost of aluminum made in the United States. Moreover, recycling saves 95 % of the energy required to produce virgin aluminum, an unusually great savings. As a result, one would expect the importance of energy subsidies to be far greater for aluminum than for other materials industries.

Koplow analyzes the aluminum smelters that buy electricity from the Bonneville Power Administration (BPA) in the Pacific Northwest. Federal subsidies to BPA, passed on in lower prices for electricity, could be important to these producers. For the BPA's customers, federal energy subsidies amounted to 5 to 13 % of the market price for primary aluminum in 1989, the year for which Koplow's data were developed, or 7 to 18 % of the price of scrap aluminum in 1994. The difference between the high and low estimates reflects the cost advantage of public power, the biggest item that Koplow counts as a subsidy. As a governmental entity, BPA can borrow money at lower interest rates than a private utility, and does not have to earn a profit; hence it can and does charge its customers less for electricity. The higher estimates include this advantage, while the lower ones exclude it.

In an era when the virtues of privatization are held to be almost beyond dispute, it is startling to stumble across evidence that public enterprises sometimes provide basic services more cheaply than profit-making private businesses. It seems perverse to describe this savings, the economic return on an earlier optimism about public investment, as an unfair subsidy. In any case, the advantage of cheap public power is only available to industries and other electricity consumers in a few rigidly defined geographical areas. It is not part of the story of subsidies to virgin material industries in general.

Excluding the local advantages stemming from public ownership of BPA, Koplow finds that energy subsidies amount to 7 % of the price of scrap aluminum—in effect, a 7 % price penalty on recycling. In other industries, where the energy saved by recycling accounts for a much smaller proportion of production costs, the barrier to recycling due to energy subsidies is proportionately smaller, likely in the range of 1 % of prices or less.

Another perspective on the issue is provided by a Tellus Institute study of state virgin material incentives in California, performed for the

California Integrated Waste Management Board (CIWMB).[13] The qualitative conclusion is the same as in the federal case: while state incentives cost California taxpayers huge amounts annually, this does not affect the competitive position of secondary materials in the California economy.

We found that three industries—crude oil, natural gas, and timber—together account for more than two-thirds of the value of raw materials produced in California, and receive virtually all of the quantifiable state subsidies and incentives. The timber industry receives preferential tax treatment, subsidized fire protection, and other timber management services, worth $70 million or 8 % of the value of timber harvested in 1990. Several provisions of the state tax code are in effect subsidies to the oil and gas industry. Depending on one's view of a local tax controversy, the total subsidy to oil and gas production might be as much as $255 million, a little under 5 % of sales in 1990.

Yet these amounts have almost no effect on recycling, for two reasons. The first is what we called the "mismatch" between virgin and secondary material production. Almost none of the subsidized virgin materials compete with the state's recycling efforts. Oil and gas are used almost entirely for fuel, while California timber is used almost exclusively to make lumber rather than paper. Thus while subsidies to oil, gas, and timber drain the state's budget and undoubtedly promote excessive use of these materials, this has almost no direct effect on recycling.

Second, even in the few cases where subsidized virgin materials do compete directly with recycled materials, the state incentives are too small to make a difference. Other factors are far more important in determining the profitability of recycling. Lumber recycling is apparently confined to unusual market niches where a steady supply of clean lumber is available, such as recycling of Hollywood studio sets, or to sporadic opportunities such as post-earthquake salvage. The supply of recyclable lumber is the limiting factor, and would remain so even if all state subsidies to virgin lumber production were removed.

A small amount of oil and gas is used to make plastics and asphalt, two areas where virgin and recycled products do compete directly. In the case of plastics we estimated that, at $17 per barrel, the price of oil represented 9 to 18 % of the price of three common plastics. So California's incentives for crude oil production, worth just under 5 % of the value of crude oil, would be less than 1 % of the value of plastics—hardly a decisive factor in the competition between virgin and recycled plastics.

The situation is similar in the case of asphalt, which is made up of a lot of rock and sand aggregate mixed with a little bitumen, a crude oil-derived product. The cost of crude oil used to make bitumen represents about 16% of the price of asphalt, so again a 5% subsidy to California crude oil production represents less than 1% of the price of asphalt.

The traditional technique for repaving roads involves scraping off the old pavement and transporting it to a landfill, then bringing in new aggregate and bitumen to make new asphalt. Alternatively, it is possible to use the old pavement in one of several recycling techniques, producing new pavement with 15 to 100% recycled content. Asphalt recycling is profitable for many California communities in part because it avoids transportation costs, both for bringing new aggregate from remote quarries and for taking old pavement to landfills. If California's incentives for oil production were fully passed on to asphalt buyers, it would become cost-effective to bring in virgin materials from only five minutes farther away. In short, asphalt recycling, like plastics recycling, is barely affected by California's virgin material subsidies.

Subsidies to virgin material production have been much greater in the past; speculation about the historical importance of subsidies is presented in Chapter 3. But the most important past subsidies have gradually been reduced or abolished. At this point, removal of the remaining incentives for virgin material production, creating a "level playing field" between virgin and secondary materials, would do little to promote recycling—with the interesting but apparently isolated exception of aluminum. Ironically, aluminum already has the highest recycling rate among common materials; the sole obvious effect of eliminating all virgin material incentives would be to increase aluminum's high recycling rate still further. Elimination of subsidies to extractive industries is generally a worthwhile objective for other reasons, but is unlikely to do much to promote recycling.

Advance Disposal Fees

Yet another potential market incentive for waste reduction and recycling, the last one that will be considered here, is an advance disposal fee: a tax on goods levied at the point of sale, based on the cost of ultimate disposal of those goods. When goods are sold, the theory goes, neither seller nor buyer takes into account the disposal cost that will later be imposed on society. Hence the prices of waste-generating products are too low, and everyone is free to generate too much waste. Collecting the disposal cost in advance, at the time of sale, would correctly raise product prices to reflect the true costs to society, leading to reduced sales of goods that eventually turn to waste.

In terms of practical applications, many states have advance disposal fees on particular products that pose problems or hazards in disposal, such as automobile batteries and tires. But across-the-board advance disposal fees covering wider ranges of manufactured products have, with one important exception, remained a matter of theory rather than practice.

The most detailed analysis of advance disposal fees is contained in another Tellus Institute study performed for the California Integrated Waste Management Board.[14] In 1990, CIWMB requested a proposal for a cost-based disposal fee to apply to all goods sold in California, including a calculation of the environmental as well as the economic costs of disposal.

Working quickly (bureaucratic constraints in California required us to complete the study in barely five months), we estimated the size of the state waste stream, then calculated costs of solid waste collection and disposal, and assigned those costs to individual product categories. Based on the fragmentary available evidence, we also developed estimates of the externalities associated with landfilling of waste and assigned these externalities to the individual products responsible for the externalities. Half of the landfill externalities, it turned out, were assigned to the handful of potentially hazardous products in the waste stream, such as oil-based paints and batteries.

Adding the monetary costs of waste collection and disposal to the estimated externality costs yielded a proposed fee for each type of manufactured goods sold in California. The fee revenues would have totaled just over $5 billion annually, about 1% of gross state product or $170 per capita. Two-thirds of that amount was the monetary cost of waste collection and disposal, which was already being paid through other institutional channels; only the externality costs, the remaining third of the total amount, represented a new financial burden.

Response to the fee proposal was immediate and overwhelming. CIWMB rejected our recommendations, and agreed to print the report only with a lengthy, hostile disclaimer bound into the front. At least one other state, Minnesota, concluded on the basis of our California study that the option of advance disposal fees could be rejected without further discussion. Rarely has economic research had such a prompt, visible effect on policymakers.

What accounted for the negative reception that our study received? In the debates in Sacramento, much was made of the practical problems of administering a comprehensive fee on a statewide basis. But a deeper difficulty was that our fee proposal was at once too large and too small. The revenue total of $5 billion was clearly too large, perhaps by two orders of magnitude, for serious consideration in the "no new taxes" mood of the 1990s. Yet at the same time the fee we would have assessed on individual products was usually too small for consumers to notice. Five billion dollars is not actually a lot when spread across the vast California economy.

Our proposed disposal fees on most nonhazardous products would have added 2 % or less to their purchase prices. For example, fees on 10- to 12-ounce glass and plastic bottles would have been 1 cent; total fees on the wrappers for a classic fast food meal, including a hamburger, French fries, and a soft drink, would have been less than a cent. Only on the items that cause identifiable environmental hazards in disposal would the fee have been large enough to cause noticeable changes in consumer behavior.

Thus the general problem was that a cost-based, across the board disposal fee raised enough money to affect the state budget and draw overwhelming political opposition, without being large enough to affect the patterns of consumer purchases of most individual goods. A fee large enough to affect fast food purchases, for instance, would have raised much bigger revenue totals, and would have been even further out of the question, politically speaking.[15]

Broad-based disposal fees were rejected in practice by almost, but not quite, everyone. Florida instituted an advance disposal fee (ADF) on containers that was in effect from 1993 to 1995. It initially imposed a one penny per container fee on cans, cartons, bottles, and jars sold in the state, rising to 2 cents per container in the second year.[16] However, not all of the 12 billion containers sold annually in Florida actually required the fee. The state established several categories of exemptions for container types and brands that meet recycling goals.

Any material which achieved a 50 % recycling rate in the state was exempt; aluminum and steel cans both met this standard from the beginning. Exemptions were also available for materials or individual brands that met recycled content standards (which varied by material) or used equivalent amounts of Florida's recycled materials in other products. Eventually, all paper milk cartons and drink boxes, virtually all soft drink containers, and all glass bottles made or filled in the United States won exemption, as did many types of plastic containers.

The Florida ADF raised a total of $45 million in its first year. As more and more packages won exemption, revenues dropped to $23 million in the second year (despite the higher per-container fee), and would have fallen even lower if the ADF had remained in effect longer. The revenues were used to fund recycling initiatives, landfill improvements, and clean water and sewage treatment programs.

Russell Martin, ADF manager at Florida's Department of Environmental Protection, says that the state was surprised at the number of applications for exemptions. Some companies were simply documenting past recycling performance, but some, Martin believes, increased their use of recycled material in order to meet the standards for exemption. In fact, so many companies wanted to buy recycled plastics in order to qualify for exemption that Piper Plastics decided to locate a new plastics recycling facility in Florida. Anheuser-Busch planned to build a glass recycling plant in the state, in part due to the ADF.[17]

In the midst of this success, the Florida legislature declined to renew the ADF in 1995. Like legislatures everywhere, they were seeking to cut taxes and programs. The high prices for recycled materials in 1995 made it seem less urgent for public policy to promote recycling. And the growing number of successful ADF exemptions may have suggested that the job had been accomplished, and industry had complied with the state standards.

It is pleasant to end the account of market incentives with a success story. Yet a little more curiosity is called for. *Why* did the Florida ADF succeed? The answer is not that the fee raised prices so much that consumers reduced their purchases or switched to less wasteful alternatives. A fee of one or two cents per container is lost in the noise of the marketplace, drowned out by the differences from store to store, or from week to week as supermarket sales come and go.

The ADF succeeded because packaging producers scrambled to meet the standards for exemption. The value of the exemption was not the savings of a penny or two—a price change too small to matter to consumers is also too small to matter to producers—but rather its symbolic meaning. Exemption came to serve as a state seal of environmental approval, conveying a marketing benefit worth far more than the modest reduction in consumer prices. Which would influence you more in the supermarket: a package of soup that sold for a penny less than a rival brand, or a package of soup that proclaimed, "THIS CONTAINER IS TAX-EXEMPT BECAUSE IT MEETS STATE RECYCLING STANDARDS"? (This is a hypothetical label for the sake of argument, not a quotation from actual Florida packaging.)

Despite the outward form of a market incentive, in other words, the Florida ADF functioned primarily as advertising for state recycling standards, and as a source of revenue. In time, any advertising campaign loses its novelty; had it survived, the ADF would have faced additional problems in maintaining its message. It functioned well at first, when some packages were exempt but others were not. This not only yielded revenue for state environmental programs, but also created a distinction between the companies that had complied with the standards for exemption and those that had not. As the packaging industry approached 100 % compliance, however, the revenue vanished, as did the distinction conveyed by exemption. Continuing the ADF would have meant maintaining the regulatory mechanism for certifying everyone's exemptions, while obtaining neither significant revenue for the state nor advertising benefits for industry.

Such problems would not arise if the ADF were a market incentive which operated primarily through correcting relative prices, as envisioned in economic theory.

The Price of Pragmatism

If the newly popular phrase, "three strikes and you're out," applied to market incentives, it would now be another theory's turn at bat. To make the preceding long story short, none of the market incentives for recycling examined here—unit pricing for waste disposal, elimination of virgin material subsidies, or advance disposal fees—accomplish much on their own. Simply getting the prices right in these areas has little effect on the prospects for recycling. One reason is that both virgin material production and waste disposal account for only a small part of the cost of most products on the market. Value added in processing, fabrication, and distribution usually dwarfs the costs of getting materials and getting rid of them, whether or not estimates of externalities are included.

Whatever the explanation, the result is that the broad theoretical argument for market incentives is of limited practical importance. A recycling program that is unprofitable today, with uncorrected market prices, would be only a little less unprofitable after an arduous campaign to correct the prices and internalize the externalities. A recycling program that is just breaking even would do only slightly better with the laboriously corrected prices. The most obvious winner from the market incentives analyzed here would be aluminum recycling, already the most profitable of common recycling efforts. As a response to the critics of recycling, "getting the prices right" is a dud, seemingly showing that recycling would be barely more desirable in an environmentally conscious world than it is today. Few recycling advocates would accept this as the theoretical basis for their views, if they understood where it leads.

It remains possible to defend market incentives for recycling on very different, pragmatic grounds. Perhaps unit pricing for garbage collection is one of the most effective ways to advertise the availability of free recycling collection. Perhaps Florida's disposal fee was the best way to advertise state standards for recycled content in containers. It is conceivable that policies masquerading as market incentives are in general a good form of advertising for environmental objectives, even when the direct effects on the market are too small to matter.

But the price of pragmatism is that the market can tell us only how to recycle, not how much or why. Once we dismiss the argument for market incentives based on grand theory, we must look for other answers to the question of why we recycle, answers that necessarily lie beyond the logic of the marketplace. The next chapter explores the reasons why the environmental motivations for recycling may be inherently incompatible with a market-oriented framework.

Notes

1. Robert Stavins et al., *Project 88: Harnessing Market Forces to Protect Our Environment* (Washington: 1988), and *Project 88—Round II: Incentives for Action—Designing Market-Based Environmental Strategies* (Washington: 1992); Frances Cairncross, *Costing the Earth* (Boston: Harvard Business School Press, 1993); Paul Hawken, *The Ecology of Commerce* (New York: HarperCollins, 1993). Hawken's views are discussed further in Chapter 9.

2. Martin V. Melosi, *Garbage in the Cities: Refuse, Reform, and the Environment, 1880–1980* (College Station, Texas: Texas A&M University Press, 1981).

3. Robin Jenkins, *The Economics of Waste Reduction: The Impact of User Fees* (Brookfield, Vermont: Edward Elgar, 1993).

4. Robert Repetto, Roger C. Dower, Robin Jenkins, and Jacqueline Geoghegan, *Green Fees: How a Tax Shift Can Work for the Environment and the Economy* (Washington, D.C.: World Resources Institute, 1992).

5. Douglas R. Bohi, *Analyzing Demand Behavior: A Study of Energy Elasticities* (Baltimore: Johns Hopkins University Press, 1981); Gary S. Becker, Michael Grossman, and Kevin M. Murphy, "An Empirical Analysis of Cigarette Addiction," *American Economic Review,* Vol. 84, No. 3 (1994).

6. James D. Reschovsky and Sarah E. Stone, "Market Incentives to Encourage Household Waste Recycling: Paying for What You Throw Away," *Journal of Policy Analysis and Management,* Vol. 13, No. 1 (1994).

7. Marie Lynn Miranda, Jess W. Everett, Daniel Blume, and Barbeau A. Roy, Jr., "Market-Based Incentives and Residential Municipal Solid Waste," *Journal of Policy Analysis and Management,* Vol. 13, No. 4 (1994). Note that their Table 4 shows that the communities with the lowest fees per bag had the greatest reduction in waste disposal, while those with an intermediate level of recycling effort achieved a greater reduction in waste than those with either higher or lower levels of effort. One town reported a more than 400% increase in recycling due to the introduction

of unit pricing; it seems likely that in this town, at least, recycling was barely underway before unit pricing began.

8. Don Fullerton and Thomas C. Kinnaman, "Household Demand for Garbage and Recycling Collection with the Start of a Price per Bag," National Bureau of Economic Research Working Paper 4670 (Cambridge: NBER, 1993).

9. Don Fullerton and Thomas C. Kinnaman, "Garbage, Recycling, and Illicit Burning or Dumping," *Journal of Environmental Economics and Management,* Vol. 29 (1995), 78–91.

10. Douglas Koplow and Kevin Dietly, *Federal Disincentives: A Study of Federal Tax Subsidies and Other Programs Affecting Virgin Industries and Recycling* (Washington, D.C.: EPA Office of Policy, Planning, and Evaluation, 1994).

11. Energy Information Administration, *Federal Energy Subsidies: Direct and Indirect Intervention in Energy Markets* (Washington, D.C.: Government Printing Office, 1992); Douglas Koplow, *Federal Energy Subsidies: Energy, Environmental, and Fiscal Impacts* (Washington, D.C.: Alliance to Save Energy, 1993). A helpful reconciliation of the two sets of estimates is included in the Alliance to Save Energy study.

12. Douglas Koplow, "Federal Energy Subsidies and Recycling: A Case Study," *Resource Recycling,* November 1994. Koplow is the author of the Alliance to Save Energy study, and a coauthor of *Federal Disincentives* (see Notes 10 and 11).

13. Frank Ackerman, Irene Peters, et al., *California's Incentives for Production of Virgin and Secondary Materials* (Sacramento: California Integrated Waste Management Board, 1993).

14. *Disposal Cost Fee Study: Final Report* (Sacramento: California Integrated Waste Management Board, 1991). For short summaries, see Frank Ackerman, "Waste Management—Taxing the Trash Away," *Environment,* June 1992; and "Advance Disposal Fees and Incentives for Waste Reduction," *New Partnerships: Economic Incentives for Environmental Management* (Pittsburgh: Air & Waste Management Association, 1994).

15. Marc Breslow, an economist who worked on the study, reaches somewhat more optimistic conclusions about the likely effects of disposal fees, but acknowledges that his results are based on very uncertain price elasticity estimates. See Marc Breslow, *Regulating Solid Waste Externalities through Tax/Fee Systems,* Ph.D. dissertation, Economics Department, University of Massachusetts/Amherst, 1993; and "Reducing Pollution and Disposal Costs by Taxing Materials," *Resource Recycling,* June 1993.

16. Russell Martin, "Improving Recycling through Market Forces," *BioCycle,* October 1994.

17. Russell Martin, personal communication, January 1996.

CHAPTER 3

More Than the Market

The annual congresses of the National Recycling Coalition (NRC), first held in 1982, now draw more than 2,000 participants each fall. Long gone are the days when enthusiasm for recycling routinely implied long hair and long hours in volunteer collection efforts; today's NRC is dressed for success, befitting its members' increasing prominence in both government and industry. Only the occasional (male) ponytail creeping out over a suit collar remains to recall the recyclers of yester-year.

State and local government officials, hordes of consultants (I speak from personal experience here) and others regularly gather at the NRC congresses and numerous other recycling conferences to trade strategies, techniques, and experience. The level of energy and commitment is remarkable, and the optimism is pervasive: unlike many other environmental groups in the 1990s, the crowds at recycling conferences sense that their cause is winning. The breadth of information and varieties of initiative on display are also astonishing. At the accompanying trade shows you can buy exotic recycled materials, subscribe to specialized recycling publications, observe deafening demonstrations of monstrous Rube Goldberg devices for sorting recycled containers, and even attend recycled-plastic-fabric fashion shows—an acquired taste with today's technology, though doubtless that will change.

The outpouring of effort reflected at these conferences, and visible in local recycling efforts throughout the year, does not arise from a careful calculation that recycling is a cost-effective waste management option. While many are working hard to make recycling pay for itself, those who work the hardest began long before there was any hope of making their cause profitable. Most would continue to advocate recycling as environmentally desirable even if it did not save money. Although recyclers naturally celebrate the occasions when they do make a profit, few have accepted profitability as the sole criterion by which to judge their success.

In this context, consider the implications of the last two chapters. The range of environmental benefits discussed in Chapter 1 provide important motivations for recycling. But as shown in Chapter 2, there is no easy way to use the market mechanism to achieve these benefits via environmentally adjusted prices. That is, the strategy suggested by economic theory, "getting the prices right" and relying on the market, would do little to boost the prospects for recycling. Such a negative conclusion would be discouraging to the many speakers who now extol market incentives at recycling conferences, but would not necessarily drive away their audiences.

However, a conceptual gap remains to be filled. If it is not to be understood solely in terms of market incentives and mechanisms, how should recycling be viewed? What is needed is a new analysis that matches the vigor of recycling in America today. The real reasons for recycling, both for the thousands of hard-core advocates and for the tens of millions of weekly participants, involve much more than the logic of the marketplace.

This chapter offers three steps toward a new theory, three reasons why conventional economics fails to understand the environmental issues raised by recycling. First, the presumption that the market selects efficient technologies is not always appropriate; current levels of recycling may reflect historical accidents and social forces, rather than an economic optimum. Second, concern for long-term environmental problems and the welfare of future generations cannot be adequately represented by market mechanisms, which are oriented to choices within a single lifetime. Finally, there are social decisions that cannot be reduced to individual consumer preferences, and intrinsically noneconomic values that cannot be translated into dollars and cents; a different kind of decisionmaking is required to address these questions.

Chaos, Typewriters, and the Choice of Technology

In economic theory, market outcomes are usually said to be efficient. Competition should allow the survival of only the fittest firms and production techniques. Hence the technologies in use at any time are assumed to be "optimal"—that is, they are the best possible choices, given the state of knowledge and available resources. As explained in Chapter 2, one can argue that prices should be adjusted to incorporate environmental externalities; competition with adjusted prices might lead to a slightly different set of winners. However, if it were still profitable, at the adjusted prices, to engage in extensive exploitation of virgin materials and landfilling of trash, one would be led to the conclusion that recycling was a suboptimal technology, not worth the effort and expense.

But what if the presumption of optimality itself is flawed? What if the technologies in use today reflect accidental events and constellations of forces that governed the market in the past? Rather than enjoying the best of all possible production techniques, we might just be stuck with the ones that our predecessors stumbled into. To understand this possibility, it will be helpful to take a look at the influence of the natural sciences on economics, and the implications of the new field of chaos theory.

Twentieth-century economic theory relies heavily on a deterministic worldview borrowed from nineteenth-century physics, in which chaotic fluctuations could not normally arise. In that worldview, physical or economic systems are assumed to be governed by natural laws and basic forces that exert relentless pressure toward a unique equilibrium. Temporary disturbances introduced from outside are soon smoothed out, and equilibrium is regained. Pour milk into hot black coffee and swirling disorder is visible only for a moment; soon the whole cup of liquid reaches a uniform color and temperature. Introduce a new commodity or technology into the market, and economic disorder is only momentary; soon competition leads to a uniformly efficient, profit-maximizing pattern of production. In the late nineteenth century, when economic theory assumed the outlines of its present form, it drew extensively on the physics of the day.[1]

The nineteenth-century equilibrium model explains many phenomena very well, and remains an important theoretical tool. Yet at the same time that economics has focused on ever greater refinements of this model, the natural sciences have explored alternative models that have the power to explain other phenomena. Some disturbances are more than temporary; some systems do not move inexorably toward equilibrium. To cite one important example, a rapidly flowing fluid can become and remain turbulent. The patterns of turbulence, as seen in rapids on a river, are qualitatively familiar, but essentially impossible to predict in detail. The earth's weather, a system of often turbulent air flows, displays the same combination of familiarity in general and unpredictability in detail.

The field of chaos theory emerged, at first accidentally, out of mathematical models of the weather. Assumptions that differed only slightly from those of traditional equilibrium models seemed to offer a better description of the weather—and turned out to imply very different patterns of behavior. In the new models, small disturbances did not always dissolve into equilibrium. In fact, different small disturbances led, over time, to very large differences in ultimate outcomes. Rhetorically, this became known as the butterfly effect: a butterfly flapping its wings could in theory cause a thunderstorm on the other side of the globe.

Chaos theory flourished in the 1980s, and has now been applied in many physical and biological sciences. Graphically, its results are displayed in the bizarre complexity of fractals, where small changes in a few simple equations can cover the computer screen with entirely new pictures of spirals, waves, and endlessly unfolding intricacies. Evidence of chaos has also been found in economics. For example, some analysts have claimed to see fractal patterns in stock market prices, an area as notoriously unpredictable as the weather.

More broadly speaking, the possibility of chaos can be taken as a mathematical metaphor for turbulent times. The small changes in underlying assumptions that turn equilibrium into chaos are just as plausible in economics as in any scientific field. The discipline of economics has long confronted messy, unpredictable reality with tidy abstractions; now it appears that the unfailing neatness of theoretical outcomes is due to the use of nineteenth century rather than twentieth century physics as a source of inspiration. In those cases where economic reality is intrinsically chaotic and unpredictable, modern theoretical models can be readily adjusted to match.

A specific application to the question of technology choice will soon reveal the point of this digression. The butterfly effect should, according to standard economic theory, be impossible to observe in the marketplace; competition should lead to the adoption of the most efficient technologies, unaffected by small amounts of initial wing-flapping. A classic counterexample presented by economic historian Paul David begins not with a butterfly, but perhaps with a typewriter salesman flapping his arms more than a century ago.[2]

David explores the persistence of the common computer (formerly typewriter) keyboard layout, often called "QWERTY" after the sequence of letters in the top row on the left. It has been known at least since the 1940s that alternative key arrangements lead to much greater productivity in typing, yet there has been no discernable movement toward adoption of these alternatives. The QWERTY layout was one of several competing options in the 1870s and 1880s, at the dawn of the typewriter era. In the 1890s it gained a slight lead in market share, and was unshakably entrenched before the turn of the century.

Once QWERTY was securely in the lead, it could never be budged. Neither monopoly power nor coercion was needed; the market made it in everyone's interest to perpetuate QWERTY. Since it was already the most popular option, every new typist maximized employment opportunities by learning QWERTY rather than any other key arrangement. Every employer of typists likewise maximized the available pool of employees he could draw on by sticking with QWERTY. Decentralized, competitive market processes thus locked everyone into use of an obviously inferior technology, a pattern which has survived throughout the twentieth century.

The mechanism that allows this persistence of suboptimal technology has been analyzed in theoretical terms by Brian Arthur.[3] He develops a general model of the technological "lock-in" process seen in the QWERTY example. The model challenges standard economic theory only on one crucial point: the assumption of decreasing returns. That is, economists usually assume that the more there already is of something, the less profitable it becomes to have even more of it. The first gourmet ice cream shop in a neighborhood will make the biggest profits; as competitors appear in the neighborhood, the market will become sated and profits per scoop or per shop will decline.

The QWERTY story depends on exactly the opposite situation (i.e., increasing returns). The more that other people use QWERTY, the more desirable it is for you to use it as well. The same is true of more than the keyboard; the existence of increasing returns characterizes the whole process of choice of computer hardware and software. Few of us are willing to be the only person in town using a particular computer or word processing program, no matter how powerful, elegant, or cheap it might be. The more that you use the same hardware and software as everyone else, the more easily you can draw on other people's skills and experience, exchange information with co-workers, and transfer your own knowledge from one computer to another.

Arthur demonstrates that "lock-in" results when there are increasing returns to adoption of a technology and when individual choices, once made, are difficult to reverse. Under these conditions, sooner or later one option will gain an unchallengeable lead, and move steadily toward a 100% market share. Small events can make a big difference in Arthur's model: an early head start in adoptions can lead to lock-in of a suboptimal technology such as QWERTY. Arthur suggests that the technologies used for U.S. nuclear power plants and for automobile engines may also be examples of lock-in to inferior techniques of production.

The image of chaos as a turbulent, fluid process may not seem appropriate for something as resistant to change as the QWERTY keyboard, or technological lock-in in general. Perhaps more fitting is the variant or successor to chaos theory, known as "complexity theory." The newer theory, of which Arthur has been a leading proponent, focuses on the ways in which simple processes can give rise to long-lasting, complex structures. The relationship between chaos and complexity is a close one; complexity may often appear at the boundary between smooth and chaotic behavior.[4] Both chaos and complexity have similarly unsettling implications for standard economic theory.

Returning to the discussion of recycling, are the conditions for technological lock-in present in the history of material use? Evidence of increasing returns in industrial production can be seen in the frequent discussion of "learning curves": the more experience a company has had with a particular technology, the lower its costs will be. Once an industry has started down the learning curve for one method of production, it will be inclined to reject untried alternatives. Existing techniques, with the benefit of experience, may be cheaper than the start-up phase of an alternative—even if, with comparable levels of experience, the new alternative would cost less.

Logging, mining, refining, and processing of virgin materials have a head start of a century or more over recycling and processing of secondary materials. The shared engineering and technical knowledge and the labor force experience found in these industries may well create increasing returns to adoption of the leading technologies. Government subsidies to extractive industries have been much larger in the past than they are today. So even though current subsidies are relatively unimportant, the history of subsidies may have helped establish the profitability of virgin material extraction, allowing or promoting lock-in to material-intensive techniques of production.

For example, in the late nineteenth century the paper industry switched rapidly from rags and other recycled fibers to virgin wood pulp as its preferred raw material (see Chapter 1). This change appeared to cut costs and allow much more efficient production: the price of newspaper dropped from 25 cents per pound in the early 1860s to two cents per pound in 1897.[5] However, prices fell in part because the industry had to pay the real cost of collection of rags, but obtained wood for almost nothing.

A series of nineteenth century federal laws and land grant policies transferred huge areas of the public domain into private hands for little or no payment.[6] Timber and paper companies were among the principal beneficiaries of this generous privatization program. Some of the generosity may have been accidental: land developers and speculators filed countless fraudulent homesteading claims, and found large loopholes in laws that purported to regulate the use of mining claims, swamps, and other lands. Large parts of the federal largesse, though, were indisputably intentional—land grants to railroads represented more than 9% of the area of the continental United States. The railroads worked closely with timber companies, often selling them large parts of their land grants at modest prices; the two industries were bound together by interlocking boards of directors and other business ties.

It is easy to imagine a more socially and ecologically conscious land management policy, involving a more conservation-oriented approach to forest management—and resulting in a much higher market price for wood. How much difference would that hypothetical alternative have made to the evolution of the paper industry? Even with higher wood prices and careful forest regulation, the industry might still have diversified into wood-based paper production, in response to the shortage of rags. If wood had been more expensive, however, its economic advantage over rags as a raw material would have been less compelling. The industry might have chosen to keep its options open by maintaining and expanding both papermaking techniques, rather than almost entirely dropping the old in favor of the new.[7] Then, in addition to the refinement of wood-based paper technology, there might have been a parallel development of more modern systems of recycled fiber collection and processing throughout the twentieth century.

Instead, there has now been more than a hundred years of development of techniques and experience in making paper from wood, combined with, until recently, a very limited role for recycled material. Significant retooling is required for modern paper mills to make increased use of recycled paper, and in the 1980s the industry initially resisted the demand for paper with high recycled content, arguing that it was unaffordably expensive. The spread of state mandates for recycled content in paper products, as well as growing consumer demand, ultimately led to the necessary retooling in many mills. But we will never know how much more easily and efficiently paper and other fibers could have been recycled if a different set of prices had prevailed during the hundred-year logging binge.

Political forces inevitably shape the choices made by the market. A century ago, the era of the robber barons pushed the market in one direction, toward exploitation of virgin raw materials that appeared almost free for the taking. Today, the era of recycling is beginning to push in the opposite direction, but with a disadvantage caused by the passage of time. Weaknesses in the current market position of recycling reflect, in part, how far we have come down the learning curves for virgin material production. Secondary material production might become similarly efficient if given an equal opportunity to grow.

However, as with the QWERTY keyboard, the technology that achieved an early lock-in could persist indefinitely—if it were sustainable. The sense of urgency about developing alternatives to extensive virgin material exploitation and landfilling comes from the belief that current patterns of resource use cannot be continued indefinitely. And the question of long-term sustainability moves beyond the market in another direction.

Buy Now, Pay Later

Among the factors motivating recycling is the idea that resource conservation is essential for economic sustainability. Suppose that future generations are entitled to resources allowing them to achieve at least our level of well-being; this provides a vague but sufficient definition of sustainability. How can the needs of the future be incorporated into contemporary economic decisionmaking? The question has frequently been raised in connection with the threat of global climate change, a well-known case in which actions taken today can produce effects that last for a long time. The use of fossil fuels, for example, releases carbon dioxide, a greenhouse gas, into the atmosphere, where it persists for decades. The result will be a gradual change in climate; the damages will mount slowly, but will be severe a century or more from now. No mechanism forces any balancing of the current benefits of fuel consumption against the future costs. In fact, the standard approach to near-future decisions breaks down when applied to far-future events, showing the need for new theoretical departures.

The standard approach is easily explained. There are many situations where current benefits lead to costs in the near future. If benefits and costs are both expressed in monetary terms, there is little ambiguity about how to compare them. Buy something now with a credit card or a bank loan, and you have to pay the money back with interest. The interest rate establishes the connection between present and future; it is the cost of enjoying your purchase now instead of later.

The same is true, indirectly, if you buy something with money you already have in the bank. Buying now means losing the interest you would have received on the money in your bank account. If a bank pays you 5 % interest, then every $1.00 that you leave in the bank brings you

$1.05 next year. As a result, you could say that $1.05 a year from now is worth the same amount to you as $1.00 today. You could use this fact to "discount" income or expenses that you anticipate a year from now: divide next year's amounts by 1.05 to find out how much they are worth today. The interest rate used in the calculation, 5%, is also referred to as the "discount rate."

Economists and business analysts constantly use this technique of discounting to evaluate projects with costs and benefits stretched over several years. Discounting is easily extended beyond one year: continuing the same example, $1.00 today is worth the same amount as about $1.10 two years from now (actually a fraction of a cent more, thanks to compound interest). To discount income or expenses that will arrive two years from now, divide by 1.05 twice. For transactions three years away, divide three times—or more concisely, divide by $(1.05)^3$.

The result of the discounting calculation (i.e., the value today) is called the "present value" of a future amount. To evaluate a project with costs now and benefits later, or vice versa, just compare the present values. An investment that costs $100 and yields $104 next year is not worth making, since the present value of the benefit, $104/1.05, is about $99, less than the cost. You would be better off putting $100 in the bank.

The process of discounting future amounts should not be confused with correcting for inflation. Interest rates are almost always higher than the rate of inflation. Suppose, with the interest rate at 5%, that the rate of inflation is 2%. Then $1.00 today buys the same amount of goods as $1.02 next year. But buying an object a year later is less valuable than buying it now, due to the lost year of enjoyment. That is why $1.00 today has the same value as $1.05 next year; leave the money in the bank and you can buy 3% more stuff next year, as the reward for waiting. In this example, 3% is the "real," "constant-dollar," or "inflation-adjusted" interest rate (all three terms mean the same thing). Economic analyses spanning many years frequently use inflation-adjusted prices and interest rates, to facilitate a focus on the real, underlying costs.

For economic decisions whose consequences span one or a few decades, discounting and calculation of present values are indispensable. For longer-term environmental issues, however, the same techniques yield nonsensical results. The problem is only in part that environmental costs and benefits may be hard to express in monetary terms (a subject taken up in the next section of this chapter). Even if monetary values for environmental outcomes are agreed upon, discounting has a disturbing tendency to show that the right response to long-term environmental risks is to eat, drink, burn fossil fuels, and be merry. The present value of the far future looks too small to worry about.

A calculator exercise serves to illustrate the paradox. Suppose that the value of a human life will always be $10 million, or 10^7, in constant dollars, somewhat more than the values currently proposed in the rather cold-blooded field of risk analysis. And suppose that the earth's population will stabilize at 10 billion, or 10^{10} people. Then the value of all human life on earth will be 10^{17}. If the real discount rate is 3% per year, then the present value of all human life 1325 years from now is less than $1.00.

That is, if you were given the opportunity to prevent the certain death of everyone on earth in the year 3325 by spending a dollar today, it would not be economically rational to do so. The logic of discounting implies that you could instead invest your dollar in something that, after 1325 years of compound interest, would be worth more than all human life. (At higher real discount rates, the epoch when the present value of 10 billion human lives is less than a dollar arrives sooner: just over 800 years from now at 5%, or less than 600 years at 7%.) This result is at once perfectly logical and perfectly absurd, proving the need for a rethinking of the economic treatment of the far future.

The resolution of the paradox is that discounting works for the near future because it is legitimate to assume that the same individual is evaluating costs and benefits now and later. However, as the time period under consideration stretches beyond a lifetime, current and future costs and benefits will not be evaluated by the same individuals. No one agent will experience both the costs incurred today and the benefits that will be enjoyed 100 years from now, let alone 1325 years. There is no one who personally can make the trade-off implied by the mathematical procedure of discounting over a century or more. Discounting is a single-observer, single-lifetime procedure, and is not necessarily meaningful for decisions spanning multiple generations.

If discounting does not apply to the welfare of future generations, then we are forced to fall back on an approach that comes naturally to many noneconomists: deciding, on ethical grounds, what we choose to leave to our descendants. We may feel that we have an essential human obligation to leave to the future a natural and built environment at least as healthy and plentiful as that which we received from the past. But there is no proof that shows this approach to be superior to any other, no formula that shows what the future needs.

The limits to objective calculation in this area are revealed particularly clearly by the work of economists Richard Howarth and Richard Norgaard.[8] They demonstrate that nonmarket decisions about the future are inescapable even between one generation and the next, let alone across centuries or millennia. Howarth and Norgaard construct a theoretical model of resource allocation between two overlapping generations, and prove that today's market prices depend on the property rights of the next generation, or equivalently, on the resources that one generation leaves to the next. Any change in the rights or resources available to future generations produces a different "optimal" market outcome today.

The more of the world's finite supply of oil that is left to future generations, for example, the less that is available today, and the higher today's price will be. This means that current market prices, interest rates, and discount rates cannot be used to determine how much to provide for the future. According to Howarth and Norgaard, causation flows the other way: current market prices depend on the logically prior, nonmarket decisions that we implicitly or explicitly make about what will be left to future generations. If we choose to leave more oil to our children, today's market price is higher; if we leave them less, today's price is lower.

There would be no problem of sustainable material use, and no need to leave anything in particular to later generations, if we could rely on a steady stream of new technologies to save us from all future resource scarcities. Many past scarcities have been overcome by the development of substitute materials; will a new *deus ex machina* emerge in time, every time? One alternative is to dismiss the problem by betting the future on the continuing success of technology. There are contemporary advocates of this approach, as will be seen in Chapter 10. More cautious approaches require us to make choices about the resources we will leave to our descendants—for example, by recycling.

Looking backward, the market cannot tell us how much our pattern of resource use is due to lock-in to the technological choices of an earlier, environmentally unconscious era. Looking forward, the market cannot tell us how much we should leave to the future, but merely reflects the values we hold and the choices we make today. The third and final examination of issues beyond the market considers the scope of inherently nonmarket environmental values in more general terms.

The Limits to Environmental Valuation

Does every value have a price? Is every public policy decision an outcome that would be reached by the market under some suitably adjusted set of prices? The affirmative answer to these questions is often taken for granted in academic and policy debates today. Yet it is impossible, from that perspective, to make sense of the commitment and beliefs that motivate recycling and many other environmental initiatives. A more promising approach is provided by several authors who have explored the limits to markets and environmental valuation.

The philosopher Mark Sagoff draws a distinction between our roles as citizens and as consumers. The two roles involve different realms of discourse. Proposals to open national parks to commercial ski resort development can be opposed by citizens who would nonetheless, as consumers, enjoy skiing there if development occurred. Citizen preferences are judgments about what we collectively should do, while consumer preferences are expressions of what an individual wants. Neither is reducible to the other.[9]

For Sagoff, the rights of future generations are not a separate issue, but an area where we must make judgments as citizens today. Almost any current decision could be justified as responding to the needs of some imaginable future population. Moreover, actions taken today help create a future in our own image, with people whose wants will resemble our own. The balance we strike between industry and wilderness will shape the preferences of our descendants, not simply respond to them. In short, we transmit values as well as resources to the future: "What is worth saving is not merely what can be consumed later; it is what we can take pride in and, indeed, love."[10]

The worth of things that matter most to us, such as love and religion, are measured not by our willingness to pay for them, but by our unwillingness to pay. Such things, Sagoff suggests, have a dignity rather than a price. It is ultimately the dignity of our natural and cultural heritage, not any calculation of quantifiable costs and benefits, that explains environmental objectives such as the preservation of national parks.

A related point has been made by the economist Fred Hirsch, who asserts that the process of turning things into marketed commodities can alter and degrade our enjoyment of them. Some things are changed for the worse by the mere fact of having a price put on them; what we experience outside the market often cannot be reproduced within it. Consensual, noncommercialized sex, Hirsch points out, seems to most people to be inherently different from prostitution. To quote his final words on the subject, "Orgasm as a consumer's right rather rules it out as an ethereal experience."[11]

Much the same could be said of buying votes at election time, which, like prostitution, is usually illegal but by no means unknown. One could survey voters about the price at which they would sell their votes;

some would give meaningful answers, from which a market price could be constructed. But the economy would not work better if that price was "internalized" through an overt, legitimate market for votes. Rather, fraud would have violated the basic norms of society, and something important would have been lost.

The analogy to environmental values is easily drawn. One could sensibly claim that environmental goals embody essential, perhaps "ethereal," human experiences, which, like consensual sex, are corrupted by being bought and sold—or that environmental standards embody basic social norms which, like electoral participation, are undermined by being bought and sold. In either case, we as citizens have to decide on the limits within which we will allow ourselves, as consumers, to buy and sell. The environmental objectives we pursue through recycling lie, in large part, outside those limits.

The argument that there are inherent limits to market valuation is also raised, in language more familiar to environmental economists, by Arild Vatn and Daniel Bromley. They maintain that "valuing (or pricing) environmental goods and services is neither necessary nor sufficient for *coherent and consistent choices about the environment*."[12] Valuation studies—surveys conducted by economists to find the dollar values that people would place on specific environmental costs or benefits—fail to produce meaningful environmental prices for at least three reasons.

In the first place, when asked by economists to put a price on an aspect of the environment, people may have trouble understanding the question. Most people do not understand the multiplicity of values provided by complex, interdependent ecosystems, and certainly have not thought about them in monetary terms. A survey is likely to make people confront the issue for the first time; it may therefore be constructing, rather than discovering, the respondents' valuations. Second, individuals may resent or reject the premise of the survey. Questions such as extinction of species are often viewed in moral terms; the attempt to elicit monetary valuations of moral issues may produce meaningless answers.

Finally, valuation imposes the "commodity fiction" on individual aspects of the environment, as if environmental goods and services could be exchanged at the margin and consumed in discrete units. In fact, many environmental functions are indivisible and must be provided or maintained in fixed proportion to each other, rendering any prices less meaningful. Surveys that artificially separate aspects of the environment often place a much higher value on spectacular big animals than on the muddy wetlands and humbler species that are crucial to the survival of the spectacle—but this does not provide useful information about how to value and preserve the ecosystem as a whole.

Environmental policymaking, as seen by Vatn and Bromley, often involves setting the norms and contexts within which individual preferences can be weighed—requiring our judgments as citizens before we can act as consumers, in Sagoff's terms. Conflict over the policy context, the clash of proposed rights and entitlements, must be resolved before preferences and valuations can be assigned. Formation of judgments about rights and social norms is in part an inherently social process, and cannot be fully comprehended in surveys of individual opinion and preference.

A final voice in this chorus of critiques examines the motives for consumer behavior. Just as some values cannot be reduced to prices, some decisions that individuals make cannot be reduced to self-interested consumer choice. In a discussion of the nature of consumer choice and behavior, Amartya Sen uses refillable bottles as an example to illustrate the possibility of alternative motivations for the same decision.[13] Suppose, says Sen, that using and returning a refillable glass bottle for soft drinks is better for the environment but less convenient for the individual than a throw-away can, and the deposit on the glass bottle is not sufficient to motivate returns. Why might a consumer still use and return glass bottles? At least four different answers are possible.

First, the consumer may simply like glass bottles, or may believe (probably incorrectly) that he himself will directly benefit from the environmental gains due to his own recycling. This case, the least plausible, involves recycling for personal, though nonpriced, gain. Second, the consumer may worry about the welfare of others, and use and return glass bottles because he feels better when the environment is better for everyone. In this case, there are positive externalities (nonmarket benefits to others) from recycling; if these externalities were internalized, perhaps through a larger deposit, the market could lead to the right outcome.

It is more difficult to capture the remaining two cases through the market mechanism. Third, the consumer may be afraid of the social stigma attached to doing the wrong thing, or afraid that others will emulate him and worsen the environment if he uses disposable cans. Such issues of social stigma and emulation do not fit well within standard economics; rather, they recall Thorstein Veblen, an iconoclastic economist of a century ago, and his analyses of conspicuous consumption. Fourth, even if the consumer thinks that as a "free rider" he could enjoy both the environmental benefits of everyone else's recycling and the convenience of personally using throw-aways, he may still feel a responsibility to recycle. The latter case, which particularly interests Sen, involves social norms that cannot be reduced to individual market choices. Even when the calculation of individual costs and benefits clearly points in one direction, feelings of social responsibility may override that calculation.

The decision to use refillable bottles is, for Sen, only a pedagogical example of his general point about the importance of behavior based on social norms. But it is an appropriate example, shedding further light on the reasons for recycling. Not only the benefits of recycling, but also the behavior motivated by those benefits, require a broader explanatory framework than the paradigm of private market choice.

⊛ ⊛ ⊛

This chapter has traveled far beyond the limits of conventional economic analysis. If current levels of virgin material use reflect historical events and learning curves rather than underlying efficiency; if the market is fundamentally incapable of making decisions about sustainability and the resource needs of future generations; if environmental values are indivisible, unmeasurable, or inherently degraded by being treated as commodities; if recycling reflects social norms rather than individual market choices—then there are ample grounds for interpreting recycling, and other environmental pursuits, in ethical and political terms that involve much more than the market.

The escape from economics is, alas, only partial. However much recycling raises ethereal, eternal, and ethical questions, it also exists in the ordinary world of budget cuts and competition. Municipal officials, if no one else, must constantly ask how much recycling costs, here and now. It is almost impossible to pin down an answer, for very practical as well as philosophical reasons, as explained in the next chapter.

Notes

1. For a thorough but dense presentation of the influence of physics on economics, see Philip Mirowski, *More Heat Than Light* (New York: Cambridge University Press, 1989).

2. Paul A. David, "Clio and the Economics of QWERTY," *American Economic Review*, Vol. 75, No. 2 (1985).

3. W. Brian Arthur, "Competing Technologies, Increasing Returns, and Lock-in by Historical Events," *Economic Journal*, Vol. 99, No. 1 (1989).

4. See, for example, M. Mitchell Waldrop, *Complexity* (New York: Simon & Schuster, 1992).

5. Judith McGaw, *Most Wonderful Machine: Mechanization and Social Change in Berkshire Paper Making, 1801–1885* (Princeton: Princeton University Press, 1987), p. 203.

6. Roger Geller, *Wasted Forests: The Virgin U.S. Paper Industry and the Federal Policies that Support It,* Masters thesis, Tufts University, 1990, Chapter 3.

7. Use of rags and wastepaper never completely vanished, and remained important at times when demand for paper was growing most rapidly; see Martin Melosi, *Garbage in the Cities: Refuse, Reform, and the Environment, 1880–1980* (College Station, Texas: Texas A&M University Press, 1981), pp. 183–184. But Melosi's account suggests that by World War I, if not earlier, virgin paper production from wood was viewed as the norm, and recycled paper production was the supplemental or backup technique.

8. Richard Howarth and Richard Norgaard, "Intergenerational Transfers and the Social Discount Rate," *Journal of Environmental and Resource Economics,* Vol. 3 (1993), pp. 337–358, and other papers cited there.

9. Mark Sagoff, *The Economy of the Earth* (Cambridge: Cambridge University Press, 1988).

10. Sagoff, *Economy of the Earth,* p. 63.

11. Fred Hirsch, *Social Limits to Growth* (Cambridge: Harvard University Press, 1976), Chapter 6 and Appendix. The quote is from p. 101.

12. Arild Vatn and Daniel W. Bromley, "Choices without Prices without Apologies," *Journal of Environmental Economics and Management,* Vol. 26, No. 1 (1994). The quote is from p. 131, italics in original.

13. Amartya Sen, "Behavior and the Concept of Preference," *Economica,* Vol. 40 (1973), especially p. 255.

CHAPTER 4

A Truck Is a Terrible Thing to Waste

While there are many good reasons to recycle, there are many bad ways of going about it. Consider the following two (true) stories. What, if anything, is wrong with these pictures?

First, a college town in the Midwest—it would be cruel to name names—has long been proud of its commitment to recycling. The town's planners knew that aluminum is a valuable material, and that curbside collection is often a sound strategy for recycling. So they assigned a truck to pick up aluminum cans from households every two weeks. Nothing else, just aluminum cans. Collecting only a small quantity of material, the truck's average collection cost came to $1800 per ton of cans, more than ten times the cost of most curbside programs. Scrap aluminum is worth a lot, but not $1800 per ton. Thus the town accomplished something that few other communities have done: it consistently lost money on recycling aluminum, the most valuable of common waste materials.

Second, the greater Toronto area, home to about one out of every ten Canadians, was desperately short of landfill space in the early 1990s. There were, of course, vast, sparsely populated spaces to the north of Toronto; there were also landfill operators in nearby parts of the United States who were willing to take Toronto's garbage. However, Ontario's environmental policy at that time called for every region of the province to make local provision for its own waste disposal needs. Despite ambitious recycling programs, the eastern, central, and western sections of greater Toronto were each required to build a massive new landfill to handle their remaining waste. This was far more expensive than shipping the waste out of the metropolitan area. The landfill proposals provoked intense controversy, but the critics did not challenge the idea of local responsibility for waste; instead, they proposed even greater levels of recycling and composting, and processing of mixed waste to reduce the need for disposal capacity.

Both stories might appear to involve needlessly expensive strategies for waste management. The expenses arise for different reasons, however, and only the first is unambiguously needless. The college town made a simple technical or planning mistake (which it has since corrected). Driving up and down the streets and stopping at each house is expensive, and a recycling truck must collect much more than aluminum cans at each stop to have a reasonable cost per ton. In this case, the town's objectives can be met far more cheaply with a better-designed program.

Ontario, on the other hand, was committed to a principle of local responsibility for the environment. It may seem remarkable to demand that the waste from one-tenth of Canada's population be handled within a minuscule fraction of Canada's land area. But it is only remarkable because we are used to the absence of local responsibility for waste, and to the availability of remote rural land for waste disposal. Ontario's policy was a comprehensible statement of principle, a political choice rather than a planning mistake. The "obvious" cheaper alternatives would have violated the province's objectives.

This is not to say that Ontario's statement of principles eliminated economic conflict and debate. Quite the contrary: local responsibility for disposal meant that more was at stake in the details of planning for waste management. An alliance of grassroots organizations fought vigorously against the proposed Toronto-area landfills, and hired a team of expert consultants (myself included) to argue the case that there were affordable local alternatives to massive new landfills.

Before the case reached its conclusion, however, a more conservative provincial government was elected in 1995. The new administration repealed the requirement of local provision for waste disposal, and the proposed landfills were left on the drawing boards. This, too, was a public choice about the environment, a change in objectives rather than a correction of a technical error. Toronto's landfill crisis vanished as a result of change in the political context, not technical improvements or the construction of new facilities.

Computing the Costs of Curbside Recycling

It is easy to spot some of the glaring mistakes in recycling, such as the truck that collected only aluminum. It is surprisingly difficult, however, to answer the next question that naturally arises: if mistakes are avoided, how much does a well-run recycling program cost? As seen in the story of Toronto, recycling does not exist in a political vacuum: a city that faces a local landfill crisis or other constraints on disposal will adopt a much more extensive and expensive recycling program than a community with ample disposal capacity. Nor does recycling exist in a stable, predictable economic environment. Regardless of the level and techniques of recycling selected by a community, the continual changes in the markets for scrap materials frustrate all attempts to calculate a "bottom line" for recycling.

Nonetheless, in a budget-conscious era, municipal officials must constantly try to estimate what their recycling programs will cost. At Tellus Institute, in response to requests from numerous state and local agencies, we created the WastePlan© computer model to perform the required cost calculations. Given a description of a community and its waste management system, the model simulates the costs of many different recycling options. The best possible software cannot, however, create certainty in an uncertain world.

To see how much is known about recycling costs and how much cannot be pinned down, consider the situation of a community that has municipal garbage collection and disposal, but initially has no recycling program. Will its waste management costs go up or down when it begins recycling? Curbside recycling will make five things happen to waste management costs:

The volume of garbage is reduced by recycling, so

(1) Garbage collection costs may decline.

(2) Garbage disposal costs are almost certain to decline.

The introduction of recycling itself implies that

(3) There are new costs for recycling collection.

(4) There are new costs for processing the collected recyclables.

(5) Revenues will be received from the sale of recycled materials.

The first two, the savings in garbage collection and disposal, are often called "avoided costs"—savings that result from not incurring costs—in contrast to the remaining three categories, which are direct costs and benefits of recycling.

Reasonably stable and reliable estimates can be calculated, we will see below, for the first four of the five categories. The last one, however, is

erratic and unpredictable, requiring continual revisions in any estimates of the overall cost of recycling. (At this point, the reader who is
not interested in the details of the first four categories can get to the
punch line more quickly by skipping ahead to the heading, "The Predictable Elements of Recycling Costs: A Summary," on page 70.)

The first and third of the cost categories, garbage and recycling collection, involve the strange economics of collection trucks. Here the
costs depend primarily on time spent in collection, which turns out to
have little to do with the quantity of material picked up from each
household.

The dominant elements of collection costs—wages and truck purchases—may both be thought of as hourly costs. This is clear in the case
of wages; for truck purchases, it is often assumed that a new vehicle has
a predictable operating lifetime. A $100,000 truck that was expected to
last for 10,000 hours of collection could be said to cost $10 per hour.
Smaller costs such as fuel and maintenance can also be viewed as
hourly costs of operation. So once the type of truck, number of workers
per truck, and wage rate have been chosen, the costs per truck-hour are
fixed. The more truck-hours that collection takes, the more it costs.

The time required for curbside collection depends very directly on
the number and location of the households being served; changes in the
volume of waste per household have much smaller effects. To see why
this is the case, imagine a day in the life of a garbage truck (the story
would be very similar for a recycling truck). The steps that depend on
the volume picked up from each household are shown in italics.

- Workers arrive at the garage, and drive the truck to the beginning of the
  collection route.
- At each stop the workers:
    get off the truck;
    pick up the bags or cans;
    put the garbage into the truck;
    return the empty cans to the curb;
    get back on the truck;
    and drive to the next stop.
- When the truck is full, usually once or twice a day, it is driven to the dis-
  posal site, where it is emptied.
- At the end of the day, the workers return the truck to the garage.

Even the steps shown in italics are not strictly proportional to the
quantity of trash per household; an average of 10 % less garbage would
not mean 10 % fewer bags or cans, nor would it require 10 % less time

to pick up the waste and toss it into the truck. However, the italicized steps, in which workers actually handle the waste, are the only ones that are affected by the quantity collected from each household. The other steps—getting on and off the truck, driving between stops, driving to and from the disposal site and garage, and emptying the truck—must be done once a day in any case, and consume most of the day. These steps have everything to do with the location of the stops, and nothing to do with how much is picked up at each one. (One partial exception to this pattern is the frequency with which the truck must be emptied. If enough material is picked up, the truck may have to make an additional daily trip to the disposal site. But small changes in the quantity collected will not usually affect the number of truck loads per day.)

With this understanding of collection trucks in mind, let us turn to the five categories of cost impacts of recycling, beginning with the two types of avoided costs.

The Meager Benefits of Avoided Costs

Recycling advocates often believe that they are saving money by reducing the need for garbage collection and disposal. That is, they assume that avoided costs play a major part in the economics of recycling programs. In much of the United States, however, the role of avoided costs is actually quite small.

Avoided garbage collection costs, in fact, are nonexistent in many communities. Recycling saves some time in garbage collection, although the percentage of time saved is much smaller than the percentage of waste recycled. However, small reductions in garbage collection time may be hard to translate into monetary savings. Suppose, for example, that recycling results in garbage trucks all finishing their daily routes 30 minutes earlier than before. This extra 30 minutes of free time may not lower the costs of recycling to the taxpayers. If, as a result of contracts or custom, workers get paid for full days of a fixed length, then slightly shorter collection routes may still require the same number of workers.

That is, costs may be roughly proportional to collection time, but "lumpy." Labor costs of garbage collection may not decline until it becomes possible to reduce the number of trucks and crews. The bigger the city, and the higher the recycling rate, the more likely it is that this goal can be achieved. In a city with 20 trucks, for example, a 5% reduction in garbage collection time (which would require much more than 5% recycling) would allow one truck to be retired, or not replaced when it wore out. The workers who accompanied that truck could then be reassigned to the recycling program. There would be no net loss of jobs; recycling collection creates more jobs than are lost in garbage collection.

In small towns, it is unlikely that recycling will reduce the number of trucks or collection workers that are needed. In general, collection schedules may be less flexible in smaller municipalities that employ fewer garbage trucks. A study done by Barbara Stevens in the 1970s found that there were economies of scale in garbage collection—that is, costs per household decreased as the size of the community increased— up to a population of 50,000, or roughly equivalently, up to the point where the town needs 5 garbage trucks.[1] Stevens attributed much of the economies of scale to the difficulties of efficiently scheduling and utilizing equipment, including a backup truck, in smaller communities.

In larger cities, there may be significant savings in garbage collection costs due to recycling. According to Peter Anderson, a consultant based in Madison, Wisconsin, the introduction of curbside recycling and a yard waste diversion program allowed Madison to cut back from 26 to 20 garbage trucks, even though the city's population grew by more than 12% in the same period. Since the city was also able to switch to a different, cheaper model of garbage trucks, the per capita garbage collection cost dropped by a remarkable 37%.[2] Although Anderson argues that many communities can achieve similar savings with careful planning, the Madison experience appears to be based on a fortuitous combination of circumstances (not only the beginning of curbside recycling, but also the diversion of yard waste and the option of buying cheaper trucks). Other communities, unfortunately, have not typically achieved cost reductions comparable to Madison's.

An estimate of typical garbage collection costs can be obtained from a recent study, also by Barbara Stevens, which surveyed a random sample of U.S. communities with populations greater than 25,000. She found that in 1993 the average annual cost of garbage collection was $68 per household in municipalities that had curbside recycling, versus $59 per household in towns that did not pick up recyclables.[3] Far from saving money, recycling appears to have added slightly to the cost of garbage collection. However, the difference is not statistically significant.[4]

The second avoided cost category, reductions in disposal costs due to recycling, is easier to analyze. It, too, is usually small. In most communities the municipal agency or private waste hauler that collects the garbage pays a landfill or incinerator for waste disposal by the ton. The price is referred to as the "tipping fee," or cost of tipping waste out of a garbage truck into the facility. In 1994, state average tipping fees at landfills ranged from $8 per ton in New Mexico to $75 in New Jersey, with a national average of \$31 per ton. Average incinerator tipping fees (in the states that have incinerators) ranged from \$20 per ton in Arkansas to \$90 in New Jersey, and were usually higher than landfill fees in the same state.[5]

The Stevens 1993 survey found that curbside recycling picked up an average of 0.22 tons of material per household per year. Keeping that amount of material out of landfills saves only about \$7 at the national average tipping fee. Even at New Jersey incinerator rates, recycling 0.22 tons of material would save only \$20 in disposal costs. The savings are larger, of course, for recycling programs that divert more waste than the average; and even though the per-household savings are modest, the city-wide totals are often important for municipal budgets.

There are at least two circumstances in which a town's avoided disposal costs from recycling are not equal to the per-ton cost at the relevant landfill or incinerator. On the one hand, some communities cannot reduce their disposal costs, as a result of so-called "put or pay" contracts with incinerators. Such contracts guarantee that the town will deliver and pay for at least a certain minimum quantity of waste; if waste deliveries fall short of the minimum, the town still has to pay the guaranteed amount. Put or pay contracts shift most of the risk associated with running an incinerator onto the towns that supply it. They also undermine the towns' incentives for waste reduction or recycling, by eliminating the possibility of savings from avoided disposal costs.

On the other hand, if a community is running out of landfill capacity and will soon need a new disposal facility, the benefits of avoiding disposal via recycling can be worth more than the current tipping fees. In densely populated areas, and in any area where there is strong opposition to new landfills, the next disposal facility will often be far more expensive than the last one. In that case, every ton of waste that goes into the old landfill not only incurs the low costs of operating the existing site; it also brings slightly closer the day when the old landfill will close and the massive investment in the new facility must be undertaken. Conversely, waste reduction or recycling postpones the new investment, as well as saving the costs of operating the old site.[6]

This issue has been particularly important in New York City, which currently sends most of its waste to the Fresh Kills municipal landfill on Staten Island. Reportedly the world's largest landfill, the 3000-acre Fresh Kills site is relatively inexpensive to operate, but will be filled and permanently closed in a decade or two—at which point the city will face vastly higher costs for any conceivable disposal alternative. New York City has sharply raised the Fresh Kills tipping fee for private waste haulers to reflect the anticipated costs of future disposal capacity. The fee increase has driven most private haulers to seek other disposal sites, preserving Fresh Kills' remaining capacity for use by the city's Sanitation Department. The city has also tried to initiate ambitious waste reduction, recycling, and composting programs, responding now to the disposal crisis lurking in the not-too-distant future, but this effort has been slowed by the impact of more immediate municipal budget crises. (In 1996, in response to demands from Staten Island residents, New York state and city officials promised to close Fresh Kills within five years. To be credible, this promise would have to be backed up by both increased funding and alternative disposal plans—neither of which was initially provided.)

For communities that face genuine landfill crises, a recycling program that delays the need for the next landfill or incinerator is valuable; the avoided disposal costs measure that value. However, most of the country is not about to run out of disposal capacity, and avoided disposal costs are correspondingly low. Far more important in most areas are the direct costs and benefits of recycling: the costs of collection and processing of recyclables, and the revenues from selling the processed materials.

The New Truck on the Block

Recycling trucks are governed by the same logic as garbage trucks: costs are dependent on the number and location of stops, but insensitive to moderate variations in the amount picked up at each stop. The basic expense of curbside collection, hiring workers and buying trucks sufficient to visit every household, must be incurred in order to pick up any recycled material—as seen in the town that collected nothing but aluminum cans. Adding the second type of material, or the third, adds nothing to the time spent driving up and down the streets.

In reality, it is not quite that easy to expand a recycling program. Collection of additional materials is not completely a free lunch, but the second helpings cost a lot less than the first. As more materials are added, the truck will fill up faster, and may have to make more frequent trips to the facility where it delivers its loads. However, the time and cost required for these trips are only a fraction of the overall collection effort.

Another cost of adding materials, in some programs, is increased sorting time. If collection workers sort the recyclables at the curb, putting them into the appropriate bins of a multi-compartment truck, then more materials require more time at each stop. To avoid spending time in curbside sorting, many programs only separate paper from all other materials, using a two-compartment truck, or collect all recyclables together, leaving the sorting to the facility where the materials are delivered.

With these qualifications, it remains true that trucks making house visits are expensive, and picking up as much as possible at each visit is generally desirable. The Stevens survey shows a mean cost for curbside recycling of $27 per household per year. Since a large part of this cost is incurred regardless of how much is collected, the cost per ton collected drops dramatically as the recycling rate increases, as seen in Table 4-1. In communities that recycled less than 10% of their waste, curbside recycling collection cost an average of $285 per ton. For recycling rates between 10% and 20%, the collection cost drops to $102 per ton, and for recycling rates over 20% the cost declines further to $93. Even with recycling rates around 20%, garbage collection remains cheaper per ton, since the garbage trucks still pick up much more material at each stop. However, Table 4-1 shows that the gap between the two rates closes as the recycling rate increases.

After recyclable materials are collected, they arrive at a sorting or processing facility. In small rural communities this can be as simple as a warehouse where materials are manually sorted into separate bins. Increasingly, however, recycling involves larger "material recovery facilities" (MRFs), which combine automated and manual sorting, perhaps some cleaning or processing, and baling or otherwise preparing materials for shipment to industries that will use them. If you bought any of the exotic machinery on sale at recycling conferences, this is where you would install it.

There is nothing like a standard design or cost for MRFs. The complexity, choice of equipment, and labor requirements all depend on factors such as the types and quantities of incoming materials, and the de-

Table 4-1
Recycling Rates and Collection Costs

| | Collection Costs (dollars per ton collected) | |
Percentage of Waste Recycled	Garbage Collection Costs	Recycling Collection Costs
0–9%	$42	$285
10–19%	$53	$102
20% +	$66	$93

Source: Barbara Stevens, "Recycling Collection Costs," *Resource Recycling,* September 1994, Table 4.

gree of sorting that occurs before the material reaches the MRF. There are important economies of scale in MRF construction and operation; facilities that are designed to handle less than 100 tons per day are much more expensive, per ton, than bigger ones.[7] A 100 tons-per-day facility might serve a population of 200,000 or more, showing the need for regional cooperation in recycling in all but the biggest cities. Cost estimates for processing recyclables at large MRFs are often around $40 to $50 per ton, though this can vary with the age, size, and technology of a specific facility.[8]

The Predictable Elements of Recycling Costs: A Summary

Of the five cost categories associated with a curbside recycling program, the first four have now been examined. Table 4-2 presents a summary of the discussion, using national average data. To recapitulate briefly:

(1) Garbage collection costs may go down as a result of recycling, particularly if the community is big enough and the recycling rate is high enough to allow transfer of trucks and workers from garbage collection to recycling. However, many communities are not at that point; it seems safer to assume zero savings in an average town's garbage collection.

(2) At the national average landfill tipping fee, every ton of recycling saves $31 in garbage disposal. Using Stevens' average of 0.22 tons of curbside recycling per household per year, this amounts to a $7 saving per household.

(3) Using the same tonnage of recycling, Stevens' $27 per household average cost of recycling collection is equivalent to $123 per ton of material.

(4) The techniques and costs of processing recycled materials vary

Table 4-2

Average Costs and Benefits of Recycling[a]

	Per Household per Year	Per Ton of Recyclables
1. Avoided garbage collection cost	$0	$0
2. Avoided garbage disposal cost	−$7	−$31
3. Recycling collection cost	$27	$123
4. Recycling processing cost	$11	$50
5. Recycling revenues	???	???
Total excluding revenue (items 1–4)	$31	$142

[a]Costs are positive; benefits are negative.

widely; $50 per ton is within the range of frequently cited cost estimates. It is equivalent to $11 per household.

The total cost, excluding recycling revenues, is thus $31 per household per year, or $142 per ton of recycled material. Note that this is a national average calculation, not necessarily applicable to any specific recycling program. Net costs of recycling will be lower in areas with higher disposal costs, since the disposal savings are worth more there. Higher recycling rates will also tend to lower costs, both by making it more likely that a community can save money in garbage collection and by reducing per-ton costs of recycling collection. On the other hand, net costs of recycling will be higher in areas where disposal costs or recycling rates are below average.

Although we have stopped for a summary of the costs of recycling, only four of the five categories have been discussed. The fifth, revenues from the sale of recycled materials, remains a line of question marks in Table 4-2. With the other lines filled in, it is possible to calculate the revenues needed for break-even: if prices paid by industry for recycled materials are higher than $142 per ton, under the average conditions shown in the table, then recycling saves money; if not, there is a net cost to the community. Even at zero revenue, recycling does not impose a crushing burden, costing each household $31 under average conditions. However, one would like to know how much of that $31 is likely to be offset by the revenues received by the recycling program.

Unfortunately, we have at this point completed the analysis of the predictable economic elements of recycling. If prices of recycled materials ever stop fluctuating wildly, it will be a dramatic change from recent history.

Scrap Markets and Commodity Futures

When materials leave a recycling facility, they enter the markets for scrap materials. The recent rise of recycling has expanded these markets, but did not create them. Scrap dealers have long been in the business of collecting materials and selling them to industry. Recycling programs will receive roughly the same prices for their materials as scrap dealers. In effect, municipalities that run recycling programs, or MRFs that process municipal recyclables, are forced to become scrap dealers themselves.

The markets for some scrap materials are well enough established that the federal Bureau of Labor Statistics (BLS) collects and publishes price data for them, as it does for many goods and services. Price indexes for four leading scrap materials—old corrugated cardboard, old newspaper, aluminum scrap, and iron and steel scrap—are shown in Figures 4-1 through 4-4. The graphs present monthly producer prices (formerly called wholesale prices) for each material from 1970 to 1995, in the form of indexes with the 1982 value arbitrarily set equal to 100.

The principal message of these graphs is that scrap prices are erratic and volatile. For the two paper products, prices were close to the 1982 level as recently as late 1993, then soared six (for newspaper) or eight (for cardboard) times higher by mid-1995, only to fall to twice the ear-

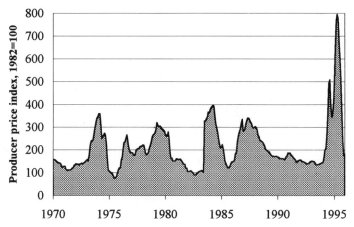

Figure 4-1
Price index for old corrugated cardboard. *Source:* Bureau of Labor Statistics.

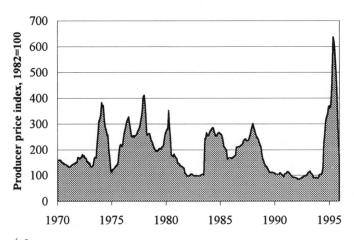

Figure 4-2
Price index for old newspaper. *Source:* Bureau of Labor Statistics.

lier level, or less, by the end of 1995. Aluminum prices "merely" doubled from 1993 to 1995, while iron and steel scrap rose by a piddling 50% or so.

Looking back at earlier years, the 1995 price spike was, in paper, the biggest ever, but hardly appears unique; wild ups and downs are the rule. In aluminum, several earlier price surges were even more dramatic than the events of 1995. The first major peak in all four graphs, in 1974–1975, was followed by a crash in prices that drove many early recycling programs out of business, as mentioned in Chapter 1. What ap-

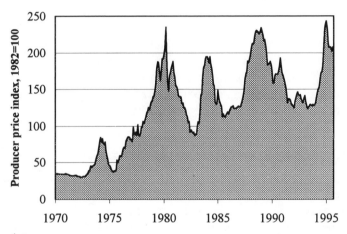

Figure 4-3
Price index for aluminum scrap. *Source:* Bureau of Labor Statistics.

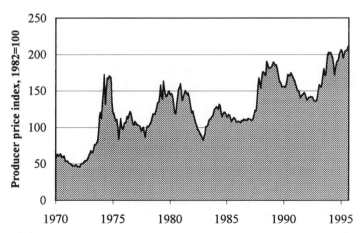

Figure 4-4
Price index for iron and steel scrap. *Source:* Bureau of Labor Statistics.

pears exceptional in the graphs is not the jagged peaks and valleys, but the relatively stable, low paper prices of 1990–1993.

The volatility of these graphs is not common to all price indexes; it is a remarkable feature of scrap prices in particular. For the sake of comparison, a fifth graph is included, from the same source, showing the producer price index for finished consumer goods. Its pattern is completely different, rising more rapidly in some years than in others, but showing none of the wild swings seen in scrap prices. The better-known consumer price index follows essentially the same pattern as Figure 4-5; a comparable graph of the consumer price index would be even smoother, eliminating most of the tiny wrinkles seen in the finished consumer goods index.

What accounts for the drama of scrap price fluctuations? Some, though not all, of the price changes match the business cycle of the U.S. economy: scrap prices are usually up when production is expanding, and down when unemployment is high and production is declining. Some industries prefer virgin materials, and turn to scrap markets only as a last resort when suppliers of virgin materials are unable to expand output fast enough to meet demand. This causes the surges in scrap prices toward the end of economic expansions, followed by crashes when recessions begin.

The story is made more complicated by the role of foreign markets; the United States is a major exporter of both paper and metal scrap. Thus business cycles in foreign countries that buy U.S. scrap will also affect prices. I have never understood why some recyclers view scrap

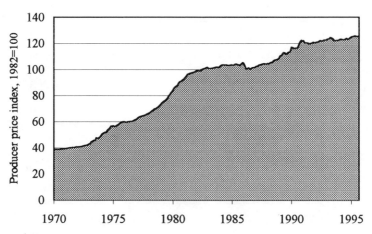

Figure 4-5
Price index for finished consumer goods. *Source:* Bureau of Labor Statistics.

exports as a sign of failure; U.S. recovered materials are just as capable of doing good for the environment abroad as at home. Mexico, a country where trees are certainly scarce, is one of the leading buyers of U.S. scrap paper. Is it any less desirable for our recycled newspaper and cardboard to be used in the Mexican paper industry, saving the dwindling supply of trees south of the border? Desirable or not, it means that the ups and downs of the Mexican economy are among the forces swaying U.S. scrap prices. The same is true for resource-poor East Asian countries such as Taiwan and South Korea, which are also important buyers of U.S. scrap materials.

Changes in scrap markets can also be caused by many other factors, including the progress of recycling in recent years. The low scrap prices of 1990–1993 reflect not only the recession in the U.S. economy, which lowered the demand for scrap, but also rapid growth in the supply of materials, as recycling programs spread across the country. In paper, where the low prices were most pronounced and prolonged, the industry was unprepared at first to use the increased supplies produced by municipal recycling efforts. Even after paper companies were persuaded to switch, in part by state laws mandating recycled content in newsprint and other paper products, several years were required for the sizeable investments in refitting paper mills to use more recycled paper. When the refitted mills began buying more scrap paper, after 1993, the prices took off.

Objective explanation, however, can take us only so far. Underlying causes do not move fast enough to explain all the price changes seen in the graphs. Lurking behind the surges in scrap paper prices in 1995, among others, there must be wilder tales to be told. One can easily imagine stories of speculative intrigue, misinformation, and panicked overreactions. In such a volatile market, fortunes can be won and lost in gambling on where the prices will come to rest.

The danger is that local recycling programs may find themselves among those whose fortunes are lost. Municipal public works and sanitation departments, traditionally the agencies responsible for waste management, are rarely skilled in commodity speculation; recyclers with backgrounds in environmental advocacy may not be much better. Yet completing the analysis of recycling, filling in the last line in the economic summary as shown in Table 4-2, seems to require an ability to predict the future of scrap prices.

One of the ways in which municipalities can lose is by signing long-term, fixed-price contracts when prices are low. Buyers of scrap materials offer, and, when they can, insist on such terms when the market is down. In 1993, just before prices exploded, New York City signed five-year, fixed-price contracts paying recycling companies $40 to $50 per ton to remove the metal, glass, and plastic containers collected by the city's recycling program. Two years later, when nearby communities were selling similar materials to MRFs for $10 to $25 per ton, New York City was still paying to have its containers removed. Fortunately, the city's separate contract for its recycled paper included payments tied to market prices, yielding a share of the profits from the 1995 boom.[9] The risks of price fluctuations are not confined to municipalities: a Boston-area MRF that signed fixed-price contracts with several cities in 1995 was forced into bankruptcy as prices fell in early 1996.

In other fluctuating commodity markets, a modicum of stability can be achieved through use of futures—contracts to buy or sell at a fixed price at some future date. By trading in futures, suppliers of materials learn what the market anticipates their products will be worth, and can obtain advance commitments for next month's or next year's price. To provide the same opportunity for recyclers, the National Recycling Coalition and the Chicago Board of Trade, the agency that administers most commodity futures trading, are working to establish markets in futures for recycled materials. The introduction of futures trading to the world of recycling began in 1995, and will take place gradually over a period of several years.

Even when it is fully implemented, however, futures trading is not a panacea for price fluctuations. At best it can smooth out anticipated price changes, such as predictable seasonal variations. Unanticipated swings in prices still provide notorious opportunities to win or lose big in futures markets. New York City, in 1993, did not anticipate the upswing in prices for recycled containers, and might have done equally badly if futures trading had been available.

The Economics of Uncertainty

The unanswered question remains central to the economics of recycling: what prices should be anticipated? In the case of paper, for example, industry is now prepared to use much more recycled material than in the past. This suggests that prices may remain above the low levels of the early 1990s. On the other hand, it is hard to believe that the peak prices of mid-1995 will become the new norm; six to eight times the 1993 prices seems implausible. A wide range of uncertainty remains between these two limits: will the new average be one and a half, two, three, or four times the old low prices? The balance sheets of recycling programs across the country depend on the answer.

The importance of shifting price predictions can be seen in the results of a massive study of waste management and recycling costs done by

Franklin Associates in 1994.[10] It assembled detailed cost and quantity estimates for many different waste management scenarios, with and without recycling. (Like many Franklin reports, this one embodies an immense amount of effort, but is almost devoid of documentation for its specific estimates other than references to earlier, often unpublished Franklin research—making it difficult to evaluate their work in any detail.) The original study, using 1993 prices for recycled materials, concluded that recycling generally was uneconomic (i.e., recycling raised the overall cost of waste management). But by the time the study appeared, prices were already on the way up. A recalculation by Franklin, using 1995 prices for recycled materials but leaving all other assumptions unchanged, reversed the earlier conclusion and showed that recycling now reduced the cost of waste management.[11]

The Franklin estimate of the average price for recycled materials rose from $46 per ton in 1993 to $165 per ton in 1995. Using these prices in Table 4-2, we would find that recycling was on average a net cost to municipalities in 1993, and a net benefit in 1995; recall that $142 per ton of revenue was needed for recycling to break even. At 1993 prices the average program would show a net loss of $96 per ton of recycled material or $21 per household per year. At 1995 prices this would become a net gain of $23 per ton or $5 per household due to recycling.

This analysis (like Franklin's) implies that an average recycling program was barely profitable at the high prices of 1995. If prices fall back to somewhere between the 1993 and 1995 levels, recycling might then lead to a small loss under average conditions. That loss might be reduced or eliminated by running a better-than-average recycling program, and in any case is likely to be swamped, in one direction or the other, by unpredictable fluctuations in prices.

There are others who have reached more optimistic conclusions, claiming that recycling saved money even at the low prices of the early 1990s. I wish they were right; it would eliminate the appearance of conflict between economic and environmental goals, and make the justification of recycling much easier. Two of the optimists who have been most important in recycling circles are John Schall and Jeffrey Morris.

Schall wrote a widely circulated paper arguing that there were economic as well as environmental grounds for supporting the solid waste management "hierarchy."[12] The hierarchy, often cited by EPA and state recycling agencies, identifies waste reduction as preferable to recycling and composting, which in turn are preferable to incineration and landfilling. Schall played the leading role in the early days of Tellus Institute's solid waste research, and his paper draws heavily on certain Tellus studies. In particular, he relies on the packaging study which is described in Chapter 5, and two extensive analyses of New York City area solid waste management options: one for the city's Department of Sanitation, and the other for the Regional Plan Association.

Schall's paper begins with a number of provocative insights about the state of waste management and recycling, and then moves into an intricate series of calculations. His goal in the calculations is to show that increased waste reduction and recycling are cheaper than business-as-usual waste management that relies heavily on disposal. Two of his key assumptions, however, have provoked controversy and limited the acceptance of his quantitative results. First, he assumes a $100 per ton disposal cost, which is perhaps plausible for long-term studies of the New York City area but far too high for the country as a whole. The higher the disposal cost, the greater the value of alternatives to disposal. Second, he incorporates the monetary values for pollution externalities developed in the Tellus packaging study in 1992 as a financial measure of the environmental benefit of waste reduction and recycling. The controversy surrounding these values, and the 1994 revision that lowered most of them, will be discussed in Chapter 5 and its appendix. Although Schall uses the pollution externality numbers as we originally intended to, I now believe that they are more useful as indicators of the relative severity of different emissions than as absolute dollar values.

Jeffrey Morris, an economist at Sound Resource Management Group (SRMG) in Seattle, takes a more conventional approach. His calculations of the costs of recycling are similar in structure to those presented earlier in this chapter, but lead him to more optimistic conclusions. A widely cited SRMG study of the economics of recycling in four Washington cities in 1992, for example, found that in each of the cities the net costs of recycling collection and processing were less than the costs of garbage collection and disposal.[13] It is perhaps the best of the studies arguing that recycling can be profitable and is therefore worth examining in detail.

The SRMG data are summarized in Table 4-3, and compared with national averages as developed above. The national average garbage collection cost (for cities with curbside recycling) and recycling collection cost are from the Stevens survey; average disposal cost is from *BioCycle*'s annual "State of Garbage in America"; and the $4 average recycling processing cost, net of revenues, is the $50 processing cost net of the $46 revenue estimate for 1993, from Franklin Associates.

Table 4-3 shows that among the four communities, recycling (collection and processing combined) is substantially cheaper than the national average only in Seattle, which is famous as an outstanding example of big-city recycling. Spokane, in contrast, spends substantially more than the national average, and the other two cities are within 10% of the norm.

Table 4-3

Garbage and Recycling Costs (dollars per ton) in Four Washington Cities

	Seattle	Spokane	Bellingham	Vancouver	National Average
Garbage					
Collection	67	101	90	85	68
Disposal	70	87	91	71	31
TOTAL	137	188	181	156	99
Recycling					
Collection	89	199	91	137	123
Processing[a]	1	−24	25	−6	4
TOTAL	90	175	116	131	127

Source: Washington data from Sound Resource Management Group, *The Economics of Recycling and Recycled Materials* (Seattle: Clean Washington Center, 1993), p. 6.

[a]Recycling processing costs are shown net of revenues.

The Washington story is not so much based on optimism about recycling as on pessimism about garbage costs. All but Seattle are 25% or more above average in garbage collection costs. And all four spend far more than the average on disposal. The SRMG study explains that Spokane and Bellingham, where disposal costs are highest, both send their waste to expensive incinerators. Seattle and Vancouver both ship their waste long distances to landfills in Oregon, involving shipping costs as well as higher than average tipping fees once the waste reaches the disposal site.

In short, the apparent cost advantage of recycling in the four Washington cities is due primarily to unusually costly garbage collection and disposal; only in Seattle is the economic performance of the recycling program substantially better than average. Morris, in response, says that the calculation of disposal costs for many communities should include $15–25 per ton for getting the waste to an out-of-town landfill, in addition to the tipping fees discussed earlier. However, disposal costs in his four Washington communities are much more than $25 per ton above the national average. He also observes that curbside recycling programs tend to be concentrated in areas with above-average disposal costs, making existing recycling efforts more profitable than the national averages would suggest.[14]

The cost advantage of recycling seen in Table 4-3 is misleading, since recycling is compared with the total costs of garbage collection and disposal, rather than the avoided costs (i.e., the amount by which recycling reduces garbage costs). All four cities presumably would have to provide garbage collection whether or not they have recycling. Therefore, in order to evaluate whether recycling saves money for the cities, the appropriate comparison is between the *total* costs of recycling and the *avoided* costs of garbage collection and disposal. This is the calculation that was labored over earlier in this chapter, culminating in Table 4-2. For disposal, a municipality's avoided costs often are the same as total costs: every ton of recycling saves the full per-ton cost of landfilling or incineration. For collection, the situation is quite different, and every ton of recycling saves much less than the full per-ton cost of garbage collection.

Suppose that we arbitrarily assume that recycling in the Washington cities avoids one-third of their per-ton garbage collection costs and all of their disposal costs—that is, each ton of recycling in Seattle, for instance, saves $22 in collection and $70 in disposal. Under that assumption, recycling saves money, barely, in Seattle ($2 per ton) and Bellingham ($5 per ton). Recycling has a net cost to the community in Vancouver ($32 per ton) and Spokane ($54 per ton), although in neither city is recycling as expensive as the national average would be under the same assumptions ($73 per ton). This is not quite the triumph for recycling that the SRMG results suggest at first glance, but it is also not bad for a year in which recycling revenues were as low as they were in 1992.

Jobs from Trash?

A final argument about the economics of recycling needs to be considered. Increasingly, recycling is being presented as a strategy for economic development, a way to create jobs and industries in the urban areas where materials are collected. Several studies have demonstrated that there are already noticeable numbers of jobs in enterprises that process or use recycled materials. For example, the 10-state Northeast region is said to have more than 100,000 jobs involving processing of recyclables and use of them in manufacturing, accounting for almost 3 % of the region's manufacturing employment.[15] A different analysis found that New York City alone has about 3,000 establishments in industries related to solid-waste management, reuse and repair, and recycling, accounting for nearly 34,000 jobs and a payroll of over $1 billion.[16] A study of recycling and employment in Baltimore, Maryland, Washington, D.C., and Richmond, Virginia, found that while 100,000 tons of waste disposal created only 23 jobs, 100,000 tons of recycling created 79 jobs in collection and processing, and another 162 jobs when the recovered materials are made into new products.[17]

Whatever the specific numbers, there are good economic reasons to expect recycling to create jobs. Money spent on recycling leads to more employment than the same amount spent on garbage disposal. Recycling is a labor-intensive activity, involving sorting and processing of waste materials. Disposal, in contrast, involves heavy equipment, large tracts of land, and very little labor. In the simplest terms, most of the money spent on recycling goes to workers in the form of wages, rather than to owners of holes in the ground.

Moreover, recycled materials are conveniently located for use in urban economic development. Virgin materials often come from remote mines, wells, and forests; recycled materials come from cities and towns. Industries whose location depends on supplies of raw materials might therefore be newly attracted to urban areas. The paper industry was originally centered in Massachusetts, close to the sources of recycled fiber in the cities of the Northeast. Having spent the twentieth century out in the woods, paper producers might be ready to return to the "urban forests" created by modern recycling programs.

There is a crucial limitation, however, to the power of recycling to boost employment. Recycling is sure to create more jobs *if* it costs the same amount as disposal. If it costs more than disposal, then the outcome is less certain. For instance, suppose a recycling program costs $1,200,000, and reduces spending on garbage disposal by $1,000,000. The increased cost will probably be paid, one way or another, by the households of the community. They will therefore have to reduce something else by $200,000; a likely candidate is consumer spending at retail outlets.

To calculate the employment impacts of recycling in this example, the jobs created by $1,200,000 of recycling must be compared with the jobs that would have resulted from $1,000,000 of disposal plus $200,000 of retail spending. While disposal creates fewer jobs per dollar than recycling, retail spending creates more. Recycling could be either better or worse for employment than a combination of disposal plus retail spending, depending on the balance between the two. If the gap in costs between recycling and disposal becomes big enough, the loss of jobs from decreased retail spending will dominate the calculation, showing that expensive recycling is worse for employment than cheap disposal.

A similar qualification applies to the benefits of using recycled materials in local industries. If it is as profitable to use materials locally as to sell them elsewhere, then there are advantages to building links between recycling programs and industries in the same area. Some recovered materials are almost sure to be used close to home: recycled glass, for example, is worth so little per ton that it is uneconomical to ship it over long distances. The same is true of compost made from yard waste, and of many recycled building materials. Other, higher priced materials, however, are worth so much more on national or international markets that it is often uneconomical to use them locally. Subsidizing local use of recycled materials would have the same problem as paying for expensive recycling programs: if the subsidy reduces consumer spending or other local expenditures, it may do more harm than good for the local economy.

The prospects for jobs from recycling and for local use of recycled materials thus depend on the balance between recycling and disposal costs. If recycling is the cheaper alternative, or even if it is slightly more expensive, then it can yield additional benefits of increased employment and perhaps strengthen local economic linkages through supplying recovered materials to industry. However, if recycling is much more expensive than disposal, the indirect economic benefits can be outweighed by the costs.

It may be unfair to judge the effort to develop local jobs and local material use solely in terms of aggregate economic benefits. Recycling as an economic development strategy is also motivated by the desire for local control and self-sufficiency. Returning economic and environmental decisions to a manageable local scale is a value in itself for many advocates of community development. If this is the objective, then it makes sense to view exports of scrap paper to Mexico as a failure. More generally, local material use then becomes an end in itself, not a means to hold down municipal costs. The goal of local self-sufficiency recalls Ontario's former policy of local responsibility for waste disposal; to follow this principle consistently, hard choices have to be made.

Local control and responsibility is an admirable principle, but not an absolute one. While some environmental problems, such as contamination of soil and water, can be addressed locally, others, such as greenhouse gas emissions and climate change, are inherently global. In terms of the economics of recycling, developing small-scale local uses for compost is an excellent idea; building small-scale local aluminum mills to make use of recycled beverage cans is not. Recovered aluminum cans will continue to be shipped long distances to the large facilities that can use them most efficiently. While recycled paper mills may gradually appear in or near urban areas, some of our recycled paper will undoubtedly continue to travel abroad and save trees in places far away.

⊛   ⊛   ⊛

In conclusion, while much is known about the economics of recycling, the bottom-line question—how much does it cost?—cannot be answered with any precision, due to the unpredictable prices for recycled materials. An average recycling program would have lost a modest amount of money at the low prices of the early 1990s, and would have made a small profit at the high prices of 1995. A better than average recycling program, or higher than average disposal costs, can lead to outcomes even more favorable to recycling. Cost-effective recycling also creates local jobs, and opportunities for local use of recovered materials; however, when recycling is much more expensive than disposal, these benefits must be weighed against the lost stimulus due to reduced consumer spending.

Recycling is almost always environmentally desirable, which is why it is worth doing even if it entails moderate cost increases. Facile justifications of recycling on the grounds that it is always profitable threaten to lose sight of the underlying environmental issues. Meanwhile, the argument about profitability hitches the fortunes of recycling to the pulsating star that shines over the scrap markets. Recycling is environmentally desirable, but it is also expensive—sometimes a little more expensive than disposal, sometimes a little less. The expense of recycling results in large part from the costs of truck collection; it is important to collect as much as possible with as few trucks as possible. From a budgetary standpoint, a truck is a terrible thing to waste.

The high cost of collection is just one of the reasons why waste reduction is often an even better idea than recycling. When the choice is available, a ton of waste prevention will usually do more for the environment than a ton of recycling; switching to a lighter-weight product can sometimes be beneficial even if it is less recyclable than the original, heavier version. This observation, and some of the paradoxical conclusions it leads to, are central to the discussions of packaging policy and of organic waste management in the chapters just ahead.

Notes

1. Barbara Stevens, "Scale, Market Structure, and the Cost of Refuse Collection," *Review of Economics and Statistics,* Vol. 60 (1978), pp. 438–448.

2. Peter Anderson, George Dreckmann, and John Reindl, "Debunking the Two Fleet Myth," *Waste Age,* October 1995. The 37% decline is my calculation from their table, which shows the total garbage truck fleet cost per year dropping from $1,939,418 to $1,225,548. The earlier figure is based on 26 of the original, more expensive trucks; the latter figure is based on 18 of the newer, cheaper trucks (the number that would have been required if the population had not grown). Both assume the same labor cost per truck.

3. Barbara Stevens, "Recycling Collection Costs by the Numbers: A National Survey," *Resource Recycling,* September 1994; and "What Does it Cost to Collect

Yard Debris?," *Resource Recycling,* October 1994. The figures in the text are my calculation from the October article, Table 1.

4. Confidence intervals and standard deviations are not reported for the figures cited here. However, note that in the September article, Table 2, very large standard deviations ($22.51 and $25.40) are reported for mean garbage collection costs for two groups of communities, each representing more than one-third of the total sample. This makes it essentially impossible for a difference of $9 in mean garbage collection costs to be significant. Oddly enough, the communities with recycling collection had more garbage per household, even after subtracting recycling (see October article, Table 1), although this, too, may not be statistically significant.

5. Robert Steuteville, "The State of Garbage in America: Part I," *BioCycle,* April 1995, and "Part II," May 1995.

6. For a rigorous theoretical analysis of this and related points, see Mark Ready and Richard Ready, "Optimal Pricing of Depletable, Replaceable Resources: The Case of Landfill Tipping Fees," *Journal of Environmental Economics and Management,* Vol. 28 (1995), pp. 307–323.

7. Ni-Bin Chang and S.F. Wang, "The Development of Material Recovery Facilities in the United States: Status and Cost Structure Analysis," *Resources, Conservation and Recycling,* Vol. 13 (1995), pp. 115–128.

8. Franklin Associates estimates operating costs of $50 per ton for a MRFs designed to handle 128 tons per day, in *The Role of Recycling in Integrated Solid Waste Management to the Year 2000* (Stamford, Connecticut: Keep America Beautiful, 1994); see, e.g., Appendix p. H-13 and Summary p. 11.

9. John Sullivan, "While Others Sell Recyclables, New York Pays to Get Rid of Them," *New York Times,* August 12, 1995, p. 23.

10. Franklin Associates, *Role of Recycling.*

11. *Resource Recycling,* September 1995, p. 4.

12. For a short form of the paper see John Schall, "Does the Hierarchy Make Sense?," *MSW Management,* January–February 1993. The longer version is John Schall, *Does the Solid Waste Management Hierarchy Make Sense?,* Solid Waste Working Paper #1 (New Haven: Yale School of Forestry and Environmental Studies, 1992).

13. Sound Resource Management Group, *The Economics of Recycling and Recycled Materials* (Seattle: Clean Washington Center, 1993).

14. Jeffrey Morris, personal communication, April 1996.

15. Roy F. Weston, Inc., *Value Added to Recyclable Materials in the Northeast* (Brattleboro, Vermont: Northeast Recycling Council, Council of State Governments, 1994).

16. The study, by the Center for the Biology of Natural Systems at Queens College, was described in Jo Thomas, "New York Starts Spinning Its Dross into Gold," *New York Times,* November 28, 1994.

17. Brenda Platt, Henry Jeanes, and Anne Kaufmann, "Recycling Boosts the Local Economy," *BioCycle,* August 1995.

CHAPTER 5

Drink Boxes, Styrofoam, and PVC

Fame of a sort descended briefly on our research at Tellus Institute in the summer of 1994, when Maine repealed its ban on the sale of juice in aseptic packaging, or "drink boxes." Not only were we cited favorably by both the industry and its critics, even *USA Today,* in its written sound bite on the issue, said, "Rehabilitation of the drink box's image came as a result of a study by the Tellus Institute, Boston, concluding the box has 'one of the lowest environmental impacts of any juice beverage container on the market,' even before recycling."[1] Dozens of reporters called to hear the revisionist account of why aseptic packaging is not really so bad for the environment. If, as Andy Warhol said, we will each be famous for 15 minutes, I can only hope that I didn't use up my whole quarter-hour bringing drink boxes back to Maine.

Four years earlier, as the Maine legislature was voting to keep out juice-in-a-box, I, like most of the Tellus research staff, would have predicted that our work would end up burying aseptic packaging rather than praising it. We were in the midst of a massive three-year study comparing the environmental impacts of all major packaging materials.[2] Sponsored by several state agencies, industry groups, and the Environmental Protection Agency, the study was motivated by widespread debate about packaging policy.

Packaging of all types accounts for about one-third of municipal solid waste—and undoubtedly for more than a third of the worrying about waste. Of the materials we throw out, it *feels* the most wasteful. Used once and then discarded, packaging seems to pass through our lives only briefly as it rushes from factory to landfill. Moreover, packaging includes some of the most easily recycled materials, metal cans and glass bottles, as well as a growing number of new, hard-to-recycle plastics and composite materials. It is no surprise, therefore, that packaging policy has been a prime concern among recycling advocates.

Although many would agree that packaging waste should be reduced, there is a basic disagreement about the nature of the problem. Is it an issue of the sheer bulk of excess packaging in general, or are some particular packaging materials uniquely bad for the environment? These two views lead to different approaches to policy. Emphasis on the overall quantity of packaging leads to proposals that address the volume of waste in general, such as mandated recycling levels, per-package taxes, or unit pricing for waste collection.

On the other hand, emphasis on particular "problem" materials leads to proposals for restrictions or bans on the guilty substances. Opposition to drink boxes was one example; it was widely believed that the convenience of this package would undermine the use of recyclable bottles and cans, and lead to a flood of trash and litter. The infamous styrofoam "clamshell" container for fast-food sandwiches was another nominee for the worst package on the market, and was abandoned by McDonald's after years of protest.

Our research was designed to determine whether packaging is all comparably bad, or whether there is a best or worst package. The conclusion, in short, is that there is indeed one clear loser, although it is neither drink boxes nor fast-food styrofoam. Among other materials, we found that in most cases, the lightest-weight package is the best for the environment.

The Price of Pollution

We set out to measure the "externalities" associated with packaging, that is, the costs imposed on society by packaging use that are not reflected in its market price. We examined glass, aluminum, steel, five types of paper, and six types of plastic, encompassing all the packaging materials that are in widespread use in the U.S. economy. For each material we compared three types of impacts: air and water pollution from the manufacturing process; monetary costs of solid waste management; and air and water pollution from the waste management process.

Our study was an example of lifecycle analysis, a new field of research that has flourished in recent years. The goal is to trace the environmental impacts of a product "from cradle to grave," that is, from production through disposal. The implicit assumptions that motivate lifecycle analysis are first, that there is a wide variety of externalities associated with a single product, and second, that it is possible to tabulate these externalities in a way that is informative and useful. The first assumption is easy to accept; the second is an ongoing challenge.

The image of lifecycle analysis as an objective, scientific process was damaged in the "diaper wars" of the late 1980s, in which rival analyses were sponsored by the makers of disposable diapers and the services that distribute cloth ones.[3] Substantively, the clash showed that disposable diapers result in more solid waste, while washing cloth ones creates more water pollution. Methodologically, it showed that the results of lifecycle analysis depend on who is asking the questions, and on the choice of impacts that are examined and emphasized. Practitioners of lifecycle analysis have begun a slow-moving process of hammering out agreement on a standard methodology, but this effort appears to be years, if not decades, away from completion.

We sought to avoid or overcome the dilemmas of lifecycle analysis in several ways. The broad sponsorship of our study, with support coming from several different industries and from consumer-oriented public agencies, helped to ensure an even-handed treatment of the entire spectrum of packaging materials. We were careful to use the same public databases for evaluation of all industries, a point which, as explained below, proved more controversial than we had expected. And our idealistic young staff hoped that, by working insanely long hours, we could document every known emission associated with packaging production, and thereby avoid any problems of selective coverage.

The attempt at all-inclusive research, however, threatened to worsen another problem with lifecycle analysis: the difficulty of interpreting the results. Studies of pollution impacts often have a mind-numbing quality. Long lists of emissions, with names that only an organic chemist could love (or remember), are matched with tiny numbers in exponential notation. In the end, very little is clear. The reader, desperately seeking meaning in the mass of data, is often tempted to add the weights of dissimilar emissions; at times the authors succumb to the same temptation. But one thing which is clear is that well-known pollutants differ by orders of magnitude in their degree of hazard. A gram of dioxin can kill quite a few people; a gram of sulfur dioxide is a minor eye and throat irritant. Adding the two, gram for gram, yields a number devoid of meaning.

While we delved into detail on more than 100 different emissions from packaging production, we also worked on developing a meaningful summary evaluation of those emissions. We weighted our emissions data by the relative health hazards of different pollutants, based on laboratory studies; this made a gram of dioxin, for example, millions of times as important as a gram of some other emissions. (However, the quantities of dioxin emitted are so minute that, even on a toxicity-weighted basis, dioxin is not the most important emission from any of the industries we studied. Other, less exotic pollutants are emitted in such vastly greater quantities that they have more serious aggregate impacts.) We then applied estimates of pollution control costs required under current regulations, as measures of the value society places on reducing emissions. The result was an implied dollar value for the hazard caused by each pollutant, allowing easy comparison of different impacts. More detail on the method, and updated values based on a 1994 revision of the data, can be found in the appendix to this chapter.

The study yielded four major conclusions, one expected and three unexpected. The result we expected was that, in every case where data were available for both virgin and recycled production of the same material, recycled production had lower environmental impacts (or, for one of the less common grades of paper, about the same impacts). The magnitude of the environmental benefit from recycling, however, differs widely by material. Aluminum recycling saves 95 % of the energy required for virgin production, and eliminates the dirtiest, most difficult processing stages. In contrast, glass and paper recycling save proportionally much less energy, and require many of the same processing stages as virgin production.[4]

For products that can be made from only one material, this first conclusion might be all that one needs to know about environmental impacts. Recycled widgets (the unspecified generic product used by economists everywhere) are better than ones made from the same virgin raw materials. In such cases, public policy might be designed to encourage or mandate the use of recycled material. For example, many states have adopted recycled content requirements for newsprint. These standards helped push the paper industry to make major investments in recycled paper mills in the early 1990s.

However, the conventional wisdom about recycling is more obviously appropriate for newspapers, which are always made of the same material, than for packaging. Choice among materials is the rule rather than the exception in packaging; almost anything can be packaged in more than one way, using more than one material. Our other, unexpected conclusions arose in the course of comparisons of the environmental impacts of different materials.

One of the unexpected results was the relative unimportance of pollution from the waste management process. Air and water emissions from new, state-of-the-art landfills and incinerators, and the emissions from collection trucks, are insignificant in comparison with manufacturing emissions. Often the waste management impacts were 1 % or less of the production impacts for packaging materials. That is to say, as unattractive as it is to live next to even the newest landfill, it might be 100 times as bad for your health to live next to a paper mill, oil refinery, or steel mill.

This is not to deny that waste management has often caused serious pollution. Old, unlined or leaking landfills, especially those that have accepted industrial as well as municipal waste in the past, have caused critical local environmental damage. The worst offenders can be found on the list of Superfund sites. But thanks to EPA and state regulations, you can't build them like that any more. The impacts of old landfills are, in every sense of the word, sunk costs.

Looking forward, there are only minimal health hazards attributable to burying packaging materials in new landfills that meet current standards. The household items that are most important to keep out of landfills are not packaging, but rather the small quantities of hazardous wastes, such as lead batteries, oil-based paints, certain cleansers, cosmetics, and household chemicals. These items account for a vastly disproportionate share of the environmental damage from landfill emissions. Separate collection and proper treatment and disposal of household hazardous wastes should be the top priority in efforts to reduce landfill impacts.

And the Loser Is . . .

The second surprising result was the identity of the material that received the worst evaluation. Production of polyvinyl chloride (PVC), the plastic coded "3" on the bottom of packages, causes emissions of vinyl chloride monomer and other carcinogenic substances. Nothing else comes close to releasing as much toxicity per ton of packaging as PVC production.

All plastics production involves manipulation and combination of complex organic compounds. But among the most common plastics, only PVC production creates and emits *chlorinated* organic chemicals. Here the packaging industry collides with another environmental controversy. The growing "toxics use reduction" movement has targeted chlorinated organics as a principal source of toxicity in industry. Greenpeace, for example, has launched a campaign for a chlorine-free economy.

Anti-chlorine forces point to the numerous chlorinated organic compounds that are notoriously dangerous pollutants. The list includes not only vinyl chloride, known to be a human carcinogen, but also DDT, PCBs (polychlorinated biphenyls), dioxins and furans, and CFCs (chlorofluorocarbons). "There are no uses of chlorine that we regard as safe," says Greenpeace researcher Joe Thornton. Established groups that favor phasing out or avoiding the use of industrial chlorine include the United States–Canadian International Joint Commission concerned with pollution in the Great Lakes, and the American Public Health Association.

In response, the industry argues that chlorinated organics are not all the same. Brad Leinhart, managing director of the Chlorine Chemistry Council, says that the many thousands of organochlorine compounds are chemically, physically, and biologically heterogeneous, and only a few have been proven to be hazardous. W. Joseph Stearns, director of chlorine issues for Dow Chemical, says, "The substantive part of this issue is that *some* organochlorines are persistent toxics, not that all organochlorines contain chlorine."[5]

More than a quarter of the chlorine used by U.S. industry goes into the production of PVC. Plastic pipe, widely used in plumbing today, is made from PVC, as is vinyl siding for houses. Other uses include numerous molded plastic consumer products, and the magnetic tape used in tape recordings. In packaging, PVC is used for water and oil bottles, snack packages, and the so-called "blister pack"—the combination of clear plastic front on cardboard backing that is often seen on drugstore and hardware items.

For the analysis of packaging, many of the complexities of the chlorine debate can be avoided. Whether or not all chlorinated organic compounds are toxic, it is clear that vinyl chloride and other emissions from PVC production are hazardous to human health. And the requirements for substitutes for PVC are different in packaging than in areas such as plumbing. All of the packaging uses of PVC could immediately be replaced by other, chlorine-free plastics. The costs would be greater in some cases, but likely only by a small amount; after all, chlorine-free plastic packaging is already widespread, and does not impose an intolerable expense on the consumer goods that use it. A switch from PVC to other materials would, according to the Tellus Packaging Study, be the most important step that could be taken to reduce the toxicity attributable to packaging.

The Vinyl Institute, representing PVC producers, has always objected to the Tellus study. They claim that our estimated emissions were necessarily out of date, because they were taken from published EPA databases. We evaluated all industries on the basis of the latest published government sources; as a matter of principle, we declined to update data

based solely on unconfirmed industry self-reporting. To our amaze-
ment, several industry groups, and consultants who had performed lifecycle analyses based on proprietary industry databases, claimed that
our reliance on public data was a controversial approach—since "everyone knew" that public data was always dated! We argued, before, during, and after our study, that scientific method requires the use of veri-
fiable data, in this case implying data in the public domain. Studies that
rely on proprietary data provided by the study's sponsor blur the distinction between research and public relations.

At about the same time that the Tellus study appeared, the Vinyl Institute published its own analysis of the impacts of production of PVC
and other packaging materials—clearly based on proprietary data and
industry self-reporting.[6] How much difference would it make if we accepted their figures on production emissions? If the Tellus emissions
data are correct, production of a PVC bottle is 10 to 12 times as bad for
the environment as production of the same size bottle from other plastics. If the Vinyl Institute data are correct, the PVC bottle is only 4 times
as bad as other plastics. That is, using Vinyl Institute emissions data
would change the numbers, but not the qualitative conclusion about
PVC versus other packaging materials. PVC would still clearly be the
packaging material with the worst impacts on the environment. It is not
surprising, therefore, that the Vinyl Institute study argues strongly
against making any attempt to evaluate the hazards implied by its emissions data.

What would a chlorine-free economy mean for packaging? The paper
industry, most of which still uses chlorine bleaching to whiten its product, would have to switch to a different bleaching process—which is
commercially available, though not yet widespread. The plastics industry would have to give up PVC bottles, and would have to develop a substitute for plastic wrap ("Saran" wrap and similar brands are often
made from a closely related chlorinated plastic, PVDC). Costs in these
areas might increase, although health costs for those affected by industrial pollution would decrease. Other packaging production processes,
including those for all the other major plastics, would be largely unaffected.

The Lighter, the Better

The last major conclusion of our study was one of the most significant
for public policy. Herein lies the rehabilitation of the drink box, along
with other surprises. When we compared *per-ton* impacts of packaging

materials we found that, as we and other recycling advocates had sus-
pected, glass was best, followed by metals and paper, while plastics in
general looked worst. But when we compared *per-package* impacts, we
found that, PVC aside, the lightest-weight packages were almost always
the best for the environment. To our initial chagrin, plastics came out
quite well in many comparisons.

Before the fact, it seemed likely that environmentally oriented research might endorse the use of glass bottles for beverage delivery. After
all, glass has a clean image. It is certainly recyclable, and its production
uses less energy and emits less pollution than the production of other
materials. If you are buying a ton of packaging material, it is true that
you do less damage to the environment if you choose glass rather than
any of its rivals.

The problem is, you aren't buying a ton of packaging, you're buying
a package. And glass bottles are heavy. Among single-serving juice containers, glass bottles weigh 10 to 12 times as much, per ounce of juice,
as plastic bottles, aluminum cans, paper cartons, or drink boxes (all of
which are somewhat similar in package weight per fluid ounce). So the
question is, are the other materials 10 to 12 times as bad for the environment, per ton, as glass?

The answer, we found, is "no." The other materials used to make
juice containers are only two to six times as bad, per ton, as glass. On
balance, therefore, the packaging impacts per ounce of juice are lower
with any of the other materials than with single-use glass bottles. (Refillable bottles, which were not included in the study, are discussed in
Chapters 6 and 7.) The higher-impact materials allow the production of
lighter-weight packages, and it is package weight, in this and many
other cases, that turns out to be decisive.

To dramatize the importance of package weight, in lectures on packaging issues, I have sometimes abruptly tossed an assortment of empty
juice containers at the audience—and then pointed out that I only had
to give advance warning to the person who caught the glass bottle. The
other containers bounce harmlessly off the heads and shoulders of the
startled observers.

For another picture of the importance of lightweight packages, consider the amount of trash that would be generated in two communities
with opposite approaches to juice containers. One allows only glass bottles, while the other allows only aseptic packaging, weighing one-tenth
as much per package. Suppose that Glasstown has an active recycling
program, recovering 80% of its glass bottles (a rate which is never
achieved in practice unless there is a deposit on the bottles), while Pa-

perville throws out all of its empty drink boxes. For every 100 juice container sales, Glasstown sends only 20 glass bottles to the landfill, while Paperville sends all 100 boxes. But 20 bottles weigh as much as 200 drink boxes. Glasstown, despite its exemplary recycling rate, generates twice as much trash.

The reason for dwelling on this issue is not that drink boxes are uniquely good for the environment; the Tellus study gave comparable evaluations per ounce of juice to other lightweight paperboard and plastic containers. Nor is it important because of the quantity of waste involved; aseptic packaging accounts for an insignificant 0.03 % of America's solid waste. Rather, the drink box story highlights the distinction between waste reduction and recycling. As desirable as recycling may be, reduction in material use and waste generation is even better for the environment.

Conventional wisdom in environmental circles has often favored recycling above all other objectives. In 1990, when Maine banned the drink box, the exclusive focus on recycling was even more in evidence than it is today. Congressman Frank Pallone (D-NJ), together with Environmental Action Foundation, Clean Water Action, and U.S. Public Interest Research Group (PIRG), presented a "Wastemaker" award to Coca-Cola for the sale of its Minute Maid orange juice in unrecyclable drink boxes.[7] The chairs of the Maine legislative committees that approved the state ban justified their action solely in terms of the nonrecyclability of aseptic packaging.[8] In a panel discussion broadcast on CNN, Allen Hershkowitz of the Natural Resources Defense Council said of the drink box, "What we have here is a classic case of a package being designed without any consideration for environmental criteria. This is by every measure an environmental failure."[9]

Hershkowitz was unique in his articulateness, but not in his opinion. What he and others evidently meant was that aseptic packaging was designed without consideration for the sole criterion, recyclability, that was then in vogue. By that one measure alone, it appeared to be an environmental failure in 1990. Even in 1994, when Maine repealed its ban, the change of heart was based only in part on recognition of the benefits of waste reduction. Also important was the industry's demonstration that aseptic packaging could, in fact, be recycled.

To recycle drink boxes, you need an industrial-sized version of a kitchen food processor. Toss in the drink boxes, fill it with water, and turn it on. In less than 30 minutes, hydraulic action will separate the paper fibers from the plastic and aluminum layers. The paper, which represents 70 % of the weight of aseptic packaging, can then be recovered, and is used to make products such as tissues and towels. This process, called "hydrapulping," is used by paper recyclers in several locations around the country.

Yet as proud as the aseptic packaging industry is of the hydrapulping process, it remains of secondary importance to the evaluation of their product. Only a few municipal recycling programs collect drink boxes and send them to a hydrapulping facility. The advantages of lightweight packaging, however, are significant everywhere, regardless of local recycling options.

Moreover, the quantity of aseptic packaging waste alone is too small to justify construction of a hydrapulper. Drink boxes constitute less than 10% of the material received at existing hydrapulping plants. Other plastic-coated paperboard containers, particularly "gable-top" milk and juice cartons, make up the vast majority of the material, without which the facilities could not afford to operate. Consequently, the decision to build (or send materials to) a hydrapulper depends primarily on plans for recycling milk and juice cartons, not on the comparatively tiny quantity of drink boxes that come along for the ride. Even plastic-coated cartons as a whole are a small part of the solid waste stream, averaging only 3.6 pounds per household per year. As a result, the decision to recycle these cartons has only a modest effect—sometimes positive, sometimes negative—on municipal recycling costs.[10]

It would be a mistake to welcome aseptic packaging back to the company of environmentally acceptable products on the grounds that hydrapulping shows it can meet the goal of recyclability after all. Recyclability is only a secondary goal, not the ultimate environmental standard by which packaging should be judged. Greater gains can often come from waste reduction. And as shown in the fable of Glasstown and Paperville, maximum waste reduction may conflict with maximum recycling. Aseptic packaging should be viewed as one of several alternatives that achieve substantial waste reduction in beverage delivery; as it turns out, many of the waste-reducing beverage containers are not widely recycled.

Food for Thought

A similar story can be told about coffee cans—and has been told at numerous recycling conferences by Tom Rattray of Procter & Gamble. You can buy a pound of coffee in a familiar, recyclable steel can, or in a vacuum-packed foil wrapper, sometimes called a "brick pack" in honor of its shape. The multi-layered foil wrapper is not recyclable, but weighs

15% as much as the can. So which generates less trash? If the can is re-cycled at a rate of less than 85%, as it (in reality) will be, then the brick pack is the winner. In terms of manufacturing impacts, too, the steel can has lower impacts per pound of packaging, but higher impacts per pound of coffee, than the foil.

One small company chose lighter-weight packaging rather than heav-ier but more frequently recycled alternatives, based explicitly on the findings of the Tellus Packaging Study. In a 1994 press release on envi-ronmental packaging, Stonyfield Farm Yogurt used the Tellus results to help explain to its customers why it had opted for yogurt cups made of polypropylene (the number 5 plastic), which is rarely recycled, rather than ones made of high-density polyethylene (HDPE, the number 2 plastic), which is more often recycled. Although recycling of HDPE bot-tles is common, the wide-mouth containers used for yogurt are made of a particular type of HDPE which many recycling programs do not ac-cept. The polypropylene yogurt container was 20% lighter than the HDPE one. Stonyfield Farm judged that recycling of HDPE yogurt con-tainers was unlikely to reach a 20% rate in the near future, so that the polypropylene option would actually generate less waste—as well as lower impacts from manufacturing.[11] Use of our study by bigger com-panies, alas, has been rare.[12]

For some types of food packaging, recycling is rarely an option, and there are limited choices of materials. Yet there still can be important differences in environmental impacts, based on differences in package design. The Tellus study looked at two examples: the packaging used to deliver fast-food burgers and microwave dinners.

For burgers we examined three options: the clamshell-shaped con-tainer made out of paperboard, the clamshell made from polystyrene (styrofoam), and the paper wrapper. Of the three, the paperboard clamshell has the highest impact. It weighs three times as much as the polystyrene version, more than offsetting paper's lower impact per pound of packaging. The best option is the paper wrapper, which bene-fits from both light weight and lower impact per pound of material.

We found nothing in the production or disposal impacts that could explain the infamy of the polystyrene clamshell.[13] The intense reactions of environmentalists to fast-food polystyrene may reflect an aversion to the fast-food industry itself (which I share, particularly after surviving the years when my children enjoyed it), combined with the high visi-bility of polystyrene litter. The problem of litter, as distinguished from proper waste disposal, is addressed in Chapter 7.

Among microwave dinners, there is a wide range of package designs. The lightest weight ones use the microwaveable tray and cover as the outer package, with no additional layers required. Others put the tray and cover inside a light wrapper, or a heavier box. The packaging materials, paperboard and plastics, are similar in impacts per pound, and all are nonrecyclable in most areas. The heaviest package of the five we bought weighed three times as much as the lightest, while all held 8.5 to 9 ounces of food. It should come as no surprise that the lightest package—the one with no extra layers—is the environmentally preferred alternative. There was no visible marketing benefit to the heavier packages, since all five were similar in size and had bright, multi-colored text and designs on top.

The examples could be continued through other aisles of the supermarket, but by this point you can carry out further studies on your own. To minimize the environmental impact of packaging, first avoid plastic containers with the number 3 (for PVC) in the triangle on the bottom. Then, to choose among other alternatives, look for the lightest package per ounce of contents. Once you have bought a package and used its contents, by all means try to reuse it, or see if it can be recycled in your community. But think carefully before you buy a much heavier container just because it makes a satisfying "clunk" when tossed into your recycling box.

Packaging Policy: Just Weigh It

The implications of this analysis extend well beyond advice to shoppers. The original impetus for research on packaging impacts came from debates about public policy. The underlying question posed at the beginning of this chapter—is packaging all equally bad, or are there particular problem materials?—can now be resolved. One material, PVC, stands out as particularly problematic, due to carcinogenic emissions in the manufacturing process. Since it is easy to replace PVC in packaging applications, it seems appropriate to tax heavily, ban, or otherwise discourage its use.

Among other materials, detailed analysis of production emissions and disposal costs leads to a conclusion reasonably close to "it's all equally bad." In almost every case, the lightest package, per unit of contents, is the one with the lowest impact on the environment. Drink boxes, fast-food polystyrene, and other plastics in general fail to qualify as unique problems requiring unique solutions. Rather than legislating the choice of material or the required level of recyclability, it makes sense to adopt policies that encourage use of the lightest possible packaging for each product.

Viewed from this perspective, some of the widely discussed policy recommendations for packaging appear a bit eclectic and unfocused. One initiative in particular deserves mention, since it appeared likely, at one time, to set the standard for state policies nationwide. Starting in the late 1980s, the Coalition of Northeast Governors (CONEG) sponsored a lengthy series of negotiations between industry and government representatives, in the hopes of reaching agreement on packaging policy. After years of meetings and discussions, a consensus was finally reached among the participants. The resulting "CONEG guidelines" call for every package to be either reused five times, reach a target recycling rate, contain a specified level of recycled content, or achieve a certain percentage weight reduction, measured from a fixed base year. The CONEG guidelines have been the basis of proposed legislation in many states, but ironically have not been adopted anywhere in the Northeast. To date the CONEG guidelines have been enacted only in Oregon, where they took effect for plastic packaging beginning in 1995.

At first glance the CONEG approach may appear admirably flexible. However, the diverse choice of objectives diffuses the impact of the policy. All of the alternatives are treated as equally desirable; each packaging producer may choose which goal to meet. But as we have seen, there is no reason to think that a high recycling rate or recycled content is as important as weight reduction. Nor is there any recognition of the fact that some packages are already much lighter than others, and therefore are environmentally preferable even without further reduction. The danger of the CONEG guidelines is that they are so flexible that they will produce little or no noticeable results, while sounding like a lot is being done.

Oregon's plastics recycling requirements may have been indirectly responsible for one positive development. The American Plastics Council, an industry trade association, chose Oregon as the site for a demonstration project in automated sorting of plastic bottles. The different plastic resins must be separated before recycling; very small percentages of mis-sorted plastics can ruin a batch of recycled material. Most recycling facilities must do this sorting by hand, one of the major bottlenecks in processing of plastics. The new equipment being tested in Oregon uses a combination of x-rays, infrared detectors, and color sensors to sort the different resins. The American Plastics Council has funded the equipment and guaranteed a minimum price for the plastic scrap that it produces for its first three years.[14]

Early reports indicate that the automated sorting system is working well, although it cannot yet sort shapes other than bottles, such as yogurt containers. However, Oregon's recycling law is responsible only for the location of the demonstration project, not its existence. Moreover, it is too early to tell whether the new automated sorting system can survive on its own without industry subsidies. The plastics industry has been experimenting with techniques for recycling its products for some time; this is not the first well-publicized demonstration project that has claimed to solve the problems of plastics recycling. Sitting on my desk is a black pencil holder whose sides proudly tell its story: it contains 80% post-consumer polystyrene, made from material collected at a recycling conference in June 1989, reprocessed at the "Plastics Again" plant in Leominster, Massachusetts, in August, and distributed to participants in another recycling conference in October 1989. "Plastics Again," the flagship of industry recycling efforts in its day, failed and closed its doors several years ago.

One can certainly hope that the latest experiment in plastics recycling will succeed—and at the same time remain skeptical about the merits of Oregon's approach to packaging policy. A simpler alternative to the CONEG guidelines suggests itself, based on the analysis presented in this chapter. To determine the environmental impacts of packaging, just weigh it. Fees or targets should be based on the weight of packaging per unit of contents. This would simplify measurement and recordkeeping, and would create an unambiguous message to industry: when it comes to packaging, less is better than more.

In the course of the 1990s, the relatively low-profile discussions of packaging policy in the United States have been overshadowed by more prominent events elsewhere. Germany, in particular, has adopted a controversial new policy, embodying the principle of producer responsibility for packaging, that has largely framed the terms of international debate. Germany's approach, its echoes in other countries, and the idea of producer responsibility are the subjects of the next chapter.

Appendix: Valuation of Pollution from Packaging

The research that forms the basis for this chapter, the Tellus Institute Packaging Study, contains estimates of the emissions of more than 100 pollutants that result from packaging production and disposal. Emissions from raw material extraction, energy production, and manufacturing processes are all included, along with analysis of disposal costs and environmental impacts, and applications of the findings to five case studies. The full study runs to 900 pages, and, not surprisingly, has been read primarily by specialists in the field. In order to make our findings comprehensible and relevant to nonspecialists, we realized that we would need a standard with which to measure the pollution due to each packaging material. Adding the weights of different emissions is clearly the wrong standard, since some pollutants matter much more than others.

One promising approach is to apply rankings of health or damage effects of pollutants, based on laboratory research. For example, suppose that pollutant A has been found to be 10 times as toxic as pollutant B per unit of weight. Then adding ten times the emissions of A to the emissions of B produces a "toxicity-weighted" sum; this is much more meaningful than the unweighted sum. The Tellus study used this technique extensively, collapsing dozens of disparate emissions into a toxicity-weighted total.

If all emissions were responsible for the same kind of environmental damage, then a single damage-weighted total would be all that was needed. However, there are multiple types of environmental damage attributable to pollution. How should the toxicity of some emissions, for example, be compared to the climate change potential of others?

Economists usually propose to answer such questions by attributing monetary values to pollution damages. The most popular technique involves what is known as "contingent valuation," essentially an opinion poll in which economists ask people how much a certain kind of environmental damage is worth to them. Criticisms of this technique are discussed in the last section of Chapter 3. Although economists like contingent valuation, others are not always impressed; the editors of the *Harvard Law Review,* for example, published a scathing critique of the contingent valuation process, entitled "Ask a Silly Question. . . ."[15]

Concerned about the limitations of contingent valuation, we used an alternative approach to valuation of emissions, sometimes called the "control cost" method. We assigned dollar values to each of several types of pollution, based on the expenditures required by current pollution control regulations. This approach, which has been developed in the context of electric utility regulation, assumes that the value of reducing pollutant emissions can be measured by the costs of mandatory controls. If regulations require spending twice as much to control pollutant X as to control pollutant Y, per pound of captured emissions, then it can be inferred that regulators believe (or at least act as if) X causes twice as much damage as Y. Emissions can thus be "priced" at the per-unit cost of currently required pollution controls.

Just as contingent valuation studies ask random samples of the population to estimate the value of damages caused by pollution, the control cost method of valuation indirectly asks environmental regulators the same question. More precisely, it infers the regulators' answers from their past behavior. The values that regulations place on pollution are arguably a better indication of society's valuation than the opinions of a random sample of people. Regulators are usually better informed than the public at large, and have been democratically chosen to represent the public on such questions; they are either elected, or appointed by elected officials. Some of the problems that could invalidate contingent valuation results, such as public ignorance of specific environmental hazards or lack of experience with complex environmental judgments, should not arise with regulators.

The 1994 Update and the Limits of Valuation

The original Tellus valuations, published in 1992, reflected work done in 1990–1991. In 1994, we had an opportunity to update and revise these valuations, using control costs as of 1993, and adding some new information that had become available. The update occurred in the course of a study, sponsored by the United Nations Industrial Development Organization, of the environmental impacts of packaging in Mexico.[16] It was a fascinating but also frustratingly incomplete research project. The incompleteness stemmed from the lack of data; even though the research team spent most of its time and effort on data collection, emissions data for Mexican industry remained sparse by U.S. standards. Based on the available data, we concluded that PVC production was again the most environmentally harmful aspect of the packaging industry, with vinyl chloride emissions per ton of PVC significantly higher than in the United States. For other materials, we found that production in Mexico was usually "dirtier" than production of the same material in the United States, in large part because electricity produced in Mexico, and used in Mexican industry, involves much higher pollutant emissions per kilowatt-hour than U.S. electricity. The principal conclusion, though, was that better data were needed for an adequate lifecycle analysis of packaging in Mexico.

The updated Tellus externality valuations appeared only as an appendix to the Mexico study. They were much lower in absolute terms, often less than half the original valuations. However, the relative rankings of packaging materials remained unchanged—our qualitative conclusions survived, even though our dollar values for externalities did not.

The principal reason for the reduction was that estimated control costs for several major pollutants were lowered in the early 1990s, as new regulations and new control techniques evolved. This process of change has continued since 1993; the cost of controlling sulfur dioxide emissions, in particular, has dropped sharply. However appealing our control cost method of valuation might appear in theory, it is of limited practical value in a period of rapid change in pollution control options, technologies, and costs.

In my opinion, it has now become difficult to interpret our valuations of emissions as actual dollar values of externalities. Indeed, the whole process of valuation of externalities as a basis for policy raises a number of practical and theoretical problems, as discussed in Chapters 2 and 3. We originally had intended to calculate the dollar values of packaging externalities as a basis for tax or fee proposals (see the discussion of Schall's work in Chapter 4). But even if packaging externalities were evaluated, and externality-based taxes were levied on individual materials, rigorous analysis of the expected effects on packaging use would remain a complex, data-intensive task—as shown in later research by Irene Peters, an economist who worked on the Tellus Packaging Study.[17] On the other hand, our qualitative conclusions about the ranking of packaging materials appear to be fairly robust, having been virtually unaffected by a major revision in control costs. At this point, I think it is more realistic to use our estimates to measure the relative environmental impacts of different materials—recognizing that the absolute importance of environmental effects is inevitably a political question, no matter how carefully it has been researched.

Since there has been some interest in our valuations, it may be useful to present the results of the 1994 revision. The complete calculations that produced these numbers are lengthy, and those who are interested in details should contact Tellus Institute. To address the detail about which we received the most inquiries, the values of numerous toxic emissions, weighted according to toxicity as described above, were tied to the control cost for lead emissions. We used an estimate of $528, in 1993 dollars, per pound of lead, based on controls at secondary lead smelters. Therefore, the inferred cost of each toxic emission is:

$$\text{Emission cost per pound of } X = \$528 \times \frac{\text{toxicity of pollutant } X}{\text{toxicity of lead}}$$

The 1994 revision was based on this and other control cost valuations. The revised externality values for U.S. packaging production, in 1993 dollars per ton of packaging material, are shown in Table 5-1. In one case, virgin production of corrugating medium, I have adjusted the published figure in an attempt to correct for incomplete data in the original study.[18]

For glass and aluminum, the two values shown in the table are for 100% virgin and 100% recycled materials, respectively. For aluminum

Table 5-1
Tellus Packaging Study Externality Values (1994 Update)

Plastics	
HDPE (high-density polyethylene)	$128
LDPE (low-density polyethylene)	$158
PET (polyethylene terephthalate)	$331
Polypropylene	$148
Polystyrene	$162
PVC (polyvinyl chloride)	$1,714
Paper	
Bleached kraft paperboard	$121
Unbleached coated boxboard	$94
Linerboard	$95
Corrugating medium	$101
Unbleached kraft paper	$96
Boxboard from wastepaper	$76
Linerboard from wastepaper	$77
Corrugating medium from wastepaper	$109
Glass and Metal	
Virgin glass	$70
Recycled glass	$48
Virgin aluminum	$928
Recycled aluminum	$76
Steel	$79

with 50% recycled content, the appropriate value is the average of $928 and $76, or $502.

For steel, we found that the steel used in cans comes exclusively from basic oxygen furnaces, where the secondary content (including in-plant scrap) must remain between about 28% and 40%; while some steel products can be made in electric arc furnaces with 100% secondary content, steel cans cannot. The value shown here for steel is an average of the nearly identical values found in the study for steel cans with the maximum and minimum feasible secondary content. Of the materials included here, steel is the one for which packaging accounts for by far the smallest percentage of total use, and of recycling; much larger differences would be found in a study of primary and secondary steel production in general, rather than of steel cans in particular.

The values presented here are for production impacts only. The original Packaging Study values included two other categories of impacts.

One of those categories, environmental impacts of disposal, turned out to be minimal, often 1 % of production impacts or less. The other category was the monetary cost of waste management, based on 1990 estimates of New Jersey disposal costs. Waste management costs vary from place to place; even in New Jersey, the 1990 estimates are no longer appropriate. Thus the production impacts alone are the figures that appear to be most relevant for broader analyses.

Notes

1. Anita Manning, "Earth Notes," *USA Today,* August 25, 1994.

2. *Tellus Institute Packaging Study,* 2 volumes, 1992. For a short summary, see Frank Ackerman, "Analyzing the True Costs of Packaging," *BioCycle,* April 1993.

3. The conflict is summarized in William Rathje and Cullen Murphy, *Rubbish! The Archaeology of Garbage* (New York: HarperCollins, 1992), pp. 156–160.

4. Data on plastics recycling, an industry still in its infancy, were not available at the time of the study. Based on more recent information, it appears that in this case, too, recycling reduces environmental impacts. For one grade of paperboard, for which data were also incomplete, it appears possible that recycled and virgin production have roughly similar impacts per ton; the figures in this case are particularly uncertain, as explained in the appendix. The absence of discussion of steel recycling is also addressed in the appendix.

5. Ivan Amato, "The Crusade to Ban Chlorine," *Garbage,* Summer 1994.

6. Chem Systems, Inc., *Vinyl Products Lifecycle Assessment* (Wayne, New Jersey: Vinyl Institute, 1992).

7. *Environmental Action,* July–August 1990. Ironically, orange juice is undoubtedly Coca-Cola's healthiest product, and the drink box is likely Coke's lightest weight single-serving package.

8. Senator Judy Kany and Representative Michael Michaud, letter to the editor in *Maine Sunday Telegram,* Portland, Maine, September 9, 1990.

9. Cable News Network transcript, November 7, 1990, 10:00–11:00 p.m.

10. Robert Steuteville, "Recycling Polycoated Packaging," *BioCycle,* March 1994.

11. *Stonyfield Farm and Environmental Packaging* (Londonderry, New Hampshire: Stonyfield Farm Yogurt, 1994).

12. However, Scott Noesson, Environmental Projects Manager for Dow Plastics of North America, has used the Tellus method of ranking pollutants to evaluate Dow Chemical's company-wide emissions. He found that carbon tetrachloride was a small part of the weight, but accounted for most of the toxicity, of Dow emissions, and reported that Dow is successfully working on reducing its carbon tetrachloride emissions. (Presentation by Scott Noesson, Recycling Congress of Ontario, October 7, 1994, in Hamilton, Ontario.)

13. Styrene emissions during production, an issue that is sometimes mentioned,

may be a more serious issue than the minor waste management implications of polystyrene packaging. However, our data showed that styrene emissions during polystyrene production are far less toxic than vinyl chloride emissions during PVC production.

14. Jerry Powell, "The PRFect Solution to Plastic Bottle Recycling," *Resource Recycling,* February 1995; and "Is Mixed Plastic Bottle Recycling Working?," *Resource Recycling,* September 1995.

15. " 'Ask a Silly Question . . . ': Contingent Valuation of Natural Resource Damages," *Harvard Law Review,* Vol. 105 (June 1992). See also the extensive literature reviewed in Arild Vatn and Daniel W. Bromley, "Choices without Prices without Apologies," *Journal of Environmental Economics and Management,* Vol. 26, No. 1 (1994).

16. Frank Ackerman, Paul Ligon, Lori Segall, and Brian Zuckerman, *Lifecycle Analysis and Legislation for Packaging Materials in Mexico* (Boston: Tellus Institute, 1994).

17. Irene Peters, *A Study of the Impacts of Material Charges on Packaging,* Ph.D. dissertation, Economics Department, Clark University, 1995.

18. The Packaging Study identified both uncontrolled and controlled emissions from each production process; valuations were based on controlled emissions. However, for the sulfite pulping process, used in virgin production of corrugating medium, no data were available on controlled emissions. The published valuations therefore in effect assume that there are no emissions from sulfite pulping, an assumption which a few alert readers have objected to. In order to make a rough correction for this error, I have assumed that the efficiency of controls—that is, the percentage reduction in each emission due to controls—is the same for sulfite pulping as for kraft pulping (the pulping method used in all other virgin paper and paperboard processes modeled in the Packaging Study). This allows an estimation of controlled emissions from sulfite pulping; inclusion of those estimated emissions raises the valuation for virgin production of corrugating medium from the published $49 per ton to the $101 per ton shown in Table 5-1. Needless to say, this makes the $101 figure less firmly based than the other valuations in the table.

CHAPTER 6

The Dot Heard Around the World

It can be sobering to see ourselves through foreign eyes. In 1995 the re-cycling consortium established by German industry published a review of packaging regulation and recycling in 25 countries around the world. After examining 24 other countries, the review ends with a section en-titled, "USA—still plenty of space for landfills." Illustrated with a pho-tograph of a Western desert landscape, the evaluation of U.S. recycling policy concludes that "people are not really aware of the waste problem in the United States. This is also reflected in the waste legislation pol-icy—both of the White House and of individual states. Low [recycling targets] . . . document the lack of interest of the legislator, industry and the general public in this environmental topic."[1]

Through American eyes, it hardly appears that Americans "are not really aware of the waste problem." But it is certainly true that the United States has been relatively unaffected by the tumultuous changes in European and worldwide recycling policy in the 1990s. Those changes, based on the notion that industry is responsible for managing the solid waste its products create, burst into prominence in Germany in 1991.

In that year the German government adopted the Packaging Ordi-nance, requiring industry either to accept all returned packaging or to provide for its collection and recycling. Industry responded by creating the Duales System Deutschland (DSD), a "dual system" for recovery of packaging separately from ordinary waste collection. DSD licenses its "green dot" trademark to manufacturers and distributors, charging license fees based on the quantity and types of packaging materials each company sells in Germany. The license fees are used to finance the collection of packaging that bears the green dot. From the very beginning, huge amounts of material have been collected, at considerable cost.

This recycling effort is important not only because Germany is one of the largest industrial economies, but also because the German legislation has been discussed, criticized, and imitated (with modifications) in numerous other countries. It has opened a new debate about the extent and implications of producer responsibility for waste. Despite some dramatic problems, DSD's management of German packaging waste has expanded our knowledge of how much waste reduction and recycling is possible—and at what price. This chapter begins with a look at the context in which Germany's new approach to packaging was adopted, then examines its problems and accomplishments, and finally reviews other countries' variations on the German model and interpretations of producer responsibility.

The German Context

Ambitious recycling efforts are popular in Germany, owing in part to the lack of space for waste disposal. The former West Germany is about as densely populated as Connecticut, while the region that was East Germany is comparable in density to New York—two states in the United States where it is hard to site new landfills, and where recycling programs are widespread. Germany's waste disposal capacity is constrained not only by the lack of open space, but also by strict regulations on landfills and incinerators, and by public opposition to incineration.

The long-term scarcity of disposal capacity grew even worse in the early 1990s. Before unification in 1989, West Germany exported solid waste to numerous low-cost, poorly regulated landfills in East Germany. After unification, Western environmental standards applied throughout Germany, and many Eastern landfills had to be closed or upgraded. Other German waste exports were blocked by the growing belief that each country should handle its own waste; France stopped accepting German solid waste in 1992.

Recycling, particularly of glass and paper, was already well underway in Germany in the 1980s. The Green Party, famous for advocacy of more controversial causes at a national level, also elected thousands of local councilors who worked to establish recycling programs in communities throughout Germany.[2] Support for recycling is not confined to the Greens; the established parties have come to adopt many parts of the Green agenda, and recycling may be one of the easiest environmental goals for them to support. It was the conservative Christian Democrats, the party in power in 1991, who introduced and passed the Packaging Ordinance.

The high cost and difficulty of disposal, combined with active environmental awareness and concern, made producer responsibility for waste a natural principle to adopt. In Germany, as in all industrialized countries, packaging accounts for a substantial share of household waste. Yet individuals have little choice about the amount of packaging that surrounds the products they buy. While some packaging is required for protection of products during transportation and distribution, many packaging decisions are made by producers for marketing purposes. If packaging is selected by producers for their own benefit, perhaps they should be held responsible for managing the resulting waste. Although this idea has been discussed in many countries, Germany was the first to act on it.

Producer Responsibility: The German Law

The 1991 Packaging Ordinance has four principal components, all designed to promote producer responsibility for packaging:

• Manufacturers and distributors are required to accept returned transport packaging, such as shipping cartons and pallets, and recycle or reuse it.

• Retailers are required to accept returned secondary packaging—that is, the outer layers of packaging that can be removed immediately after purchase, such as the cardboard box containing a tube of toothpaste. Distributors are required to accept returned secondary packaging from retailers, and recycle or reuse it.

• For primary sales packaging—for example, the toothpaste tube itself—the same rules apply as for secondary packaging, unless industry establishes a collection and recycling system that meets strict government quotas for recovery of each type of packaging material. Intermediate quotas were set for 1993, the first year of required collection. Higher quotas took effect in mid-1995: 72% recovery of glass and metal packaging, and 64% for paper and cardboard, plastic, and composite packaging.

• A deposit/refund system is required for beverage, detergent, and paint containers. Beverage containers can be exempt if the industry maintains

1991 levels of refillable bottle usage in each state, and nationwide averages of 72 % refillable usage for beverages other than milk, and 17 % for milk.

For transport and secondary packaging, the ordinance quickly had the desired results. Early reports described a growing interest in reusable transport packaging, and a rapid decline in the use of secondary packaging, within the first year. (Transport packaging is a substantial category, accounting for roughly one-third of all packaging; secondary packaging, on the other hand, is less than 1 % of all packaging.) Likewise, the beverage industry has maintained the levels of refillable usage required for exemption from deposits.[3]

Most of the attention and controversy has focused on the requirements for primary packaging, by far the largest category. In this case the take-back option was impossibly expensive and unwieldy. In practical terms, industry had to create a packaging collection and recycling system that could meet the government quotas. The result was the DSD.

To ensure the collection and recycling of packaging, DSD signs three sets of contracts. First, it licenses the use of the green dot symbol on packaging, and collects license fees from producers. Packaging bearing the green dot is exempt from the take-back requirement of the law. Second, DSD pays private waste haulers and municipal waste management agencies to collect packaging separately from other waste and to sort it for recycling. Finally, DSD contracts with industry organizations which guarantee that the collected materials will be recycled. In most cases DSD sells the materials to industry, and reduces the license fee for each material by the amount of the sales revenue. For plastics, however, DSD must pay the industry to recycle the packaging, and raises the license fee on plastics to cover the cost.

Stumbling into Success

The story of German recycling was widely reported in 1993, when DSD was just getting underway and was experiencing a number of serious problems in its first attempts to carry out its mandate. It is worth revisiting now, when a few years of experience have solved some, but not all, of its problems.

The good news is that DSD was an immediate success at recycling. From a few pilot programs in late 1991, it grew into a multibillion-dollar enterprise that collected and recovered over half of Germany's primary packaging in 1993, and two-thirds in 1994 (see Table 6-1). It met

Table 6-1

Packaging Use and Recycling (thousands of metric tons) in Germany

	Packaging Used in 1993[a]	Quantity Recovered in 1994[b]	Percentage	Quantity Recovered in 1995[b]	Percentage
Glass	3,477	2,474	71%	2,590	75%
Paper and cardboard	1,667	1,177	71%	1,178	71%
Plastics	890	461	52%	530	60%
Steel cans	628	354	56%	370	59%
Beverage cartons	202	78	39%	87	43%
Aluminum	92	29	31%	41	45%
TOTAL	6,957	4,574	66%	4,796	69%

Sources: Data for 1993 and 1994 from DSD press release, May 9, 1995; preliminary 1995 recovery data from *Handelsblatt,* January 24, 1996, p. 19.

[a]Packaging use data for 1993 were the latest available; if the downward trend of 1991–1993 continued, actual 1994 and 1995 packaging use would be slightly lower (and percentages recovered slightly higher) than shown here.

[b]"Quantity recovered" includes only amounts ultimately recovered for recycling; DSD collections in 1994 (including contaminants and incorrectly sorted material) totaled 4,935 thousand metric tons.

the mandated quotas for all materials except aluminum in 1993, and for all materials in 1994. More than 80% of German households were sorting their waste soon after the program started.

The bad news was extensively reported soon after DSD began. One area of criticism involves costs, while another concerns DSD operations.

Although the green dot system and DSD are sometimes said to impose huge burdens on the German economy, the costs actually appear modest on a per capita basis. In 1994 DSD spent a total of 3.3 billion deutschemarks (DM), or almost $2.4 billion.[4] For Germany's 80 million people this was about DM 40 ($29) per person. This expenditure resulted in the recycling of 4.6 million tons of material, at an average cost of DM 720 per ton. In the absence of recycling, the same material would have been landfilled at an average cost of DM 211 per ton, or incinerated at an even higher cost.[5] Therefore, at least 30% of DSD's costs would have been spent in any case, to get rid of the material one way or another. The net social cost imposed by the Packaging Ordinance is the remaining 70 % of DSD's costs: about DM 510 per ton, or DM 28 ($20) per person.

By U.S. standards these costs are high—but so are the resulting recycling rates. Few U.S. communities have yet matched the 66 % recycling of packaging which Germany achieved on a nationwide basis in 1994. The one material for which recycling rates are higher in the United States is aluminum, which is much less common and less valuable in Europe than in America.

The optimists who appeared in Chapter 4, arguing that recycling is almost always profitable, have their counterparts in Germany. Erich Staudt, a German economist, projects that DSD's collection and recycling could soon be saving money for the average household, for two reasons. First, landfill costs, already astronomical by American standards, may rise even higher as new environmental regulations take effect. This would make recycling more of a bargain by comparison. Second, the reduced volume of household waste disposal, due to the high level of recycling, could allow a change from weekly garbage collection to once every two weeks. The combination of intensive recycling and less frequent garbage collection would be cheaper than sending all household waste to ever-more-expensive landfills.[6] However, the grounds for this optimism have not yet materialized: most communities have not switched to less frequent garbage collection, and the avoided disposal costs alone are not enough to make recycling save money.

DSD's most widely publicized operating problems were results of its hurried startup, and are somewhat distinct from the more serious ongoing questions raised by German packaging policy. Problems have arisen in each of DSD's major relationships—with packaging manufacturers, waste haulers, and recycling industries.

The problems with packaging producers, while critical in the beginning, were the easiest to remedy. The license fees paid by manufacturers were initially set too low to cover the costs of collecting packaging, and many producers were slow to sign up and pay their license fees. After narrowly avoiding bankruptcy in the middle of 1993, DSD revised its license fees to reflect the actual cost of collecting each type of packaging, and increased pressure on manufacturers to license the green dot and make prompt payments for it. DSD now generates a small surplus in order to repay the debts it incurred in 1993; repayment is scheduled to be completed by 1998.

The contracts with waste haulers and municipal agencies for collection of recyclables turned out to be more expensive than anticipated. Before the Packaging Ordinance, Germany had little experience with curbside recycling collection. Collection of glass and paper took place largely through dropoff sites; individuals brought glass and paper to the numerous public collection bins. Recovery rates were fairly high for dropoff programs; about 50 % of the country's glass packaging was being recycled by the late 1980s.[7] Recycling of materials other than paper and glass was limited by comparison.

The new collection system sponsored by DSD built upon the existing dropoff system for glass and paper, increasing the number of containers to one for every 500 people in many places. Since glass and paper account for almost three-fourths of German packaging (see Table 6-1), and have the highest recycling rates thus far, they account for most of the total tonnage. The remaining packaging types—cans, plastic, and composite packaging—are collected together, either through new dropoff collection bins or through curbside collection of recycling bins or bags put out by households.

Setting up a new collection program is bound to be expensive, especially when it collects relatively small quantities of material from each household. The problem was compounded by DSD's initial decision to pay for collection on a per-ton basis. This gave the waste haulers no incentive to monitor or discourage collection of inappropriate materials, which may have accounted for as much as 20 % to 40 % of early collections of cans and plastics. Part of the solution to DSD's 1993 financial crisis was a renegotiation of the contracts with waste haulers, setting a fixed per capita ceiling on payments for residential collection. This eliminated any incentive for overcollection, and in fact gave haulers an incentive to promote appropriate sorting of recyclables.

It appears likely that DSD's collection costs were inflated by the haste with which its program began, and the monopoly conditions it offered to its contractors. In less than two years, DSD had to arrange for collection in every community in Germany; one waste hauler or municipal agency was given an exclusive contract in each location. The haulers presumably could see that there was more pressure for immediate, comprehensive service than for cost-cutting. Competition was largely absent, and everyone knew that DSD was in a hurry to make a deal. In response to DSD's 1993 financial crisis, the waste haulers accepted lower payments than they had originally been offered. This confirms the suspicion that a more competitive bidding process would lead to lower costs in the future.

Proposals to reorganize and streamline collection continue to be debated. The process is far from perfected, and is likely to undergo further change. Yet it is also far from a state of crisis. An independent public opinion poll found that 75 % of German consumers were satisfied with the services offered by DSD in 1995, up 11 percentage points from 1993.[8]

Plastics Reduction

While many well-publicized problems have been solved, or could easily be, other problems continue to plague the German recycling system—particularly in its management of plastics. Recycling of plastics has been difficult and inadequate from the beginning, and is only slowly expanding. Although plastics make up only one-eighth of German packaging, they account for more than half of DSD's costs, because they are both expensive to collect and expensive to recycle.

After packaging is collected and sorted, its recycling is guaranteed by industry associations. When sufficient capacity is not available in Germany, the industry associations contract with foreign firms for additional recycling. For 1993 the government had set modest interim quotas, but collection immediately exceeded those quotas and overwhelmed the recycling capacity of German industry, particularly for paper and plastics. German wastepaper exports flooded European markets, driving down prices and provoking angry protests from scrap dealers and recyclers in other countries who lost revenue as a result.

The situation was even worse in the plastics industry, where recycling had barely begun and worldwide capacity was limited. In the years just before DSD began nationwide collection, Germany recycled about 30,000 tons of plastic in 1991 and 40,000 tons in 1992. For 1993 the government's quota called for recycling 84,000 tons, a quantity that German industry could have handled. However, DSD recovered an astonishing 280,000 tons of recyclable plastics in 1993, seven times the amount recycled in the previous year. In 1994 plastics recovery rose again, to 460,000 tons; in 1995 it reached 530,000 tons.

At first, most of this material was either stockpiled for future recycling, or exported to firms that claimed, often dishonestly, that they would recycle it. Some French "recyclers" pocketed the payments for accepting German plastics and dumped the material into French landfills. Numerous shipments of plastics were sent to developing countries, where recycling, if it occurred at all, often involved hazardous working conditions—and where, out of sight of the German public, it was all too easy to burn or bury the "recycled" plastics. Despite DSD's increasing vigilance in inspection of the firms that agree to recycle its plastics, the news media continues to discover stockpiles of recovered plastic hidden in warehouses around the country. An apparently endless succession of frauds, usually involving foreign incineration or landfilling, have been committed by firms that are allegedly recycling plastics. Recycling fraud will, in fact, be endlessly tempting to unscrupulous entrepreneurs, as long as DSD continues to pay firms to accept material that has no market value.

Problems such as the German recycling glut are addressed by the European Union's Packaging Directive, adopted in 1994 as part of the gradual effort to harmonize individual countries' regulations. In the new Europe, it is possible to have too much of a good thing: perhaps for the first time anywhere, regulations seek to discourage excessive recycling. The Packaging Directive sets a maximum as well as a minimum recycling target; if countries want to adopt higher standards than the maximum, they must show that they have sufficient domestic recycling capacity to handle their own materials. By 2001 each country is to recover, through incineration and recycling combined, at least 50% and at most 65% of its packaging; at least 25% and at most 45% must be through recycling. (Using terminology that may be puzzling to some recycling advocates, incineration is counted as "recovery" of the energy content of materials.) Germany's 1995 recycling quotas, which do not permit incineration, exceed the European Union standards for every material. Therefore, maintaining those quotas will require a demonstration that Germany has the capacity to recycle its own wastes.

While some capacity expansion will be needed for other materials, the real problem arises in plastics. There are two principal methods for recycling plastics: mechanical recycling, in which used plastics are ground into pellets and then remelted; and chemical recycling, in which plastics are heated to high temperatures at which they can be broken down into simpler molecules. Chemical recycling, in effect, turns plastics back into oil (or into simple hydrocarbon compounds that are usually derived from oil.)

In the past, most plastics recycling in Germany and elsewhere has relied on the mechanical method. But there are limits to what can be accomplished with mechanical recycling. When applied to mixed plastics, it produces a low-grade product known as "plastic lumber," for which there are very limited markets. Mechanical recycling yields a valuable product only when it is applied to a very pure waste stream consisting of a single resin. In the United States, the numbers identifying different types of plastic packaging are an aid to sorting. But even with such a labeling system (which Germany does not have), it would be hard to meet the German quota of 64% recovery of plastic packaging through mechanical recycling alone. The United States has not yet approached this level for the most commonly recycled plastics, let alone for plastic packaging as a whole.

More than half of Germany's plastics recycling, therefore, has taken the form of chemical recycling. Only a handful of facilities are involved. One plant is operated by the leading electric utility. Another, attached to a refinery, was originally designed to convert coal into oil during World War II; it produced little oil, at high cost, during the war, and has operated since then only during the energy crisis of the 1970s. A third is a pilot project created by BASF, a major petrochemical company, in the hopes of expanding to handle much of DSD's recovered plastics in the future. All are engineering successes but economic failures; at today's prices, the same products can be obtained far more cheaply from oil.[9]

In 1995, DSD found a controversial new method for lowering its costs: it began supplying recovered plastics to the steel industry, where the material serves as a reducing agent, removing oxygen from iron ore. Iron ore consists largely of iron oxides; in the first stages of steelmaking, the oxygen must be removed from the ore to yield pure iron. This is done by bringing carbon monoxide (CO) in contact with molten ore; CO combines with oxygen in the ore to produce carbon dioxide (CO_2). Carbon monoxide is obtained by heating hydrocarbon fuels such as coke, heavy fuel oil, or, in the distant past, charcoal. A steel mill that uses fuel oil is DSD's first customer; it has been able to substitute granulated waste plastics for oil without making any modification in its blast furnaces.[10]

The use of waste plastics in the steel industry has been criticized for failing to recycle the recovered material into new plastic goods, and for providing a subsidy to the steel industry.[11] The process seems dangerously close to incineration, which is forbidden under the Packaging Ordinance; like an incinerator, a blast furnace turns plastics into carbon dioxide and water vapor. One could argue that the processes are different, since blast furnaces use plastics for chemical reduction as well as combustion—but the distinction is a subtle one. Perhaps a better argument is that the use of plastic waste in blast furnaces does not necessarily encourage incineration of other wastes, but rather displaces a use of fossil fuels that will go on as long as there is a steel industry. Still, it is a far cry from turning old plastics into new, which was DSD's original objective. The high costs of plastics recycling evidently drove DSD to seek a face-saving retreat from its initial goals.

Because plastic waste replaces oil in steelmaking and requires no new equipment, it is, comparatively speaking, a bargain. Once the use of plastics in the steel industry was underway, DSD canceled its previously announced plans to have BASF build a huge new chemical recycling facility. While DSD has paid plastics recycling subsidies of DM 1000 per ton to existing recycling enterprises, and projected a cost of at least DM 650 per ton at the planned BASF plant, the steel industry receives only DM 200 per ton. Thanks in part to the steel industry connection, the fraction of DSD's recovered plastics that was processed in Germany jumped from 55 % in 1994 to 83 % in 1995, and was projected to reach 90 % in 1996.[12]

In plastics, as in other materials, Germany has demonstrated that it is possible to recover huge quantities of potentially recyclable packaging—and that it is a mistake to begin doing so before the capacity to process those materials becomes available. It is too soon to tell whether this will be remembered as a minor error of timing in launching an important innovation, or as evidence that a slower, more cautious approach was needed.

Do Refillable Bottles Help the Environment?

The high green dot license fees—almost $1.00 per pound of plastic packaging, and about half that much for beverage cartons and aluminum cans[13]—have prompted moves toward waste reduction as well as recycling. From 1991 to 1993 the amount of packaging used in Germany dropped by a million tons. While transport and secondary packaging accounted for part of this reduction, more than half of it was in primary packaging. This massive reduction in material use and disposal is quite likely the most important environmental benefit of the green dot system.

In the American context, we have seen that waste reduction and recycling sometimes lead in opposite directions: the lightest-weight containers, which are the least environmentally damaging to produce, are often less recyclable than the heavier alternatives. Naturally, the same conflict can arise in Germany. The merits of rival beverage containers have been extensively debated there as well, with some differences in both the options and the outcomes.

The leading beverage container options in Europe are not the same as in America. Aluminum cans are relatively rare in most countries (and banned in Denmark). Refillable glass bottles, on the other hand, are alive and well throughout Europe. And aseptic packaging—the "drink box"—has a much larger share of the market than in the United States. The study of U.S. packaging, described in Chapter 5, found drink boxes to be one of several lightweight options which had the lowest environmental impacts per ounce of beverage. However, that study did not include refillable bottles, since they have become relatively rare in the United States today. The key question for Germany, and much of Europe, is the comparison between lightweight, single-use beverage containers and heavy, refillable glass bottles.

The Packaging Ordinance requires the beverage industry to maintain historical levels of refillable bottle usage, or else to adopt a deposit/refund system. This requirement was the first aspect of the Packaging Ordinance to draw a formal challenge from the European Union. In late 1995 the European Commission notified the German government that its quotas for refillable detergent, paint, and beverage containers constituted an obstacle to trade among countries of the European Union. As a result, Germany must prove its refillable quotas are based on objective environmental criteria, rather than just historical market shares.[14]

Advocacy of refillable containers has an intuitive appeal: surely conserving material by washing and reusing bottles must be better than using a new container every time. But while this is certainly true for storage containers that never leave your kitchen, it overlooks the environmental costs of transporting heavy bottles to and from the brewery or bottling plant. Shorter travel distances and larger numbers of uses per bottle make refillables look better; longer distances and fewer trips per bottle do the opposite.

A detailed study by the Fraunhofer Institute, in Munich, compared the environmental impacts of the leading alternatives for milk and beer delivery in Germany. It suffers from the same disease that afflicts life-cycle analyses in the United States: the results are all but impossible to summarize, since the study catalogued hundreds of individual impacts for dozens of scenarios but offered no overall evaluation or bottom-line comparison. Indeed, in this case, the authors argued at some length against any attempt to draw summary conclusions from their study. However, one can safely say that they found that neither refillable bottles nor lightweight pouches and cartons are obviously superior under all circumstances. Their results shed some light on the conditions that make refillables better or worse than single-use containers.

For example, the study found that the "energy breakeven point" for milk delivery occurs between 18 and 25 trips per bottle, and between 100 and 200 km of travel distance. With more trips and shorter distances, refillable bottles use less energy overall; with fewer trips and longer distances, single-use containers become more energy-efficient.[15] In the case of beer, refillable bottles used 50 times each, with a travel distance of 100 km, were superior to single-use cans and bottles by almost every measure. For nitrogen oxides (NO_x), an important pollutant emitted by motor vehicles, 50-trip refillable bottles were still the best (emission-minimizing) option when traveling as far as 250 km, but became the worst at a travel distance of 600 km.[16]

Although the study did not compare these numbers to typical conditions in Germany or elsewhere, the German environment ministry has apparently concluded that refillable glass bottles are best for beer, while refillable bottles and one of the single-use containers, pouches, are equally good for milk. However, industry groups have contested these conclusions, arguing that the government used the wrong average travel distances and number of trips per bottle.[17]

In general, it seems more likely that the conditions favoring refillables will be found in Europe than in the United States. The European combination of high population density, smaller countries with more local breweries and bottling plants, and more continuing experience with returning refillable bottles, all point toward shorter travel distances and more trips per bottle. In contrast, America's low population density, high concentration of ownership in brewing and bottling, and acceptance of single-use disposables as the norm point toward long travel distances and fewer trips per bottle if refillables were to be reintroduced.

In an environment where refillable bottles are still widely accepted, it is not surprising that there are efforts to extend the scope of reusable containers. Several German cities, including Frankfurt, Dresden, Kiel, and Kassel, have imposed municipal taxes on disposable containers and utensils, aimed at fast food and beverage outlets. In some cases the taxes are as high as 10 pfennigs (7 cents) per plastic utensil, and 40 to 50 pfennigs (28 to 35 cents) per disposable cup, dish, or container. In some but not all cities, items bearing DSD's green dot are exempt. Soon after a court upheld the municipal taxes, McDonald's announced that it had chosen Frankfurt as the site for a large-scale trial of reusable containers and cutlery.[18]

Variations on a Theme

Germany's green dot was heard around the world; proposals inspired by it have been introduced in legislatures from Poland to Argentina.[19] The first three countries to adopt recycling programs influenced by the German example were Austria, France, and Belgium. All three have enacted laws establishing producer responsibility for management of packaging waste. All allow producers to transfer that responsibility to an industry organization similar to DSD; in each case that organization now licenses the green dot symbol for use in its own country. All three of the "second wave" systems also share one major modification of the German model: they allow incineration as well as recycling of the recovered packaging, thereby avoiding Germany's difficulties and expenses in the area of plastics recycling.

Austria's packaging laws resemble Germany's in most respects. Even the green dot license fees for packaging materials are quite similar in the two countries, as shown in Table 6-2. Austria differs in setting quotas for the total tonnage of packaging that can be delivered to landfills, rather than for the percentage of each material that must be recovered; the landfill quotas decline rapidly over the course of the 1990s, imparting a growing urgency to waste reduction, recycling, and/or incineration. Austria allows industries to opt out of the national recycling consortium if they establish their own recycling systems, an option which the makers of beverage cartons have accepted. And Austria, like a number of European countries, has even higher requirements for refillable bottle usage than Germany.

France and Belgium have made more substantial changes in the German model, aiming to hold down costs both by increasing packaging recovery rates more gradually and by maintaining closer ties to existing local waste management agencies. Their green dot fees are in most cases one-fifth to one-tenth of the German or Austrian levels (see Table 6-2).

Table 6-2
Green Dot License Fees (U.S. dollars per kilogram of packaging)

	Germany[a]	Austria[b]	France[c]	Belgium[d]
Glass	0.11	0.12/0.02	0.01	0.01
Paper, paperboard	0.28	0.28	0.06	0.03
Steel cans	0.40	0.54	0.02	0.05
Aluminum	1.07	0.68	0.10	0.08
Plastic	2.10	2.01/1.29	0.10	0.46/0.38
Cartons (composite)	1.20	NA	0.06	0.26

Source: Fees in effect as of December 1994, from DSD, *Packaging Recycling Worldwide;* converted to dollars using exchange rates as of October 27, 1995.

[a]Excludes small (less than $0.01) per-package charges.

[b]Higher glass fee is for single-use; lower for refillable bottles. Higher plastic fee is for small containers; lower for large containers. Beverage cartons are collected separately from green dot system.

[c]Excludes volume-based fees.

[d]Higher plastics fee is for HDPE; lower is for PET and PVC.

In France, a 1992 law called for recovery of 75 % of packaging by 2002, allowing ten years to accomplish roughly what Germany did in four. Each packaging industry is given a choice of establishing a deposit system, introducing an individual collection system, or paying a fee to support local collection and sorting systems. Most industries have chosen to pay the fee and joined Eco-Emballages, the French analogue to DSD.

Eco-Emballages is gradually signing recycling contracts with municipalities throughout France. Each community is offered one of three standard introductory contracts, depending on local circumstances. The introductory contract is followed by a longer-lasting one in which the municipality agrees to reach 50 % recovery of packaging within a short time, and 75 % within six years. Eco-Emballages reimburses the municipalities for their collection and sorting services, and also guarantees that their recovered materials will be bought at fixed prices. By the end of 1994, communities with a total population of 14 million, almost a quarter of France, had signed up with Eco-Emballages.

The approach to producer responsibility and packaging recovery is even more determinedly gradual in Belgium. A 1993 law imposed "eco-taxes" on packaging—unless reuse and recycling targets, specified separately for each material, were met. While ongoing parliamentary debate led to delays in the effective date for the taxes, Belgian industry set up FOST PLUS, similar to DSD or Eco-Emballages, to promote recycling. The government's recovery targets differ from those in other countries both in covering fewer materials (for example, only three leading plastics, rather than all plastic packaging), and in assuming that recycling will spread only gradually across the country, reaching 100 % of the population for the first time in 1998. By 2000, the government targets call for 41 % of all packaging to be recycled, and 32 % to be incinerated.

FOST PLUS is proceeding along much the same lines as Eco-Emballages, signing contracts with regional organizations throughout Belgium to support their collection and sorting of packaging. An interesting innovation is that FOST PLUS uses its green dot license fees to pay the regional organizations the "material chain deficit" for collected materials. The material chain deficit is defined as the gross costs of collection and sorting, minus any waste management savings achieved as a result of packaging collection, minus any revenue from the sale of recyclables. That is, the material chain deficit is the change in local waste management costs resulting from recycling—the same measure that was analyzed in Chapter 4. If industry pays the material chain deficit, local waste management agencies have the same net costs they would have experienced in the absence of recycling.

Easing into Producer Responsibility

While preserving the concept of producer responsibility for packaging waste, France and Belgium are seeking to lower the costs by allowing 6–10 years to phase in nationwide collection, integrating new initiatives closely with existing local waste management agencies, and accepting incineration as well as recycling of the recovered material. Even though these newer packaging management systems are just getting started, it is already clear that the French and Belgian versions, rather than the German original, are the models that other countries find most attractive. A Canadian proposal for "packaging stewardship," for example, has many similarities to the French and Belgian systems; although supported by some Canadian industry groups and widely debated in both Manitoba and Ontario, it has failed to win adoption in either province.

The new European approaches to packaging have had even less influence in the United States than in Canada. (The European green dot systems should not be confused with the small, voluntary eco-labeling schemes that have appeared in the United States; some of these attempts suffer from the "lifecycle analysis disease" of excessive, nearly indigestible quantities of information, and none has yet won widespread acceptance.) In the current political climate, it seems likely that any product stewardship initiatives in the United States will be at least as cautious as the Canadian, French, or Belgian systems.

Yet this is a case in which caution could be self-defeating. Germany's rapid success in waste reduction and recycling might be a consequence of its high fee levels, precisely the feature that the gradualists seek to avoid. In Chapter 2, the analysis of incentives for waste reduction and recycling suggested that many U.S. incentive proposals were too small to have a noticeable effect on producer or consumer behavior in the marketplace. The same charge could be levied against the French and Belgian green dot fees. Perhaps the much higher German and Austrian fees, far above the level that seems realistic to propose in most countries, are what is required to create a significant market incentive. Only after a few years' experience with the variety of European green dot systems will we find out whether gradual, lower-cost alternatives are as effective in recovering material as the original German "big bang" approach.

As popular as it is to lower the costs of packaging recovery, it is worth remembering that those costs have never been back-breaking. Even in Germany, the per capita cost of DSD in 1994 was $29 gross, or $20 net of disposal cost savings. The costs in France and Belgium will likely be only a small fraction of that amount; if the gradual approaches do succeed in promoting waste reduction and recycling, they will show that it can be done at a very modest per capita cost. Before dismissing the German model, it should be recalled that it was Germany's initiative that opened up the discussion of producer responsibility and inspired the potentially more cost-effective alternatives in other countries.

The notion of producer responsibility for packaging, as embodied in the European green dot systems, reflects the beginning of a shift in paradigms of waste management. At the turn of the twentieth century, urban waste removal was an urgent matter of public health and sanitation, due to the prevalence of organic wastes (see Chapter 8). Collection and disposal of waste was an essential public service, not surprisingly financed through local taxes. At the turn of the twenty-first century, the problems of organic waste and sanitation have not vanished, but have subsided in relative importance, while the issues of production and disposal of manufactured consumer goods have become more prominent.

The rise of manufactured products and the resulting wastes raise new questions of responsibility: are the decisions that cause the disposal of packaging and other discarded materials made by producers or by consumers? While both certainly play a part, it is often the case that consumers are free to choose only among a narrow range of options that are offered in the marketplace; those options are chosen by producers, who bear no responsibility for the waste that their products may cause.

Adopting a principle of producer responsibility for waste would not mean that somebody else mysteriously pays for waste management; the costs imposed on producers would surely be passed along to consumers in the form of slightly higher prices. However, it would mean that people would pay for management of waste in their roles as consumers of waste-generating goods, rather than as taxpayers supporting public sanitation. The increased costs might not have much effect on consumer choices among the existing alternatives—but responsibility for these costs might lead producers to expand the range of waste-reducing or easily recyclable alternatives available on the market. Germany is beginning to apply the concept of producer responsibility to products other than packaging; in a few years, the issues that have been addressed in this chapter may apply more broadly to recycling of consumer goods in general.

To most Americans, producer responsibility sounds like an unfamiliar new idea. Yet although it is rarely expressed in these terms, there is already one important instance of producer responsibility for solid waste in the United States. Several states have enacted "bottle bills," requiring bottlers of beer and soft drinks to charge deposits on each can and bottle, and to refund the deposits when the containers are returned. The economic and environmental impacts of bottle bills are the subject of the next chapter.

Notes

1. *Packaging Recycling Worldwide* (Köln: Duales System Deutschland, 1995), pp. 77–79.

2. E. Gene Frankland and Donald Schoonmaker, *Between Protest and Power: The Green Party in Germany* (Boulder, Colorado: Westview Press, 1992), p. 169.

3. See Bette K. Fishbein, *Germany, Garbage, and the Green Dot: Challenging the Throwaway Society* (New York: INFORM, 1994); and DSD, *Ecological Optimization of Packaging* (1992).

4. Based on the October 1995 exchange rate: $1.00 = DM 1.40.

5. Erich Staudt, "A Comparison of the Cost Structure and Fees for Domestic Waste Disposal and Recycling," (Ruhr-Universität-Bochum, abridged version, 1993), p. 9.

6. Staudt, "Comparison of Cost Structure," p. 18.

7. Justine Burt, *Green Light for the Green Dot?* (Master's thesis, Tufts University, 1994), p. 60, based on glass industry sources.

8. The survey, by the Emnid Institute, was reported in *Plastics and Rubber Weekly* No. 1614, December 19, 1995.

9. *Handelsblatt,* May 29, 1995, p. 9; Michael Lindemann, "Plastics Waste Strikes Oil," *Financial Times,* February 15, 1995.

10. "Hochofen als Müllofen salonfähig," *Süddeutsche Zeitung,* September 13, 1995; *Handelsblatt,* September 28, 1995, p. 27.

11. See, for example, *Süddeutsche Zeitung,* August 21, 1995, p. 15.

12. Ralph Tarres, "Nachfrage übersteigt das Angebot—BASF verzichtet auf den Bau einer Recycling-Anlage," *Die Welt,* August 4, 1995; "Duales System schlägt BASF-Offerts aus," *Süddeutsche Zeitung,* August 4, 1995; "Kunststoffrecycling im Inland steigt auf 83 Prozent," *Süddeutsche Zeitung,* July 15, 1995.

13. See Table 6-2; note that it expresses fees in dollars per kilogram.

14. *Europe Environment,* January 23, 1996.

15. A. Günther and W. Holley, "Aggregierte Sachökobilanz-Ergebnisse für Frischmilch- und Bierverpackungen," *Verpackungs-Rundschau* Vol. 46, No. 3 (1995), pp. 53–58.

16. German Environment Ministry (BMU) press release, September 21, 1993.

17. For the government's view, see the discussion of the Fraunhofer study results in *Wir und unsere Umwelt* (a BMU publication), No. 3 (1995), p. 4. For industry criticism, see *Handelsblatt,* November 3, 1995, p. 18.

18. Hanna Gieskes, "Plastikgabeln unerwünscht: Immer mehr Kommunen erheben eigene Steuern auf Einweggeschirr," *Die Welt,* June 30, 1995; "Frankfurt's Decision Taxes McDonald's," *Plastics and Rubber Weekly,* July 7, 1995.

19. This section is based largely on DSD, *Packaging Recycling Worldwide.*

CHAPTER 7

Bottle Bills, Litter, and the Cost of Convenience

Once upon a time, as I was reminded by an early Disney cartoon, empty beverage containers were not trash. The cartoon, from the "Silly Symphony" series, was the result of a foray into the children's section of a local video store, desperately seeking something that would entertain both me and my preschool daughter. As it turned out, the video offered more historical interest for me than amusement for my daughter.

Cartoons were an unfamiliar art form in the 1930s. The Silly Symphonies translated well-known children's stories into the new medium, showing characters emerging from storybooks onto the screen. In the one we watched, Old King Cole climbed out of a book, partied around like a merry old soul, and then, as the clock struck twelve, headed home, retreated into his book, and shut the cover. But before the cartoon faded away, King Cole offered one last proof of his essential humanity: briefly stepping back out of the book, he winked conspiratorially at the camera, set his empty milk bottles out on the front porch for the milkman, and then finally retired for the night.

In the 1930s, everyone knew that children's stories came in books and packaged beverages came in refillable glass bottles. Both of these ideas had to be unlearned in order to unleash the consumer society of the late twentieth century. Today, of course, one-way bottles, cans, and cartons are as commonplace as children's cartoons. My daughter understood neither the need for Old King Cole to live in a book nor the meaning of his empty milk bottles.

Americans now buy more than 150 *billion* beverage containers every year. About three-fourths of these hold soft drinks or beer. The rest are split evenly between milk and all other beverages—principally juice, bottled water, wine, and liquor. Although some types of beverage containers are recycled at impressive rates, more than half of the total still ends up in the trash. By the early 1990s, refillable bottles carried less than 5% of our beverages, and their share of the market continues to decline.

A Brief History of Disposable Containers

In the beginning (of the twentieth century, that is) almost all beer and a lot of soda was consumed in bars or restaurants, and did not involve any retail containers. When beer and soda were packaged, they came in heavy, refillable glass bottles. The bottles were valuable, and bottlers charged deposits on them to ensure their return.

The first disposable beverage cans, made of steel, appeared on the market in the 1930s. But the familiar refillable glass bottles were cheaper, and can sales were slow until World War II. The war years are often remembered as a high point of recycling; many Americans responded to patriotic appeals to save and recycle material to support the war effort (see Chapter 1). Yet at the same time, the government helped to supply vast quantities of beer and soda to the troops, inadvertently teaching a key group of young consumers to appreciate disposable beverage containers. Histories of the leading producers, Anheuser-Busch and Coca-Cola, reveal the importance of the new pattern of wartime distribution.

The beer industry, dominated by German-Americans, had been attacked as unpatriotic during World War I. Anxious to avoid another round of slurs such as "rats in the vats," the beer companies tried to advertise their loyalty in World War II. A prominent member of the Busch family enlisted—and Budweiser was sent off to war in olive drab cans. In 1944 Anheuser-Busch shipped the equivalent of just over 600,000 barrels of beer, one-sixth of the year's output, to domestic and overseas military camps.[1] During the war, the government shipped more than a billion cans and a half billion nonrefillable glass bottles of beer to soldiers overseas.[2]

Coca-Cola had no fears about its popularity; on the contrary, it was widely accepted as an emblem of home for homesick soldiers, who drank five billion bottles during the war. Initially Coke was shipped to the armed forces from a bottling plant in Iceland, but demand soon overwhelmed the supply. In 1943 General Dwight Eisenhower asked the War Department to establish ten additional Coca-Cola bottling plants closer to the front lines. The War Department provided machinery and personnel, usually employing soldiers who had worked for Coca-Cola before the war. By the end of the war the government had built 64 bottling plants worldwide, which were then turned over to the company without cost.[3]

After the war, refillable glass bottles were still cheaper than cans, and continued to dominate the market: in 1947, 100 % of packaged soft drinks and 86 % of beer was sold in refillable bottles, with deposits and refunds established and administered by the individual bottlers.[4] Demand from veterans helped keep the beer can alive. In the immediate postwar years, veterans bought more than a third of all beer sold in cans.[5] During the 1950s, one-way containers made major inroads in beer but not soda. By 1960, refillables still accounted for 95 % of soft drinks and 53 % of beer containers.

The cans that World War II veterans learned to love were made of steel, and quite heavy by today's standards. Men of a certain age (you know who you are) will recall the days when crushing an empty beer can with one hand required enough strength that it served as a youthful gesture of machismo. But by the mid-1960s the times were changing, in this as in so many other ways. The first aluminum beer can had appeared in 1958. Pull-tab tops were added in 1962, eliminating the need for can openers. Further advances in canmaking technology allowed production of stronger, lighter-weight cans over the next few years. By 1967, Coke and Pepsi, as well as many brands of beer, were available in aluminum cans.[6]

Lighter-weight, nonrefillable glass bottles appeared on the market as well, bearing the initially unfamiliar message, "No Deposit–No Return." As a result of the rising market share for both cans and no-deposit bottles, refillable glass bottles accounted for only 49 % of soft drinks and 26 % of beer containers in 1969–1970.

By 1970, in other words, half of soda and three-fourths of beer containers were being thrown away, ending up, at best, in trash cans and ultimately in landfills. All too often the fate of these containers was even worse, with bottles and cans tossed along roadsides, on beaches, farms, parks, and elsewhere. Beverage containers were a highly visible type of litter, one which had been virtually nonexistent just 20 years earlier.

The Birth of the Bottle Bill

The appearance of single-use containers soon led to interest in public policy responses. By far the most common and most controversial proposal has been to require bottlers to collect deposits when containers are sold and refund them when containers are returned. Formally known as beverage container deposit legislation and commonly referred to as the "bottle bill," this approach has been adopted in nine states (with a modified version in a tenth, California) and in almost all of Canada. In most states, deposit containers can be redeemed at any retail outlet that sells them, or at special redemption centers. Retailers sort the empty containers and return them to the bottlers, who reimburse the retailers for the deposits.

Vermont passed the first bottle bill in 1953, banning nonreturnable beer bottles as well as requiring deposits. But the law expired in 1957, as the container industry successfully argued against its renewal.[7] The first bottle bills that survived were adopted in 1972 in Vermont and Oregon, this time without the ban on nonreturnables. By the mid-1980s they had been joined by seven more states: Maine, Massachusetts, Connecticut, New York, Delaware, Michigan, and Iowa. All apply deposits to beer and soft drinks, and most cover carbonated water; some states include other beverages as well.[8]

Bottle bill proponents in other states were defeated by increasingly well-funded and well-organized industry opposition. Florida's advance disposal fee, discussed in Chapter 2, was a compromise between bottle bill supporters and opponents. So, too, was California's unique container redemption law. The state's 1982 referendum on the bottle bill prompted one of the acrimonious, big-budget media campaigns for which California politics has become famous. Supporters of the bill remember it as the "year of the smear," as the industry's most effective ads, in the final week of the campaign, showed interviews with five supposedly randomly chosen Oregon shoppers who complained about the high cost and inconvenience of their state's deposit legislation. In fact, all five worked for a beverage distributor or a supermarket chain, and were paid for their appearances. Genuinely random polls found that more than 90% of Oregon residents approved of the bottle bill.[9]

The California compromise, enacted a few years after the failure of the referendum, assigned a state redemption value to beverage containers. The state rather than the bottlers was responsible for collecting the redemption value at the time of sale and for refunding it when containers were returned. While eight of the bottle bill states have deposits of five cents (Michigan charges ten cents), the California redemption value is 2.5 cents per container.

Although polls show three-fourths of the population favors bottle bills,[10] and advocacy groups have continued to push for the idea, California was the last state to adopt beverage container legislation. Proposals for a national bottle bill have regularly been introduced in Congress, often by Massachusetts Representative Ed Markey, but have rarely received serious consideration. Yet interest in the question continues to surface. President Clinton's 1992 election platform called for a national bottle bill; so for the first two years of his administration, when the Democrats had a majority in Congress, there was recurrent speculation in Washington about the possibility of a White House initiative on the issue.

At the same time, new questions about bottle bills had arisen among local recycling advocates. As curbside recycling programs expanded in the late 1980s and early 1990s, they received much of their revenue from processing and selling beverage containers, particularly aluminum cans. It seemed possible that a bottle bill would undermine the profitability of local recycling programs, by skimming off their most valuable materials.

In this context, I directed a study in 1994–1995 that analyzed the economics of bottle bills and explored options for making the redemption process more cost-effective. To date the results of our research have been published only in draft form, although detailed comments have been received from some reviewers in the bottling and container industry, and others.[11]

Effects on Recycling Programs

We began by examining the impact of a bottle bill on municipal recycling programs. To aid our analysis we created a simple computer model of a typical community recycling program. We first assumed the community was in a non-bottle bill state and then considered how it would be affected by the introduction of a bottle bill.

A community recycling program is likely to lose money when a bottle bill is introduced since most of the aluminum cans and other beverage containers would then be redeemed for deposits rather than set out for the recycling truck. But the community's garbage collection and disposal costs would also be reduced, since people will redeem some containers that were formerly thrown out as well as ones that were formerly recycled. Could the garbage disposal savings equal or outweigh the recycling losses? The answer depends, in part, on the amount by which the disposal tonnage is reduced. It also depends on the cost per ton of disposal—the "tipping fee"—at the local landfill or incinerator.

To present our results we introduced the concept of the "breakeven tipping fee." Holding everything else constant, we calculated the disposal cost per ton that would be required to make the disposal savings equal the recycling losses. This measure can be used to compare many different waste diversion proposals; the lower the breakeven tipping fee, the more economically attractive the proposal. If the breakeven tipping fee for a proposal falls below the current cost of disposal, the community could save money by implementing the proposal.

For a typical community with a curbside recycling program, our initial calculations found that the breakeven tipping fee for the introduction of a bottle bill is $86 per ton. Disposal costs of this magnitude are found only in some parts of the urban Northeast and scattered other high-cost regions. Elsewhere in the country a bottle bill, under our initial assumptions, would indeed increase municipal waste management costs.

We then considered alternatives and modifications that might make a bottle bill more attractive. Our initial calculation made the conservative assumption that the community would not experience any savings in collection costs due to the bottle bill. It should come as no surprise (after reading Chapter 4) to learn that truck collection costs are crucial to the analysis. If the community can reduce collection costs as a result of the bottle bill, perhaps by using fewer recycling trucks when the volume of curbside recycling decreases, the breakeven tipping fee may fall as low as $41 per ton. Disposal costs at this level or higher can be found in many parts of the country.

Another possible modification holds even greater promise. Our initial calculations assumed that the curbside recycling program lost all beer and soda containers when the bottle bill was introduced. However, experience in bottle bill states shows that some deposit containers are still set out for curbside recycling collection. The deposits on those containers are the key to the reconciliation between the bottle bill and local recycling.

In most bottle bill states a material recovery facility (MRF) or other recycling center can only collect deposits if it separates the deposit containers it has received and presents them for redemption. At least one Massachusetts MRF does this, and it seems likely that many facilities in bottle bill states do the same. But this imposes the costs of an extra, labor-intensive sorting process on recyclers. California has a much more efficient approach: recycling programs can collect the estimated redemption value for the beer and soda containers they receive, based on periodic sampling of the incoming material stream; separate sorting on a daily basis is not required.

If recycling programs receive 4% of all deposit containers, and can collect the five-cent deposits on these containers through a California-style mechanism with minimal sorting costs, then the conflict between the bottle bill and curbside recycling vanishes. The deposits more than make up for the loss of other materials; the breakeven tipping fee is zero or negative. That is, the municipal recycling program comes out ahead due to the bottle bill, even without any credit for reduced disposal costs.

This finding resolved the first question we addressed, concerning the relationship between bottle bills and local recycling. But the broader question of the costs and benefits of a bottle bill proved more difficult to tackle.

Dead Cows and Flat Tires

Although many facts about bottle bills are in dispute, two things are certain. First, deposit/refund systems achieve much higher recovery rates than other recycling programs: 85 to 90% redemption rates are common, compared with 40 to 60% recovery of containers in well-run non-deposit programs. Second, the high recovery rates are achieved at high cost, since a separate recycling system must be created to handle a relatively small tonnage of material. If viewed solely as a waste management strategy, the bottle bill would look hopelessly expensive.

However, bottle bills did not arise as waste management options alone. They were designed in part to hold back a rising tide of litter, not just to promote recycling. The appropriate fee or deposit should be greater for litter-prone materials, since they impose greater costs on society.[12] Since no one guzzles down a six-pack of peanut butter and tosses the empties along the roadside, there is no need to spend as much on recovering peanut butter jars as on beer or soda containers. But how serious is the litter problem? How much should be spent on controlling it?

Astonishingly little is known about the extent of litter, the damages it causes, or even the cost of existing litter control programs. Some states spend about $1 per capita on litter control, while others spend much less. Tourist-oriented communities sometimes spend substantial sums at a local level. Volunteer efforts to "adopt a highway" or clean up a park are widespread.

The few existing studies of litter even disagree about how to measure it. Some report the weight of litter, others the volume, and still others the number of littered items. Beverage containers loom largest in the overall litter problem when measured by volume. By weight, the occasional heavy items account for the bulk of litter, while by number of items, cigarette butts and other small bits of trash predominate. Thus the soft drink industry can cite item-count studies to show that bottle bills cause a "statistically insignificant" reduction in litter, while the federal Government Accounting Office found that bottle bills lead to litter reduction of 10 to 40 % by weight and 40 to 60 % by volume.

The damage done by litter includes, most obviously, its ugliness. Many people go to great lengths and expense to visit parks and beaches that are litter-free, providing indirect evidence of the importance of the aesthetic dimension of litter. But there are also more direct, physically damaging impacts of litter to consider.

For example, bottle bills reduce the number of children's accidents. If you were in a bottle bill state, the reason was not hard to see. When my older daughter was a toddler, before the Massachusetts bottle bill, our local playgrounds were covered with broken glass. By the time my younger daughter was a toddler, the bottle bill had swept the playgrounds clean (of glass, at least). While I never had to take anyone to the emergency room for glass cuts, statistics show that plenty of other parents did. Outdoor glass-related injuries treated at Children's Hospital in Boston fell by 60 % in the year after Massachusetts enacted its bottle bill, while other childhood accidents remained constant or increased slightly.[13]

Broken glass is bad for tires, too. Bicycles, cars, lawn mowers, and other vehicles can get flat tires from broken bottles. Tire punctures are also part of the little-known but potentially serious problem of litter damages on farms. Undoubtedly the classic description of this issue can be found in the 1981 Congressional testimony of Ed Fielder, a Maryland dairy farmer.

> There's four basic costs that the throwaway containers bring to the farmer. The first is equipment damage. We use a lot of large machinery that has a lot of soft rubber tires on it. . . . A throwaway bottle will go right through those tires and ruin that tire because there's no way under the sun of patching a large tractor tire once it has a sizable hole in it.
>
> [Second, when a tire is ruined,] you're down for 6 or 8 hours with that machine. In the critical time of planting, when you have 2 or 3 weeks to get your crops in, of harvest, when you have a month to get your crops in, your downtime is worth $100 to $500 an hour. An hour. It doesn't take very many hours of a big tire being flat to cost you a lot of money.
>
> The third thing is lost feed. We have a lot of fields close to the roadways and we have a lot of ground close to the road. We harvest alfalfa for silage. . . . All you have to do is hear one glass bottle or

one steel can or aluminum can go through the harvester and into the wagon and back to the woods that load of silage goes because you can't feed it to a cow once it's got glass in it. . . .

The worst thing, the very worst thing that can happen is when you don't hear that bottle go through and you don't hear that can go through. Then the cow is going to eat it. . . . And it causes death, a very slow and agonizing death.[14]

Numerous anecdotes in a similar vein can be provided by the Pennsylvania Farm Bureau, which has frequently supported bottle bill proposals.[15] A less colorful, more academic study assessed the impacts of beverage container litter on Virginia farms in 1985, estimating damages of between $1.8 million and $6.4 million in that state alone.[16] On the other hand, rival experts can be found who insist that there is virtually no farm damage attributable to beverage containers.

It is difficult to place a precise value on the childhood accidents, tire punctures, and farm damages caused by litter. But this does not mean that litter reduction is valueless, as is often implicitly assumed in analyses of the bottle bill. For whatever reasons, people place a great deal of importance on litter and visual pollution. The concerns about fast-food styrofoam, discussed in Chapter 5, are only understandable in terms of litter, since these packages cause negligible environmental impacts of other types. Similarly, the surprising passion felt by many city dwellers about removal of graffiti from public places suggests the importance of visual pollution. If we cannot adequately measure the importance of these issues, the fault may lie in the measures rather than in the belief that the issues are important.

Redemption Costs: Less Than Meets the Eye

When we turned from the benefits to the costs of bottle bills, we found that nothing new had been written in almost a decade. Most authors simply quote, sometimes at second or third hand, a few early studies— particularly the Food Marketing Institute (FMI) surveys of retail redemption costs in 1980 and 1986. These surveys seem to imply redemption costs of about 4 cents per container at today's prices. However, the FMI studies are not only out of date, but also assumed labor costs that, even today, are well above average for the workers involved in redemption.

Both surveys examined in great detail the time required for a supermarket clerk to sort the returned containers. But then both surveys apparently adopted unusually generous wage rates, inflating the estimates of redemption costs. The 1980 survey assumed an hourly labor cost of $12.00, while the 1986 survey assumed $11.50. Corrected for inflation, the earlier figure is equivalent to $21.00 in 1993 dollars, while the later figure is equivalent to almost $16.00. In fact, hourly labor costs, including wages and benefits, in retail food stores averaged only $10.00 in 1993.[17] In response to our report, the principal author of the 1986 study has said that the wage rates in the two surveys were always meant as examples, not as national averages.

An estimate of redemption costs based on the 1986 study, but recalculated in 1993 dollars at an hourly labor cost of $10.00, comes out to 3.1 cents per container. Even this is probably too high, because it assumes no gains in efficiency since 1986, a year when many of the state bottle bills were in their infancy. Based on informal observation while shopping in Massachusetts supermarkets, I am convinced that there have been great gains in the efficiency of container redemption in the last decade. Both the 5 seconds of labor per container and the nonlabor costs included in the 1986 study may now be too high. Stores have reorganized and streamlined their handling of redemption, and some large-volume locations now use "reverse vending machines" which accept empty containers, scan their bar codes, and give customers refunds or store credit slips. Unfortunately the scope of our work did not include primary research to measure changes in redemption efficiency.

Since the average American buys an incredible 480-odd beer and soda containers per year, those pennies per container add up quickly. Making only modest adjustments for efficiency gains since 1986, we estimated the annual cost of a bottle bill at $17.50 per person; with greater assumed efficiency gains, our estimate dropped to $13.40 per person.[18] Under a traditional bottle bill system, these are the costs that should be weighed against the benefits of reduced littering and increased container recycling.

It may be possible to do even better than a traditional bottle bill. Most of the costs of a bottle bill result from the need to sort the redeemed containers and return them to the bottlers. But the California redemption system largely eliminates this sorting process. The fact that the state, rather than the bottlers, originates the deposits means that in California the redeemed containers only have to be sorted by material type, not by brand. Once the redemption agent has settled accounts with the state, the containers can be recycled by the most efficient means possible, without further sorting or shipping.

For those who have followed the debates on reorganization of medical care, the California redemption system could be viewed as a single-payer system for container deposits. And just as Canada's single-payer health care system eliminates many of the billing and administrative costs that plague American medicine, so does California's single-payer redemption system eliminate many of the inefficiencies of traditional bottle bill systems. Even an extremely critical review of the California system, done for the National Soft Drink Association, implies that the annual cost is about $6.00 per person.[19] Our research, based on a different analysis by a California environmental group, estimated that a California-like redemption system (stripped of a few idiosyncratic features of the actual California system)[20] would cost $2.70 per person. At these levels it is easy to believe that the combination of litter reduction and increased recycling are worth the modest price.

The Inconvenience of Cleaning Up

Two major objections remain to be considered, one typically raised by economists and the other by environmentalists. Economic analyses of deposit legislation have frequently focused on the assumed inconvenience of container redemption. The best-known studies, by Richard Porter, conclude that the evaluation of a bottle bill depends on the relative weight given to litter prevention versus the inconvenience of redemption. This approach has been elaborated further by other economists.[21] However, lack of meaningful data on inconvenience costs has often led directly to a lack of meaningful results.[22]

A common-sense approach might suggest that the inconvenience cost is due to such factors as the time and expense required to drive to redemption sites. But based on the experience of living in a bottle bill state, it appears to me that most consumers redeem containers only infrequently, and almost always do so as part of normal shopping trips. Very little labor is required to put empty cans and bottles into the car when you are already on the way to the supermarket.

The fact that people do not always return their cans and bottles for redemption is sometimes cited as evidence that the inconvenience cost must be significant. But failure to return deposit containers is not necessarily evidence of consumer opposition to the bottle bill. Office workers eating lunch outdoors in Boston in the summer are often happy to give their empty bottles to the occasional homeless or low-income person who is collecting them, thereby promoting recycling, preventing litter, and helping a needy individual in a single gesture.

Something similar may have indirectly occurred in a large lecture course I taught at the University of Massachusetts. I was astonished at the number of students who drank soda during the class and left the empty cans in the classroom. Yet the room was always free of cans the next day. Staying late one day, I discovered that one low-income student came through the classroom building on a daily basis to pick up the deposit containers. At a nickel per can, she made quite a few dollars a week for comparatively little effort.

One moral of this story is that the bottle bill's role in litter reduction does not depend on everyone—or even most people—returning containers. There just has to be one in every crowd. In a more equitable society, with no homeless people scavenging in the parks or low-income students combing through classroom debris, another approach to litter reduction and container redemption might be needed. But this is not yet a pressing, practical problem with the bottle bill. It would be delightful to face this and other dilemmas that would be caused by rampant economic justice, but the prospect unfortunately appears remote.

The mechanism that led one student to pick up everyone else's cans is easy to understand. The more complex question concerns what went on in the other students' minds. What message were they sending when my words of wisdom inspired them to drop their soda cans on the spot? Clearly they were communicating that the inconvenience of redeeming a can was worth more to them than the five-cent deposit. But they knew they would be coming back to the same classroom frequently (or so I hoped). Presumably they enjoyed finding it relatively free of trash when they arrived. If asked, they, like the Boston office workers at lunchtime, might well have been glad that the deposit inspired someone else to pick up the empty cans.

In short, it is impossible to infer from anyone's behavior that they feel burdened by the inconvenience of the bottle bill redemption mechanism. Those who discard cans and bottles in public places could equally well feel liberated by the seemingly automatic removal of the litter they find it convenient to create.

A Last Stand in New Hampshire

The environmental objection concerns the effect of a California-style redemption system on the use of refillable bottles. Recall that interest in bottle bills arose as refillable usage declined after World War II. Refillable bottles are profitable only if they are reliably returned to the bottlers for reuse. A traditional bottle bill requires that the redeemed containers be returned to the bottlers, which facilitates the continued use of refillables. But the greater efficiency and lower cost of a California-style system results precisely from the fact that redeemed containers are not returned to the bottlers. Would the wider adoption of such a system hasten the demise of any surviving usage of refillable bottles?

Much of the story of refillables in the United States is told in *Case Reopened: Reassessing Refillable Bottles,* a report from INFORM, a New York-based environmental research organization.[23] It documents the precipitous decline in sales, identifies the market niches in which some small bottlers continue to sell refillables, and describes a number of environmental benefits of reusable containers. The Tellus bottle bill research led us to explore a different question. We wanted to know whether there was any remaining mass market use of refillable bottles that might be harmed by California-style redemption.

In soft drinks there is apparently nothing left to lose. The decline in refillable soda bottles did not get underway until the 1960s, but went rapidly once it began. A major regulatory change, the Soft Drink Interbrand Competition Act of 1980, was justified in part as a means to protect the use of refillable bottles. The passage of the act increased profits and concentration of ownership in soft drink bottling, but the decline of refillables continued unchecked.[24] We found no evidence of mass marketing of refillable bottles by major soft drink companies today.

The situation was not quite as bleak in beer; data supplied by the Beer Institute showed that refillable bottles were just over 5 % of all beer containers in 1993. Usage varied widely by state, from close to zero in most Southern states to more than 20 % in Massachusetts and Vermont. Statistical analysis of the state data showed that refillable rates tended to be higher both in bottle bill states and to a lesser extent in states whose neighbors have bottle bills; this makes sense since marketing and distribution decisions are frequently made on a regional, multistate basis. No other geographic or demographic factors explained any of the variation in refillable rates.[25]

One place where refillable beer bottles have survived is in bars and restaurants. In "on-premise" consumption, the staff rather than the customers collect the empty bottles, and can easily return them to the distributor at the time of the next delivery. A further statistical analysis showed that on-premise consumption could account for all refillable beer bottles sold in 46 states; in many states refillables were between 20 % and 60 % of bar and restaurant sales. But in the four New England bottle bill states (Massachusetts, Connecticut, Maine, and Vermont) refillable sales were well over 100 % of on-premise beer consumption. If individual consumers still bought and returned refillable bottles in large numbers anywhere in the United States, this was the place to look. And finally we found what we were looking for.

To get there you take the expressway fifty miles north of Boston. At the end of the exit ramp for Merrimack, New Hampshire, is a massive Anheuser-Busch brewery and bottling plant which supplies almost half of all the beer sold in New England. When we visited the plant in late 1994 it was producing 175,000 cases of beer daily, about one-third of which—nearly 60,000 cases every day—was in refillable glass bottles. (About half of the plant's beer was in cans, and most of the remainder was in barrels or kegs.) To distribute this much beer throughout the region, 100 trucks left the plant every day; typically, 40 to 50 of them returned with cases of empty bottles to be washed, sterilized, and refilled.

Inside the plant, the bottle-filling area looked like the results of a model train builder's imagination gone wild. Two separate high-speed production lines conveyed bottles and cardboard cases (which are also refillable) up, down, and around a cavernous warehouse, along an intricately winding path that led to a long sequence of customized machines. The first machine removed the cases of empties from shipping pallets; later machines opened the cases, removed the bottles, washed, refilled, capped and labelled them, reinserted the bottles into cases, and stacked them on pallets. On one line, bottle removal was done by a coordinated array of 120 plungers pulling the empties out of five cases at a time.

My personal favorite was the machine at the end of the line, the "palletizer." It slides a group of seven cases at a time onto a shipping pallet mounted on an enormous spring. The weight of the cases pushes the spring down just enough so that the next layer of seven cases can slide on top. The eighth layer depresses the spring far enough to release the pallet, which rolls slowly down to the loading dock, bearing its tower of 56 filled cases, as another empty pallet takes its place.

The bottle-filling operation was designed in the 1970s, when the technology for handling refillables may have been of more widespread interest. One production line fills 1000 bottles a minute, the other almost 700, with virtually no labor involved. Only a handful of workers are needed for trouble-shooting. On the day we visited, the only operation routinely being done by a worker was inspection of the empty bottles and removal of the occasional nonrefillable.

According to plant manager Rodney S. Hansen Jr., refillable bottles are profitable for Anheuser-Busch nationwide; the company's costs would increase by millions of dollars a year if they vanished entirely (the exact numbers are proprietary information). However, outside New England, Anheuser-Busch sells refillables only to bars and restaurants, since the consumer demand for them has vanished. The New England plant still sold two distinct types of refillable bottles: the heavy "longneck" bar bottles, which are also used in other regions, and a lighter "family return bottle" (FRB) for home consumers in the bottle bill states.

Longnecks are designed to withstand 25 or more uses, while FRBs averaged about four uses in New England in the early 1990s. However, the lightweight FRBs cost only slightly more than single-use bottles, and would save money for Anheuser-Busch even if used only twice. The INFORM report describes FRB sales by a number of very small local breweries around the country, but Hansen believed that his was the only plant operated by any of the leading beer companies that still sold refillables for home consumption. His major competitors in New England sell longnecks to bars and restaurants, but not FRBs to individuals.

It was a fascinating vision, showing that even in the United States in the 1990s, mass production and distribution of refillable bottles could be efficient and profitable. And we were among the last visitors to see it. A few months later, in early 1995, the Anheuser-Busch plant in New Hampshire discontinued the sale of FRB refillables to retail stores, and switched one of the two refillable bottle lines to filling single-use glass bottles. Sales of longneck refillables to bars and restaurants continue in New England, as in other regions of the country—but mass marketing of refillable bottles to individual consumers has ended.

The problem, according to Hansen, was not with the cost of production. Anheuser-Busch would still make more money selling refillables than single-use containers, if consumers would buy them. However, beer distributors and retailers were increasingly reluctant to handle refillables, due to increasing consumer resistance. When all the other brands offered only cans and one-way bottles, even the nation's largest beer company could not maintain the market in refillables. In 1994, 32% of the beer leaving Anheuser-Busch's New Hampshire plant was in refillable bottles; for 1996, that figure is projected to drop to 14%.[26]

Two Roads to Redemption

For those who favor bottle bills and deposit systems, there is a choice to make. Two roads to redemption diverge; two routes lead in very different ways to recovery and reuse of the materials used to make beverage containers. In terms of existing models, one road leads to Denmark, the other to California.

While the use of refillables is common throughout Europe, it may reach a peak in Denmark. Aluminum beverage cans are banned in Denmark, and refillable glass bottles are the norm. Deposits are high, and return rates reportedly hover around 98–99%, implying that each bottle could be used 50–100 times (although bottlers often retire old, scratched bottles for cosmetic reasons, well before 100 uses). Distances from bottlers to consumers are short, due to the size of the country. Thus Denmark offers a perfect example of the conditions under which refillable bottles are good for the environment, as discussed in Chapter 6. The beer industry is alive and well in Denmark; there is no evidence that Danish consumption of beer has been crushed by the burden of returning heavy glass bottles.

The intuitive appeal of the Danish solution stems from the nature of the alternative. It is hard to imagine that it is rational to crush, recycle, and remake America's 150 billion beverage containers annually, rather than washing and reusing at least some of them. (Just another step in this direction leads to questioning the health and nutritional implications of American levels of beer and soft drink consumption, an important issue that lies beyond the scope of this book.)

But however attractive Denmark looks on some level, the evidence keeps mounting that you can't get there from here. As ownership of bottling and brewing in the United States has become increasingly concentrated in the hands of a few corporations, average travel distances from bottlers to consumers have become quite long. Declining experience with refillables has meant that return rates, and hence the average number of trips per bottle, have dropped. Under these circumstances, a return to refillables might not even be environmentally desirable, unless it were accompanied by both a change in consumer habits and revival of a network of local bottling plants around the country.

Alternatively, if the mass market for refillables is gone beyond recovery, then the California model may be more appropriate. As this chapter has argued, a streamlined version of California's redemption system could offer a low-cost method for reducing litter and ensuring high levels of recycling of our billions of cans and bottles. It economizes by avoiding returns to bottlers, and instead facilitates crushing and recycling of redeemed single-use containers. Under existing American conditions—long distances to bottlers, and (by European standards) low rates of return—such a redemption system may even be better for the environment than use of refillables.

The traditional bottle bill, as implemented in the other nine deposit states, is not nearly as expensive or inconvenient as its critics sometimes suggest. The cost is hardly unbearable, apparently under $20 per capita. Yet the California model is definitely cheaper, and loses nothing except the incentive to return the empties to the bottlers.

The process of returning the empty bottles to the bottler was arguably important as long as the traditional bottle bill was encouraging significant usage of refillables. But, as suggested by the tale of Anheuser-Busch in New England, that time is rapidly passing. The cluster of New England bottle bill states was likely the last chance for mass marketing of refillables in the United States. It combined a high population density, a longstanding pattern of use of refillables, and return rates that remained high by American standards. There was, in addition, a leading producer quite profitably selling refillable bottles. Even under these uniquely favorable circumstances, the market for household use of refillables could not be sustained.

There is a sobering lesson here for bottle bill advocates. Americans are apparently determined to buy new beverage containers every time, but there is still a great deal that can be done to ensure efficient recovery of the used ones.

Notes

1. Peter Hernon and Terry Ganey, *Under the Influence: The Unauthorized Story of the Anheuser-Busch Dynasty* (New York: Simon & Schuster, 1991), pp. 181–182.

2. David Saphire, *Case Reopened: Reassessing Refillable Bottles* (New York: IN-FORM, 1994), pp. 130–131; the statistics cited here are based on Congressional testimony by an Anheuser-Busch executive.

3. Thomas Oliver, *The Real Coke, The Real Story* (New York: Random House, 1986), p. 20.

4. These figures, and subsequent ones on refillables' market share, are from Container Recycling Institute, *Refillable Bottles: An Idea Whose Time Has Come, Again* (Washington, D.C., 1993), p. 54.

5. Saphire, *Case Reopened*, p. 131.

6. William F. Hosford and John L. Duncan, "The Aluminum Beverage Can," *Scientific American*, September 1994.

7. Louis Blumberg and Robert Gottlieb, *War on Waste* (Washington, D.C.: Island Press, 1989), p. 238.

8. For example, wine, liquor, and juice are covered in Maine, wine and liquor in Iowa, liquor in Vermont, and packaged cocktails in Michigan.

9. Blumberg and Gottlieb, *War on Waste*, pp. 226–228.

10. Presentation by pollster Peter Hart at the National Recycling Congress, Portland, Oregon, September 1994.

11. Frank Ackerman, Dmitri Cavander, John Stutz, and Brian Zuckerman, *Preliminary Analysis: The Costs and Benefits of Bottle Bills* (Boston: Tellus Institute, 1995). Although written for EPA's Office of Solid Waste, the draft report does not represent EPA opinion, policy, or guidance.

12. Ian M. Dobbs, "Litter and Waste Management: Disposal Taxes Versus User Charges," *Canadian Journal of Economics,* Vol. 24 (1991), pp. 221–227; see also the discussion of Fullerton and Kinnaman in Chapter 2.

13. M. Douglas Baker, Sally E. Moore and Paul H. Wise, "The Impact of 'Bottle Bill' Legislation on the Incidence of Lacerations in Childhood," *American Journal of Public Health,* Vol. 76 (1986), pp. 1243–1244.

14. U.S. Senate Committee on Commerce, Science, and Transportation, hearing to consider *Beverage Container Reuse and Recycling Act,* 5 Nov. 1981 (Y4.C73/7.97–83).

15. Personal communication, Jan Carson, Pennsylvania Farm Bureau, October 1994.

16. Daniel B. Taylor and John B. Hodges, "Impacts of Beverage Container Litter on Virginia Farms," *Virginia Agricultural Economics,* September–October 1985, Table I.

17. U.S. Department of Labor, Bureau of Labor Statistics, *BLS 790 Establishment Survey,* 1993. This figure includes estimated benefits at 29% of wages, which were omitted from the Tellus draft report. The 29% ratio is for all retail employees in 1993, from BLS press release USDL 95-225 (benefits for food store employees are not tabulated separately). Subsequent figures that depend on labor costs have been corrected to include the estimated benefits, and thus differ slightly from the Tellus report.

18. The higher estimate assumes 3.1 cents per container of retail and bottler costs, 489 containers per person, and 85% redemption. The lower estimate reduces retail and bottler costs by one-third. Both estimates include the cost to consumers of unclaimed deposits and the cost of reimbursing recycling programs for the deposit containers they receive, as discussed above. See Ackerman et al., *Costs and Benefits of Bottle Bills,* for details; figures reported here incorporate corrected labor costs, as explained in Note 17. The study used mid-1994 prices for recycled materials, intermediate between the lows of the early 1990s and the peak prices of 1995 (see discussion in Chapter 4).

19. R.W. Beck and Associates, *Review of the Waste Diversion Aspects of the California AB2020 Program* (National Soft Drink Association, 1994), p. E-9, estimates the annual cost at $187.2 million, while the state has a population of about 30 million.

20. In particular, we did not assume continuation of the processing fee, a complex and frequently changing mechanism which requires the container and beverage industries to subsidize recycling of their containers. The processing fee appears to be the most controversial aspect of the California redemption system, and a state commission has recommended drastic simplification or elimination of the fee: Little Hoover Commission, *Beyond Bottles and Cans: Reorganizing California's Recycling Efforts* (Sacramento, 1994).

21. Richard C. Porter, "A Social Benefit–Cost Analysis of Mandatory Deposits on Beverage Containers," *Journal of Environmental Economics and Management,* Vol. 5 (1978), pp. 351–375; and "Michigan's Experience with Mandatory Deposits on Beverage Containers," *Land Economics,* Vol. 59 (1983), pp. 177–194. For appli-

cations of Porter's approach in an international context see the discussion of deposit-refund systems in D. W. Pearce and R. K. Turner, "Market-Based Approaches to Solid Waste Management," *Resources, Conservation and Recycling,* Vol. 8 (1993), pp. 63–90; and Inger Brisson, "Packaging Waste and the Environment: Economics and Policy," same volume, pp. 183–292.

22. For example, Michael Naughton, Frederick Sebold, and Thomas Mayer, "The Impacts of the California Beverage Container Recycling and Litter Reduction Act on Consumers," *Journal of Consumer Affairs,* Vol. 24 (1990), pp. 190–220, estimate two-parameter "inconvenience curves" based on only two data points, one from California and one from New York.

23. Saphire, *Case Reopened* (1994).

24. Allan W. Vestal, "Public Choice, Public Interest, and the Soft Drink Interbrand Competition Act: Time to Derail the 'Root Beer Express'?," *William and Mary Law Review,* Vol. 34 (1993), pp. 337–391.

25. This section is largely based on Frank Ackerman, Deborah Salon, Lori Segall, and Brian Zuckerman, *Refillable Bottle Use in the Beer Industry* (Boston: Tellus Institute, 1995). This, too, was done for EPA, but does not represent EPA opinion, policy, or guidance.

26. Personal communication, Rodney S. Hansen, Jr., February 1996.

CHAPTER 8

Organic Waste and the Virtue of Inaction

 ————————————————————————————————

> Decades of intensive government research finally achieved miracu-
> lous breakthroughs and launched a multibillion-dollar industry.
> Today the industry's products, often made from exotic new high-
> technology materials, shape the life of every American community.

This description, familiar from breathless accounts of computers and
biotechnology, is equally applicable to lawn care. And since grass clippings, leaves, and other yard trimmings account for more than one-
sixth of municipal solid waste, the story of the lawn is an important part
of the tale of waste and recycling.

The lawn as we know it today is largely a twentieth-century American phenomenon, as chronicled in a remarkable history by Virginia
Scott Jenkins. Before the Civil War, grass was either cut with a scythe
or grazed by animals, and lawns—as distinct from pastures—were rare.
The first lawn mower was patented in 1868, and the first lawn sprin-
kler in 1871, making lawn care technologically possible on a large scale.
The goal of a "green velvety carpet" around every house gradually
spread across the country as the middle classes moved out from the central cities. But utilitarian pasture may have remained more common as
late as 1896, when a writer noted, "There is a good deal to be said for
. . . keeping cows out of the streets altogether," while lamenting that
most towns had been unable to do so.[1]

American lawns began as imitations of the lawns and gardens found on aristocratic estates in England and France. They gained an additional impetus from the introduction of golfing to the United States in 1888. But grasses that were imported from Europe flourished only in the Northeast and Midwest. (The leading American lawn grass, the plant that we call Kentucky bluegrass, is an Old World native, called "June grass" or "smooth meadow grass" in England.) In 1917, the Department of Agriculture and the U.S. Golf Association began a collaborative research project on turf-growing. Government research continued, with interruptions, for decades; a massive effort after World War II finally produced grass varieties that grow well in the South and West. Today, very similar green lawns can be found from coast to coast, across wide variations in rainfall and temperature.

The environmental costs of lawn care would be hard to believe if they were not so familiar. As of the 1980s, American lawns received more fertilizer than all the food crops in India, while the ever-larger power mowers that trimmed our lawns caused 100 deaths and 20,000 emergency room visits in a single year. Vast amounts of water are used on lawns, even in arid regions where water is a scarce resource. An ongoing proliferation of chemicals, many later found to be toxic, have been spread on lawns to control weeds and pests. Lawn care is typically a male activity, with industry advertisements often invoking the image of a "war" on the enemies of lush green uniformity—and the connection has sometimes been more than rhetorical. Products of chemical warfare research during World War II were sold after the war as insecticides, as documented by Rachel Carson in her 1962 classic, *Silent Spring*. More recently 2,4-D, a probable human carcinogen which is the active ingredient in Agent Orange (the defoliant used in the Vietnam War), has been sold as a weed killer. It has proved no more effective in achieving a final victory over crabgrass at home than it did over Communism in Vietnam.

One obvious conclusion is that there would be great environmental benefit to putting less effort into lawn care, and replacing it with more acceptance of the natural and regional variation in our yards, parks, and open spaces. But there are powerful prejudices against change in the institution of the American lawn. Meanwhile, all this lawn care produces an annual total of 35 million tons of grass clippings, leaves, and other organic matter that must be disposed of.

Organic material behaves differently from other waste: it decays. Pottery, glass, and metal objects can remain intact for many centuries, and plastics look likely to do the same. But organic waste—including food scraps and paper products as well as yard waste—decomposes over a period of time ranging from months to decades. This process of decay offers an opportunity to turn organic matter into compost, restoring nutrients to the soil and reducing disposal requirements. However, when organic matter decays under the wrong conditions it can give rise to undesirable by-products such as methane, one of the greenhouse gases that contributes to the threat of climate change.

Pigging Out

Lawns are new, but organic waste management is probably as old as agriculture. In preindustrial societies, food accounted for most of the material passing through the average household, and food scraps accounted for most of household solid waste. Food waste was managed by what we might now call "mixed waste composting"—and in many parts of the world, the preferred composting device had four legs and a snout. Pigs are a remarkably effective mechanism for turning all manner of food scraps and plant wastes back into food.

Feeding waste to pigs was common in medieval Europe. French waste management may have claimed a royal victim in 1131, when King Philip died in a riding accident after his horse struck an unattended pig on the streets of Paris.[2] Seven hundred years later, the world had changed in almost every respect; but Charles Dickens still warned New York City pedestrians, "Take care of the pigs."[3] In 1842, the year of Dickens' warning, there were an estimated 10,000 pigs roaming the streets of New York, some belonging to low-income households, but some running wild. To a large extent, the pigs were the waste management system of the day. Household waste was often thrown into the streets, and New York's pioneering program of municipal street sweeping was still 50-odd years in the future.

By the beginning of the twentieth century, pigs had vanished from the urban landscape, and organized garbage collection was fast becoming a normal feature of municipal life. Yet interest in feeding garbage to pigs lingered on. During World War I the government encouraged it as a patriotic means of increasing the nation's food production. Many cities separated their wet garbage and sold it to pig farmers in the 1920s and 1930s.

However, pigs fed on garbage turned out to be particularly prone to trichinosis and other diseases. After a major swine epidemic in the mid-1950s, new public health regulations prohibited the use of raw garbage as animal feed. Cooking the garbage before feeding it to pigs does eliminate the threat of disease, but also eliminates any profits from this mode of disposal; as a result, the practice has been abandoned.

Other uses of urban organic waste have been tried in the past. Bones, mainly from slaughterhouses, and manure from city streets, in the days of horse-drawn transportation, have been sold as fertilizer.[4] There was a brief flurry of interest, beginning around 1890, in a process known as "reduction," which involved cooking mixed organic waste in order to recover grease and other marketable by-products. The stench from reduction plants was evidently horrendous, and the residues appeared noxious; by 1914 this method of disposal was on the way out. Philadelphia's reduction plant, one of the last survivors, was closed in 1959.[5]

Thus, although many methods of recovering organic waste have been employed in the past, all had died out before the rise of modern environmental concern about waste and recycling. Meanwhile, the composition of organic waste has changed; the era of recycling is also the era of the lawn. Food waste has not vanished, of course, but the volume of yard waste is now much larger. The new mix of organic wastes confronts a new set of options for reducing discards and recovering valuable materials—particularly through composting.

Home Remedies and the Cost of Composting

In recent years composting has spread almost as quickly as recycling, with more than 3,000 yard waste composting facilities in operation in 1994. As with curbside recycling programs, most composting facilities are new since 1988, when *BioCycle* magazine first published its annual survey.[6] Indeed, in many places, households are now required to compost or otherwise manage their own yard trimmings. At least 25 states have banned landfilling of some or all types of yard wastes. Many communities have three trucks collecting material from households on a regular basis: one for garbage, one for recyclables, and one for yard waste.

But despite the similarities, there are important differences between recycling and composting. Recycling produces valuable, marketable industrial materials, while composting produces only a low-grade relative of fertilizer, often described as a "soil amendment" to distinguish it from real fertilizers. Thus recycling can be integrated into an industrial economy, although, as seen in Chapter 4, fluctuating prices for raw materials render the profitability of recycling nearly unpredictable from year to year. Composting, on the other hand, has little relationship to industry, and is probably too small, and located in the wrong places, to be of much use to agriculture (although there is debate on this point). Compost itself has limited market value; some facilities provide it free to gardeners who want to improve their soil, or to municipal public works and maintenance departments for roadside use. Others, particularly those that receive relatively clean waste streams and can produce high-quality compost, are able to sell their product for a predictable, albeit modest, price.

Yet composting, with its lower-valued product, may be the more consistently profitable process. The range of available technologies and options is broader in composting, and the process is simpler. A pile of old newspapers or plastic bags, if left alone, does not turn itself into anything more valuable (as I myself have proved experimentally, more than once); a pile of old leaves starts turning itself into compost within a few weeks. Unlike the recycling of industrial material, composting organic material is something you can do at home. Since "home remedies" for organic waste avoid the expenses of both collection and disposal, they are often cheaper than alternatives that involve collection systems.

How much organic waste can be diverted by the various strategies for composting, and at what cost? Our research group at Tellus Institute conducted a study of this and related questions about organic materials management.[7] We focused on three types of material which together comprise one-third of all municipal solid waste (MSW): yard trimmings (18% of MSW), food scraps (7%), and mixed paper waste that appears uneconomical to recycle (9%). All paper and paperboard products are a much larger category, 41% of MSW; but many are readily recovered through recycling programs that yield a higher-value product than compost.

We examined five principal strategies for handling organic wastes.[8] For each strategy we calculated the cost per ton of waste, and compared it with the avoided disposal cost—that is, the amount that would have been paid to bury or burn the waste in the absence of the composting program. We also estimated the quantities of waste that could be handled by each option.

Undoubtedly the simplest program for organic waste is what is often called "grasscycling." Rather than bagging grass clippings and setting them out for collection, householders are encouraged to leave grass clippings on the lawn. This provides an excellent source of nutrients for the lawn, saves effort, and diverts a significant portion of the waste stream. It offers a rare opportunity to help the environment through inaction. The only technical obstacle to grasscycling is that very heavy grass clippings can smother a lawn. In areas where this is a problem, it may be necessary to get a new "mulching mower" that creates finer clippings, or to install a mulching attachment on an existing mower (a $20 to $40 purchase)—or to mow more often.

Grass clippings, which alone account for an astonishing 7% of all MSW, have not always been bagged for disposal. As recently as the

1940s, the majority of households probably "grasscycled." The advent of power mowers, which blew grass clippings across driveways and sidewalks, created the widespread desire to clean up the cut grass; by the 1960s, many new mowers came with automatic collection bags attached. Today, grasscycling programs simply ask people to return to past lawn management practices. Several early municipal grasscycling efforts reported substantial results with almost no effort or expenditure. We found that even if a municipality bought every participating household a $20 mulching attachment every five years (a hypothetical program, not one we saw in practice), grasscycling would remain one of the lowest-cost options for organic waste management. Although some resistance to change should be expected, we estimated that at least 60% of all grass could be handled by grasscycling programs.

Another option that requires only slightly more effort is home composting. With a simple bin, usually placed in the backyard, households can compost many types of food and yard waste. A modest amount of technical knowledge is required to avoid unpleasant odors; for example, avoid meat and dairy products, and if composting grass, be sure it is mixed with other materials. But with a bit of education, and a composting bin—both of which are often provided by municipalities—anyone can turn household organic waste into compost suitable for spreading on a garden or lawn. Although more elaborate home composting devices are available on the market, they are unnecessary. When you pile up organic waste, compost happens. Skillful use of a simple composting bin makes the process of decay neater, faster, and better-smelling; but the process would occur without the use of any equipment.

The principal expense of a typical home composting program is the cost of the bins, often $25 to $50 apiece. The largest home composting effort in North America is in metropolitan Toronto, where several years of vigorous promotion have led to participation by 25% of the area's single-family households. Based on the costs of the Toronto program and other early efforts, home composting appears only slightly more expensive, per ton of waste diverted, than our estimate for grasscycling. We projected 20% participation by households in 1–4 unit buildings as a modest, feasible goal for home composting nationwide.

A third strategy can achieve additional composting at a low cost but is not, strictly speaking, something that individuals can do at home. Commercial and institutional wastes often contain a high proportion of compostable material. Supermarket and restaurant waste, for example, includes a lot of food waste, which (along with any unrecyclable paper and cardboard packaging) can easily be composted. Institutional cafeterias and food services, in schools, hospitals, prisons, and elsewhere, generate large quantities of food scraps on a daily basis. Any institution with large grounds to maintain is likely to produce a steady stream of yard waste. In all such cases, an on-site or nearby facility could compost the material while avoiding the costs of ordinary waste collection and disposal services.

Only fragmentary information was available on the costs of commercial and institutional composting. Based on the handful of cases where costs could be documented, it appears that commercial and institutional composting may be even less expensive per ton than grasscycling and home composting. Due to the lack of data, it is hard to document how much potential there is for expansion of commercial and institutional composting. Regulatory barriers have inhibited progress in this area; even small on-site institutional composting systems are often forced to undergo the same permitting and siting process as large commercial landfills.

Gadgetry and Chemistry

Other, better-known strategies for composting can handle greater quantities of material, but at higher costs. Municipal yard waste programs, which have given rise to the thousands of composting facilities around the country, could potentially handle almost all yard trimmings. A wide range of technologies and equipment can be employed; an adequate description of the diversity of municipal composting programs would involve an odyssey through specialized worlds of gadgetry and chemistry.

In brief, there are two steps to a municipal program: collection of yard waste and operation of the composting facility. Particularly in smaller communities, collection may not be provided, and residents may have to bring their own yard trimmings to the facility. In larger communities where curbside collection is offered, bags of yard waste may be picked up by conventional garbage trucks. Alternatively, special-purpose vehicles may be used, such as vacuum trucks that can pick up loose piles of leaves that have been raked to the curb.

The range of variation is even greater in facility operation. The simplest composting sites just deposit leaves in long piles, or windrows, and turn the piles over periodically with front-end loaders. High-technology facilities also deposit waste in windrows, but take additional steps in order to accelerate the composting process and improve the quality of the final product. This may require such devices as customized windrow turners, screening equipment to remove contaminants, and wood chippers or tub grinders to reduce the size of brush.

The most frequent operating problem at composting facilities is an offensive odor. This often results from using excessive amounts of grass, a material which contains too much nitrogen and not enough carbon for odorless composting. The problem is much easier to avoid when grass clippings are mixed with enough leaves, brush chips, or paper. However, facilities that accept grass clippings year-round may receive so much grass that it is difficult to keep the compost piles odor-free; some municipal programs have banned grass clippings for this reason. (Grass-cycling really is a better idea.)

With all this variety, costs are bound to vary as well. Using survey data on a number of communities, we concluded that collection is much more expensive than facility operation, and that on average, yard waste collection and composting costs $27 per ton more than garbage collection and disposal of the same material. These calculations are based on national averages, including a landfill tipping fee of $31 per ton (see Chapter 4); in high disposal cost regions in the Northeast and elsewhere, municipal composting programs may save money. Drop-off programs, which avoid the costs of collection, can save money in most of the country, but generally receive much less material.

The final approach which we considered, mixed waste composting, could potentially handle all organic waste. Its operating problems, however, have limited its popularity. Mixed waste composting facilities accept all of a community's solid waste, and separate it into recyclable materials, organic materials for composting, and a residue for landfilling. The organic material is sent to one or a series of enclosed vessels, where the speed of composting, odor generation, and quality of the final product can, at least in theory, be carefully controlled. In 1994 there were 20 facilities operating in the United States; eight were in Minnesota, where state policy calls for rapid reduction in both landfilling and incineration.

The problem is not only that the elaborate equipment required for in-vessel composting is expensive. Even worse, the equipment does not always perform as advertised. Severe odor problems have forced the shutdown of several mixed waste facilities, including some new, seemingly advanced-technology ones. Moreover, the quality of the finished compost is often quite low. Contamination from heavy metals and organic chemicals found in other waste, or from pieces of glass and plastic that remain in the compost, limits its use. Unlike the higher-grade, widely accepted compost made from municipal yard waste, compost made from mixed solid waste is often usable only for low-end applications such as landfill cover (the soil a landfill uses to cover each day's waste) or land reclamation projects.

The cost of mixed waste composting appears to be about $8 per ton higher, on average, than our estimate for municipal yard waste programs. But that $8 difference is not the reason why yard waste programs have swept across the country while mixed waste composting faces increasing resistance. Unless the operating problems can be resolved, mixed waste composting will remain an unattractive alternative.

The Composting Supply Curve

The five options discussed above can be combined into a single picture of least-cost methods for diversion of organic waste, as shown in Figure 8-1. For each option, the vertical axis measures the net social cost per ton of waste diverted—that is, the cost of the composting strategy net of the avoided garbage collection and disposal costs.

For the first three options, the net social cost is negative; that is, they save money as well as helping the environment. The costs of commercial and institutional composting, grasscycling (including mulching attachment purchases), and home composting (including bin purchases), are all less than the waste management savings that result from these programs. The horizontal axis measures the percentage of the organic waste stream that is diverted by each program. The first three, the ones that are cheaper than disposal, together can recover about a quarter of all organic waste, even under our cautious assumptions. The quantity would be even greater under the believable alternative assumptions of more than 60% participation in grasscycling, more than 20% participation in home composting, and broader commercial and institutional composting potential.

Greater diversion of organic waste is available, as Figure 8-1 shows, at a greater price. The graph may be thought of as a "composting supply curve," showing the cost of each level of diversion. Add in the full potential of the ubiquitous municipal yard waste composting programs, and more than half the organic waste stream could be recovered, including virtually all of the yard trimmings. The net social cost for this additional diversion rises to $27 per ton.

But even at this point, more than half of the food waste, and virtually all of the mixed paper, remain untouched. To go farther and capture the remaining organic matter, one could embark on mixed waste composting. This final step, however, imposes not only higher costs, but also troublesome operational problems that have scared many communities away. This portion of the curve is shown with a dotted line in Figure 8-1, expressing tentativeness about its feasibility with current technology. A better route to recovery of additional organic matter might be efforts to expand the scope of home composting and commercial/institutional food composting programs beyond the modest levels assumed here,

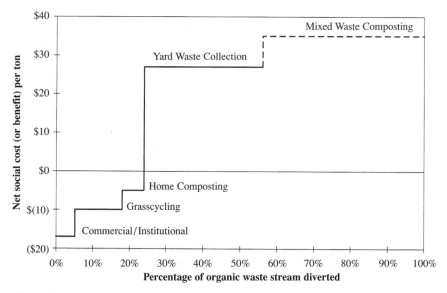

Figure 8-1
Cost of increasing levels of organic waste diversion.

combined with expansion of paper recycling programs to encompass the lower grades of mixed paper.

The composting supply curve shown in Figure 8-1 offers a definite answer to the question of the economic costs and benefits of recovering organic materials. It is in sharp contrast to the uncertainty about recycling revenues found in Chapter 4. However, the environmental benefits of material recovery may be better documented for recycling, as discussed in Chapter 5, than for composting. The environmental gains from composting can be described in general terms, but little has been done to quantify them.

Compost is a valuable soil amendment; it provides some of the nutrients needed by growing plants, and improves the retention of water in the soil. The resulting reduction in water requirements may be one of the greatest benefits from the use of compost. For a comprehensive analysis of benefits, one would need to identify the alternative to compost use. Compost might, for example, partially replace purchases of fertilizer or other soil amendments. If the production and application of chemical fertilizer could be reduced through use of compost, then emissions from fertilizer manufacturing, and pollution of soil and groundwater from fertilizer run-off, would be reduced as well. On the other hand, compost might not replace anything; that is, it might be applied in places where no other soil amendment was under consideration. It would then result in increased plant growth, yielding a very different type of benefit.

Most composting technologies, with the exception of mixed waste composting, are low-energy, low-impact processes. If odors are successfully controlled, there are few other drawbacks. Contamination of compost, making it undesirable or unsafe for use, can result from incomplete separation of organic from inorganic wastes; this is particularly a problem in the case of mixed waste composting. Ironically, contamination can also result from composting grass clippings from chemically treated lawns. Yet these problems are manageable, and do not outweigh the benefits of composting in general.

One of the broadest environmental issues related to composting is its indirect impact on global climate change. This does not arise from the operations of composting facilities themselves, which appear quite benign. Rather, it results from the alternative fate of organic waste—if it does not end up being composted, it is likely to be landfilled. Most studies, though as we will see, not quite all, have concluded that landfilling organic waste causes an increase in greenhouse gas emissions.

Heating with Gas

The greenhouse effect is by now familiar to many people. The glass windows of a greenhouse, or a parked car, allow light to enter but block the escape of heat; so when sunlight strikes the objects inside and warms them up, the heat is kept in. Some gases in the earth's atmosphere, including carbon dioxide, methane, and others, function in much the same way as window glass. The pollution caused by industrial growth has led to steadily rising greenhouse gas emissions, gradually thickening the atmospheric "window" and threatening to keep more heat inside. Since greenhouse gases persist in the atmosphere for more than a century after emission, we are now engaged in turning up the temperature for our great-grandchildren.

By far the largest contribution to climate change is made by carbon dioxide emissions from combustion of fossil fuels. But other gases and other activities that cause emissions also have an effect. Landfill methane accounts for 4% of greenhouse gas emissions in the United States, the most important nonenergy contribution to climate change potential.[9] Methane, the principal ingredient in natural gas, is a much more potent contributor to the greenhouse effect than carbon dioxide. A molecule of methane (CH_4) has 22 times the climate change potential of a molecule of carbon dioxide (CO_2).

From a climate change perspective, therefore, the critical question about organic waste is, what makes the process of decay result in carbon dioxide rather than methane? The answer is the presence of oxygen. Under aerobic conditions (i.e., when enough oxygen is available), decay happens relatively promptly, and most of the carbon released by the decaying material combines with oxygen to form CO_2. Turning or otherwise aerating a compost pile ensures that aerobic decomposition takes place, improving the smell and speed of composting as well as reducing greenhouse gas emissions.

In a landfill, however, no air reaches the waste more than a few feet below the surface, due to the pressure from new layers of waste and the daily covering of dirt. Under the anaerobic (oxygen-deprived) conditions found inside a landfill, decomposition is much slower than in the open air, and much of the carbon eventually combines with hydrogen to form methane. Landfill excavations by William Rathje and his co-workers at the University of Arizona's Garbage Project have dramatized the glacial pace of anaerobic decay, digging up newspapers that are still readable after more than 30 years in a landfill, T-bone steaks that are virtually indistinguishable from new ones, even under a microscope, after 15 years underground, and so on.[10]

While Rathje's "garbage archaeology" has produced some of the most entertaining anecdotes in the field of solid waste, it also has a serious side. Organic matter in landfills decays over an uncertain period of time that may be measured in decades. The waste that is buried today, along with the waste of recent years, will continue to decay for many years to come. And when decay does occur, much of the carbon comes out of the landfill as methane, 22 times as bad for climate change as if it emerged as carbon dioxide. (Methane emissions sometimes pose more prosaic problems as well; landfill methane has been known to travel underground, collect in nearby buildings, and cause explosions.)

A partial remedy may be on the way. New EPA regulations, adopted in early 1996, will force most landfills to install methane recovery equipment—systems of pipes that can potentially collect 70% to 90% of a landfill's methane emissions. Virtually any use of the recovered methane will reduce climate change impacts; even flaring the gas (i.e., simply burning it when it is emitted) converts methane to carbon dioxide. Of course, it is all the better if the energy from methane combustion can be captured and used. At large enough landfills, the volume of gas may make it profitable to burn the methane to generate electricity or steam, or even to purify it and sell it as natural gas, as is done at New York City's huge Fresh Kills landfill.

As the methane recovery requirement takes effect, the harmful effects of landfill methane will be reduced, though not completely eliminated. Meanwhile, interest in greenhouse gases has given rise to a minor industry of studying the relationship between waste and climate change. In Canada, the government agencies Environment Canada and Natural Resources Canada sponsored a study that compared the greenhouse gas emissions attributable to various waste management strategies. It found that reuse and recycling led to a reduction in emissions (with the exception of the energy-intensive process of rubber tire recycling), since they reduced energy use in manufacturing. Composting caused modest greenhouse gas emissions; incineration somewhat more; and landfilling was the worst. In combination with landfill gas recovery, many scenarios for diversion of waste away from landfills would be effective in reducing Canada's greenhouse gas emissions.[11] In the United States, an extensive EPA study of similar questions (in which I and other Tellus researchers played a small part) was still underway in early 1996.

The focus of research attention on climate change has led to a curious argument about the management of organic wastes, one that finds hitherto unsuspected benefits of landfilling. The conventional wisdom has long held that landfill methane emissions are an important source of greenhouse gases; the revisionist account now suggests that landfilling some organic wastes might reduce the total production of greenhouse gases. The basis for the revision is that a few laboratory attempts to reproduce the landfill decomposition process have concluded that more than half of the carbon in organic waste never decomposes, but instead remains in the landfill indefinitely.[12]

If some waste never decomposes, and if, in the future, methane recovery equipment is installed at most landfills, then it could be the case that burying organic waste would reduce greenhouse gas emissions. The argument goes like this: growing plants absorb carbon from the CO_2 in the atmosphere; then, when the plants turn into organic waste and are landfilled, much of the carbon is kept out of circulation, or "sequestered," indefinitely in landfills. Decomposition does convert some of the carbon to methane, but methane recovery captures most of that, and combustion turns the captured methane into carbon dioxide—which is no more harmful than it was before it was absorbed by the plants. On balance, therefore, growing plants and then burying them might reduce atmospheric carbon.

Although it is ingenious, this argument rests on two unproven conjectures. The first is that laboratory experiments, lasting a few weeks or months under controlled conditions, can accurately reproduce what will go on inside a landfill over the course of decades. This seems inherently improbable; how can a brief experiment determine with certainty what those anaerobic microbes will do, if given additional decades to digest Rathje's newspapers? It is crucial for this analysis to distinguish between materials that never decompose in landfills and ones that ultimately will decompose, even 50 or 100 years from now. If the bacteria are planning to eat the landfilled newspapers and emit methane at some future point, there is no benefit, from a climate change perspective, to the delay. On the contrary, delayed methane emissions will come at a time when atmospheric greenhouse gas concentrations will probably be higher than at present, and hence the damage from additional emissions will be greater. The difficulties encountered in evaluating outcomes far in the future, discussed in Chapter 3, are particularly relevant to the threat of climate change.

The second conjecture is that methane recovery equipment will be installed and will succeed in recovering most landfill methane. While the methane recovery requirement is now on the books, there is little experience to date with its implementation. It remains to be seen how rapidly and thoroughly it will be carried out, and how effective it will be in practice. Such details are relevant, because if methane emissions are even slightly greater than projected, then the putative benefits of landfilling organic material will disappear.

A bit of algebra will demonstrate how difficult it is to obtain any net climate change benefits from landfilling. Consider a cycle of growing plants and then landfilling them. At the beginning of the cycle, all the carbon that will be absorbed by the plants is in the atmosphere as CO_2, with an average climate change potential of 1. At the end, a fraction s of the carbon is sequestered in the landfill, with no climate change impact; a fraction c is emitted as CO_2; and a fraction m is eventually emitted into the atmosphere as methane, with a climate change potential of 22. The fractions must add up to 1:

(1) $s + c + m = 1$

or equivalently

(2) $s = 1 - c - m$

The average climate change potential is 1 at the beginning of the cycle, and $22m + c$ at the end. Landfilling is only beneficial if the potential is less at the end than at the beginning, or

(3) $22m + c < 1$

Since c cannot be less than zero, this implies that m, the fraction of the landfilled carbon eventually emitted as methane, must be less than 1/22, or about 4.5%. More generally, equation (3) means that

(4) $21m < 1 - c - m$

or, recalling equation (2),

(5) $21m < s$

That is, the amount of carbon sequestered indefinitely must be more than 21 times as great as the amount emitted as methane in order to achieve any net benefits from landfilling. If methane recovery systems are less than completely effective, this condition may be impossible to achieve. (This exercise has ignored the additional carbon emissions resulting from any equipment used in growing, harvesting, collecting, and landfilling the material, all of which make the impacts slightly worse.)

If one goal of greenhouse gas reduction policy is to sequester carbon, there are better places to put it than in a landfill. It might be possible, for instance, to promote the use of wood for long-lived products such as houses and home furnishings, attempting to reverse the trend away from wood in the construction and furniture industries. Growing more trees to use for these purposes would remove carbon from the atmosphere; but instead of being buried as trash, it could be turned it into durable goods that people need.

The story of organic waste highlights the importance of waste reduction and material recovery, in two respects. First, there are some easy opportunities to discard less, as in grasscycling. Systematic approaches to waste reduction are pursued more broadly in the next chapter. Second, material use cannot always be reduced; it is also necessary to carefully recover the materials we do use, as in the different approaches to composting, or in the sequestration of carbon in valuable products rather than in landfills. Rethinking the use and reuse of biomass resources will be crucial in the creation of a sustainable future economy, as described in the concluding chapter.

Notes

1. Virginia Scott Jenkins, *The Lawn: A History of an American Obsession* (Washington, D.C.: Smithsonian Institution Press, 1994); quote is from p. 32.

2. Martin Melosi, *Garbage in the Cities: Refuse, Reform, and the Environment, 1880–1980* (College Station, Texas: Texas A&M University Press, 1981), pp. 7–8.

3. As cited in Susan Strasser, *Waste and Want: Disposal, Recycling, and American Consumer Culture* (New York: Metropolitan Books, 1998).

4. See Benjamin Miller, *The Fat of the Land: New York's Waste* (New York: W.W. Norton, 1996), for an account of these and other uses of New York City wastes.

5. Melosi, *Garbage in the Cities,* p. 217.

6. Robert Steuteville, "The State of Garbage in America, Part I," *BioCycle,* April 1995, and "Part II", May 1995.

7. Lori Segall, Frank Ackerman, Dmitri Cavander, Paul Ligon, John Stutz, and Brian Zuckerman, *Organic Materials Management Strategies* (Boston: Tellus Institute, 1994). This report is the source for the following discussion of composting techniques and costs, except where otherwise noted.

8. Of the seven strategies analyzed in the report, this account combines the very similar discussion of commercial and institutional composting, and omits the option of residential source separation, a European import that has proved neither cost-effective nor popular in America. See Lori Segall, "Source Separated Organics Programs in Europe," *Resource Recycling,* July 1993.

9. *Inventory of U.S. Greenhouse Gas Emissions and Sinks: 1990–1993* (Washington, D.C.: EPA, 1994), Table ES-1, p. ES-3.

10. William Rathje and Cullen Murphy, *Rubbish! The Archaeology of Garbage* (New York: HarperCollins, 1992).

11. *Estimation of the Effects of Various Municipal Waste Management Strategies on Greenhouse Gas Emissions* (Don Mills, Ontario: Proctor & Redfern, 1994).

12. See, for example, Jean Bogner and Kurt Spokas, "Landfill CH_4: Rates, Fates, and Role in the Global Carbon Cycle," *Chemosphere,* Vol. 26, Nos. 1–4 (1994), pp. 369–386; and recent research by Morton Barlaz at North Carolina State University.

CHAPTER 9

The Hidden Utility

The environmental goals that motivate recycling are often best served by less rather than more recycling—that is, by preventing the generation of waste in the first place. This theme emerges at several points in the preceding chapters, from the surprising benefits of lightweight packaging (Chapter 5) and the reduction in packaging inspired by Germany's green dot system (Chapter 6) to the cost-effective opportunities for organic waste reduction through grasscycling and home composting (Chapter 8). The "hierarchy" of integrated waste management, advocated by the EPA and many state agencies, places waste reduction at the pinnacle, the most environmentally desirable approach of all.

But waste prevention is different. Unlike ordinary waste management options, it is not something that can be done to waste after collection; it is not a destination to which the garbage truck or recycling truck can be sent. Rather, waste prevention requires intervention and change in the waste-generating practices of household and business life, prior to the point at which materials are discarded. Waste management agencies are ill-equipped for this task; despite widespread rhetorical support for waste prevention, in practice local initiatives other than grasscycling remain rare.

Remarkably similar issues arise in connection with energy conservation. Here, too, avoiding the need for energy is usually better for the environment than producing additional fuels or electricity—but energy suppliers have not traditionally been in the business of promoting con-servation. Since the financial stakes are higher and the public debate has gone on longer in energy, it is not surprising that more has been ac-complished in energy conservation than in waste prevention. In partic-ular, many electric utility companies now invest in conservation mea-sures, as well as electricity generation and distribution. Utility conservation efforts are referred to as "demand side management" (DSM), to distinguish them from conventional investments in elec-tricity supply.

Can the analogy with DSM suggest new approaches to waste preven-tion?[1] This chapter is an exploration of that question. It begins by re-viewing the rise of electricity conservation and analyzing the role of public utilities in general. It then turns to a more detailed examination of the potential for waste reduction. The chapter concludes with a dis-cussion of the recent trend toward deregulation and enthusiasm for competition, where, for better or worse, the parallel between electricity and waste management is continuing.

The Birth of the Negawatt

Energy conservation burst into public prominence amid the oil crises and price increases of the 1970s. The sense of crisis began with the oil embargo but soon spread to energy in general. At the same time that oil was becoming scarce, the leading domestic alternatives to oil, namely coal-fired and nuclear power plants, faced escalating costs and intense environmental opposition. Against this backdrop, it was easy to see that a lot of energy was being wasted, and consequently that there were many cost-effective opportunities for conservation. Homes could be kept equally warm, for example, with less fuel and more insulation. If viewed as an investment, additional insulation often yields a high re-turn in the form of reduced heating bills. Amory Lovins popularized this approach by arguing that it is frequently cheaper to deliver "ne-gawatts" of conservation than megawatts of electricity. Lovins and many other analysts identified countless places where low-cost ne-gawatts could be found.

One might suspect, depending on how much time one has spent in economics classes, that higher energy prices alone would lead to the right amount of conservation. In fact, many energy-saving investments were made quite quickly in response to higher prices in the 1970s, par-ticularly by industry. But households and small businesses often did not take obvious energy-saving steps, at times even failing to make expenditures that would pay for themselves in a year or less.

In some cases the obstacle to conservation is a structural one. Insulation of rental housing is a famous example, in which existing market institutions make it unlikely that anyone will invest in seemingly cost-effective conservation measures. Although tenants often pay their own heating bills, this is not enough of an incentive; typically tenants have one-year leases, and hence will not make investments in insulation that take more than a year to pay for themselves. But landlords will also be reluctant to insulate, since there is little chance of recouping the investment through increased rents; prospective new tenants will not recognize the greater level of insulation as grounds for paying higher rent. Old, poorly insulated rental housing offers many low-cost opportunities for energy savings, but a third party must intervene in order to realize those savings.

In other cases, people fail to make conservation expenditures that would benefit themselves directly. Even in owner-occupied housing, many profitable energy-saving investment opportunities are routinely overlooked. A number of studies found that the barriers to cost-effective conservation included public ignorance of available options, inability to evaluate vendors' claims for energy-saving products, and lack of access to funds to make the necessary investments. By the early 1980s, there was widespread agreement that structural and institutional changes would be needed to realize the full potential for conservation.

Two principal changes to promote conservation were ultimately enacted: states modified their utility regulations to encourage electric companies to invest in and profit from demand side management measures; and federal energy efficiency standards were established for new electric appliances and for new buildings (via building codes). Though inspired by the events of the 1970s, both of these changes took most of the 1980s to get underway.

Utility regulations were modified on a state-by-state basis, largely in the early and mid-1980s, to allow utilities to spend money on carefully selected conservation measures—and to charge their customers for the cost of these measures plus a normal rate of profit. Further financial incentives were frequently included, giving utilities a share of the money saved by the conservation measures in addition to their usual rate of profit. Detailed calculations had to be made, both before and after the fact, to ensure that utilities selected the measures most likely to be cost-effective, and implemented them successfully. But the utilities were ideally situated to overcome the barriers to conservation: they were presumably well-informed, able to evaluate rival products and claims, and certainly able to finance the needed investments. Many states called for utilities to engage in "integrated resource planning," a process which puts the new demand side management options on an even footing with conventional sources of supply, and allows selection of the combination of resources that meets customers' needs at the lowest cost.

Federal efficiency standards were required by a law passed in 1978; normal bureaucratic and legislative delays combined with foot-dragging by the Reagan administration meant that the standards first took effect in 1988, with tougher standards implemented in 1990 and 1993. For refrigerators, the biggest users of electricity in most households, the energy efficiency of new models almost tripled from 1973 to 1993.[2] Few people will rush out and buy a new refrigerator solely for this reason— although, for those who enjoy detailed calculations, the energy savings make it cost-effective (and environmentally beneficial) to replace your old model somewhat earlier than you otherwise might. But in time, all old refrigerators will pass away; as they are replaced with new models, household electricity use for refrigeration will continue to decline for years to come. The new standards remove the guesswork and technical calculation from the process of buying appliances: it is no longer necessary to decipher cryptic labels to figure out which models are energy-efficient.

Both of these innovations were having a noticeable impact on energy consumption by the early 1990s. In 1993, U.S. electric utilities spent $2.8 billion, or 1.5% of their operating revenues, on DSM programs, thereby reducing annual electricity use by 1.6% and summer peak demand by 6.8%. The energy savings, 44 million megawatt-hours, were already the equivalent of the output from 6 to 8 large coal or nuclear plants—and the potential growth of DSM was by no means exhausted. The savings from appliance and building code efficiency standards are of roughly similar size; existing and likely future efficiency standards are expected to cut residential energy use 7% by the year 2015.

If It's a Good Idea for Electricity . . .

It is hard to find another industry that has prospered by selling the absence of its principal product, in order to lower its customers' costs. Farmers do receive federal subsidies at times to plant fewer acres of crops, but the subsidies are designed to raise farm prices. For a complete analogy to utility DSM, farmers would have to be free to plant additional acres, but then conclude that it is more profitable to reduce the demand for food, perhaps by sponsoring diet workshops for consumers. This, of course, does not occur.

DSM is possible for electric companies because they, unlike farmers, are regulated public utilities. Despite the name, "public" utilities are usually private, profit-making businesses; but they operate in a unique, regulated market environment. Utilities provide basic services in which there is a natural monopoly; even the most fervent advocate of competition does not want to wake up one morning to find large numbers of rival electric companies, or telephone companies, each installing their own lines on his street. A single provider, having at least a local monopoly, is far more efficient. But an unregulated monopoly would be able to charge exorbitant prices and provide indifferent or discriminatory service. Utility regulation is designed to prevent such abuses, while ensuring that the company can remain in business.

Utility regulation rests on a bargain struck between a company and its customers. The company agrees to provide service to all paying customers in its service territory, and to submit all proposed price increases and major investment decisions to state regulators for prior approval. In return the state, on behalf of the customers, grants the utility a monopoly in its service territory, and agrees to accept prices that allow the utility to recover its costs plus a reasonable rate of profit on its operations.

All markets rest on political institutions that define the rules of ownership, property rights, and allowable competitive behavior.[3] Utility regulation is unusual only in making the underlying political assumptions explicit—and hence more susceptible to change. Since regulatory approval is required for major utility investments, it is possible for society, via its regulators, to incorporate environmental criteria as well as pure cost minimization into a utility's objectives. When the rules had to be changed to allow a novel type of investment in energy conservation, it was comparatively easy to do so.

If this is a good idea for electricity, it might be good for other resources as well. In a wide-ranging environmental critique and policy analysis, Paul Hawken calls for an extension of the public utility concept to many new areas.[4] For Hawken, business is the cause of most environmental problems, as he explains in detail; but business is also essential to the resolution of those problems. To convert capitalism from problem to solution, Hawken offers two major proposals: "green taxes" on pollution, and creation of new public utilities to manage environmental resources in the public interest. A salmon utility might be created in the Pacific Northwest, for example, charging a fee on all salmon caught in the region and using the revenue to protect endangered habitats and increase the salmon population. Even more ambitiously, an oil utility could be charged with selling the nation's oil. Just as in the case of electric utility DSM, an oil utility could decide to spend money on promoting oil conservation rather than on exploration and extraction. Increasing automobile fuel efficiency would yield "negabarrels" of oil at lower cost to society than Arctic drilling; an oil utility could realize such savings, while unregulated private oil companies cannot. In areas where oil is used for residential heating, Hawken's oil utility might find it profitable to invest in insulating rental housing.

Solid waste management already has many of the characteristics of a public utility.[5] It is an essential service: for sanitary reasons, we all want to ensure timely collection of both our own waste and our neighbors'. Solid waste collection is a natural monopoly: while not quite as absurd as rival electric lines, rival garbage trucks cruising the same street in pursuit of customers would still impose substantial, needless costs. A local garbage collection monopoly can collect a community's trash with fewer trucks and lower costs than a competitive collection industry. Finally, disposal facilities have important economies of scale, meaning that it is cheaper to build a few big ones than a lot of little ones. Community opposition to siting new waste management facilities makes it all the more desirable to plan carefully for the minimum amount of required capacity, rather than allowing competition between numerous landfills.

In many ways, therefore, waste management resembles a public utility more than a competitive industry. When waste management services are provided by private firms, as is increasingly common, it would make sense to apply the same regulatory framework to them as to other utilities. Waste management is in effect a public utility, although one that is hidden from view by its different regulatory treatment.

While waste disposal faces many regulations, the majority address only the environmental performance of waste facilities. Rarely have the economic standards of utility regulation been applied to waste management. At a statewide level, New Jersey and West Virginia have regulated private waste collection firms as public utilities, although New Jersey has now abandoned the practice. (In West Virginia, regulation in part plays the role of state-sponsored instruction in accounting for numerous small, rural waste haulers.) In other areas, economic regulation of waste management is a piecemeal, local affair.

One small step toward utility-like treatment of solid waste is the practice known as "flow control." When waste is collected by private firms, municipalities sometimes control the flow of waste—for instance, by requiring waste haulers to separate recyclables and deliver them to a specific recycling center or to send all the town's garbage to a particular disposal site. Flow control may be necessary to ensure a big enough flow of recyclable material to justify building and operating a recycling plant. But even this modest form of economic regulation of waste management has been blocked by the deregulatory movement of the 1990s, as we will see below.

Wasting Away

The analogy between waste management and electricity suggests that waste prevention should be comparable to DSM. But the analogy is far from perfect. The potential for waste prevention depends on the specific types of waste involved; some are much easier to prevent than others. Consider, first, the easy cases, all but one of which have already been introduced. We have seen that grasscycling and home composting can eliminate disposal of much of yard and food wastes, while packaging policies or standards could reduce the amount of packaging waste. The easy option which has not yet appeared is the leading opportunity for business waste prevention; it also involves packaging, specifically transport packaging such as cartons and pallets.

The potential for material conservation in the business sector is documented by the EPA's "WasteWi$e" program, a voluntary corporate partnership to promote waste reduction. Nearly 370 companies, many of them very large ones, joined WasteWi$e in its first year, 1994. In that year the WasteWi$e participants reported that they had prevented the generation of 240,000 tons of solid waste. More than half of that amount, 138,000 tons, was achieved by reducing or reusing transport packaging. Examples included reuse of corrugated cardboard cartons and wooden pallets, introduction of reusable plastic shipping cases to replace single-use cardboard ones, and reduction of the dimensions of standard pallets and cartons. Corrugated cardboard was the leading material conserved by WasteWi$e waste prevention activities, at 106,000 tons, while wood, largely for pallets, accounted for 44,000 tons.[6] Thus if you ask business where it can most easily reduce solid waste generation, transport packaging is the answer.[7] (Similarly, German business quickly reduced its use of transport packaging after passage of the 1991 Packaging Ordinance, as described in Chapter 6.)

Adequately addressing the areas discussed so far would be an immense accomplishment. Yard and food waste, amounting to about a quarter of municipal solid waste, could be substantially reduced by programs to promote grasscycling and home composting, much like utility DSM programs. In most of the country, municipal investment in these programs would be a cost-effective alternative to waste collection and disposal. Packaging, one-third of solid waste, could be reduced by policies that encourage weight reduction; here the more apt analogy is to energy efficiency standards. In the case of transport packaging, business may find it profitable to carry out significant reduction without any change in public policy.

Yet even though this agenda of organic waste and packaging reduction is still far from completion, it is natural to wonder what more could be accomplished. Almost half of all solid waste is neither packaging nor organic waste; and even a successful policy of packaging weight reduction would leave large amounts of packaging in the waste stream. The remaining wastes, unfortunately, appear more difficult to reduce.

It is true that there are many little things individuals can do about waste reduction; my favorite source on the subject is the *ULS* ("Use Less Stuff") *Report,* a lively bimonthly compendium of hints for the waste-conscious.[8] There are more organized, programmatic options as well. In offices, increased use of double-sided copying and growing acceptance of electronic mail as an alternative to paper memos can save some paper. In communities, households can be encouraged to eliminate unwanted junk mail, by sending requests to the Direct Marketing Association's Mail Preference Service. Perhaps more years of experimentation and analysis will develop programs with broader waste reduction potential in these areas, comparable with utility DSM. But the results to date are quite modest compared with the potential of grasscycling, home composting, or transport packaging reduction. There are surprisingly few other reduction programs that have yet demonstrated the potential for a significant impact on the aggregate quantity of waste.

It is not merely a coincidence that organic material and packaging are the easiest areas in which to reduce waste. Most municipal solid waste consists of manufactured goods; the purchasers and users of these goods, in homes, stores, and offices, have little to say about material use in manufacturing, where the decisions that generate waste are made. While households in the past were intimately involved in production as well as consumption, today the yard and the kitchen are the only places where most American households produce material objects. Even these production processes are constrained by the available technologies and inputs, and by social pressures such as community standards about lawn care. Nonetheless, the household's role in yard and kitchen production results in a greater degree of control over waste generation in these areas than in others.

In the case of manufactured goods that are brought into the household, a change in packaging need not affect the underlying nature of the product. Juice is juice, and soft drinks are soft drinks, regardless of which of the many packaging options is used to deliver them. Thus it is possible to contemplate changes and reduction in packaging, without raising the more difficult question of the choices and uses of products themselves. To go deeper into waste reduction, it is necessary to change our relationship to the things inside the packages.

Waste reduction is limited by the fact that most wastes are only by-products of much larger decisions about the use of materials. In the case of office paper, the original paper purchase can cost ten times as much as management of the resulting paper waste, while the expense of storing, laser printing or photocopying, and mailing the paper can be a hundred times as great as the cost of waste management. Efforts to reduce office paper consumption, therefore, will be driven by attempts to economize on the costs of purchase and use, rather than waste disposal.[9] Thus waste reduction, beyond the "easy" areas noted above, may get less attention as a waste management option than as part of a broader discourse on conservation of energy and materials (which is the subject of Chapter 10).

Life After Conservation

Public commitment to resource conservation has not survived unscathed through the political and economic turmoil of the 1990s. The pressure for deregulation, which promises lower prices but also threatens to reverse environmental gains, can be seen in both electricity and waste management, continuing the parallel between the two areas.

By the time that DSM programs and efficiency standards were beginning to save noticeable amounts of electricity, in the early 1990s, the market for electricity had changed in ways that made the short-run economic argument for conservation look much weaker. The development of small gas-burning power plants, combined with a drop in the price of natural gas, allowed the cost of new supplies of electricity to fall to 3 to 5 cents per kilowatt-hour (kWh) in many cases. A decade earlier, when many DSM programs were proposed, planners expected that conservation would be competing with electricity that cost 10 cents per kWh (in 1993 dollars) to generate. While some DSM programs remain cost-effective even at the lower prices, there was certainly more potential for savings when the anticipated price of electricity was higher.[10]

Another factor creating difficulties for DSM was the movement toward increased competition in the electric industry. In the past it was taken for granted that the natural monopoly of utilities applied to all stages of electricity supply, including generation, transmission, and distribution to customers. However, one of the responses to the energy crises of the 1970s was federal legislation that very successfully encouraged non-utility generators to produce electricity and required utilities to buy from them. The resulting diversity of sources means that utilities no longer have a monopoly on generation. Moreover, the current surplus of generating capacity in many parts of the country makes utilities eager to sell power to each other (or each other's customers) if the opportunity arises—and less eager to sell conservation.

Your electric company will, for the foreseeable future, retain its monopoly on local distribution. But the largest (i.e., industrial) electricity customers have shown growing interest in opening up the supply of electricity to full-blown competition, an idea that wins support from advocates of deregulation. If competitive electricity supply is eventually extended to residential customers, it might resemble the competition between long-distance phone companies today. Your electric company might play the role of your local phone company, which provides the local aspects of your service and connects you to the long-distance carrier of your choice.

The results of competition in phone service may provide a glimpse of the brave new world of competitive electricity supply. Rates are lower, especially for those who use their phones a lot and shop carefully for bargains; activities such as making decisions about phone service and deciphering phone bills take more time than they used to; and there are an incredible number of commercials. Someday the endless pitches for AT&T, MCI, and Sprint could be joined by "Almost heaven: bringing you the warm glow of coal from the hills of West Virginia," or "Too cheap to meter: accept our introductory gift of 100 free kWh and find out why nuclear power is the answer to your energy needs."

One early attempt at retail promotion of electricity has already appeared. The Tennessee Valley Authority (TVA), which produces electricity from many nuclear and other power plants as well as from hydroelectric facilities, sponsored a series of television ads in 1995. One showed an empty chair in front of a flickering television, saying that since TVA electric rates are low, "it costs less to leave this commercial on while you grab a snack." Another, promoting electric heating, claimed that TVA rates were so low that the only way to get cheaper electricity is "to make it yourself." Tennessee consumer groups and congressional representatives quickly objected that the ads were spending millions of dollars to encourage people to waste energy. But TVA officials defended the advertising campaign as an "integral part" of their strategy to remain competitive in the face of deregulation of the electric industry.[11]

What is missing from this commercialized energy future is a natural role for conservation. None of the competitive suppliers of electricity would have the obligation to provide universal service, the foundation on which utility DSM was built; none would profit by investing in services to customers in order to avoid expensive future power plants. Instead, all would scramble to sell more energy, building power plants whenever the market could bear it. Conservation would look just as appealing to competitive electricity producers as diet workshops do to farmers.

There is less scope for deregulation of waste management, because there was less regulation to begin with. But the trend is in the same direction. In 1994 the U.S. Supreme Court ruled in favor of a private waste hauler's challenge to a municipal flow control scheme, on the grounds that flow control interferes with interstate commerce. In *C&A Carbone v. Town of Clarkstown* the Court overturned the local law which had required that all waste from Clarkstown, New York, was to be delivered to a facility designated by the town. The designated facility had been built for the town by a private operator, after state regulation had forced the town to close its old landfill. The town made a commitment to deliver at least a fixed quantity of waste to the new facility; the local law requiring its use was designed to fulfill that commitment.[12]

The six-member majority of the Supreme Court held that Clarkstown's requirement discriminated against out-of-state waste facilities, and suggested that the town could meet its objectives through subsidies to its new waste facility. The three dissenting members of the Court recognized that the town had created a local monopoly to perform a public service for the community (in terms quite similar to the discussion of public utilities above), and argued that this did not discriminate against interstate commerce in intent or effect.

Although the decision rests in part on the details of one local ordinance and might not apply to all flow control arrangements, it nonetheless has a tone of generality and precedent. It immediately created uncertainty and reluctance to build facilities that depend on flow control throughout the field of municipal waste management. Several proposals to clarify the legal status of flow control have circulated in Congress, though none had been adopted by the end of 1995. A minimal proposal, and perhaps also the maximum that is acceptable to congressional conservatives, would confirm the legality of flow control arrangements that were in place prior to the Supreme Court decision, but would not allow new ones to start up.

If interstate competition in local waste management services is constitutionally protected and takes precedence over plans and financial commitments made by local governments, then waste management planners may be an endangered species. In particular, planning for recycling or waste reduction, unless it immediately saves money, could be challenged as interfering with interstate commerce. And activities that do save money could be left to the marketplace, unaided by public planning. The clash between recycling advocates and the free-market "anti-recyclers" would be decisively settled, in favor of the latter. Perhaps retail competition, after advancing from your telephones through your electric wires, will conquer your garbage can as well; will out-of-state waste incinerators advertise that "the answer is blowing in the wind"?

Competition: Pro and Con

Local solid waste planners might be expected to be supporters of flow control. But Kay Martin, long-time director of solid waste planning for Ventura County, California, is passionately opposed to it. In her view, flow control is part of the failed strategy of building big, expensive waste management facilities, which then (as in Clarkstown) need a steady inflow of waste to remain profitable. It is better, says Martin, for government to minimize waste management infrastructure, and instead gently guide the market into finding sustainably profitable forms of recycling and resource use on its own.[13]

Consider the gap between this view and a more traditional advocacy of waste management planning and flow control. The two are separated by profound differences of philosophy and perspective. The anti-flow control, pro-competition side places a priority on avoiding the mistakes of government planning, while assuming that the market routinely gets the right answer to the questions of resource allocation. The traditional utility or waste management perspective focuses on resource needs and environmental objectives that cannot be achieved by the unregulated market at an acceptable cost, but can be directly addressed by public planning.

The distinction again appears more clearly in the analogous discussion of energy conservation. Recall that the original motivation for utility DSM programs was the discovery that many cost-effective investments in energy conservation were not being made by the market in response to higher prices alone. This implied a need for planning and public initiative, even to achieve one of the stated goals of the market: satisfying consumers' desires at the least possible cost. But as enthusiasm for the market and deregulation has spread, the original finding that the market fails in the case of energy conservation has come under attack.

The clash of rival perspectives can be seen in two published evaluations of the same DSM program, largely consisting of introduction of more efficient commercial lighting, run by Massachusetts Electric Company.[14] One analysis simply compares the cost of the program to the cost of the energy that was saved; this approach finds that the benefits far exceed the costs. The other analysis assumes that the market was efficient (i.e., was making consumers as happy as possible) to begin with, and in that context estimates the costs and benefits of introducing energy conservation. This approach finds that the costs are much greater than the benefits, indicating a failure or an undesirable program. From the latter perspective, the DSM program only looks successful because its hidden costs have been ignored.

The debate between these two positions, which is likely to be heard more widely, is not about the facts; the two analyses in this case use the same data. Rather, it is a difference of underlying beliefs about the market, and methods for measuring its performance. If it is possible for the market to make mistakes, such as failing to achieve the full potential for cost-effective energy conservation, then it is conceivable that a policy such as DSM might correct those mistakes. In that case the obvious comparison of program costs versus energy or resource savings can be used as the measure of success. By this measure, the Massachusetts Electric DSM program, like many others, is a solid success.

On the other hand, if the market is always efficient in satisfying consumer desires, then it is rare for any public policy to make consumers better off. From this perspective, the evaluation of any nonmarket initiative must include the substantial dissatisfaction it provokes among the formerly blissful populace.[15] To give an air of specificity to this dissatisfaction, hidden costs of change can be imagined; the negative analysis of Massachusetts Electric DSM cited the potential disruption and delays associated with new innovations, risk and uncertainty about the actual performance of the innovation, and other hypothetical hidden costs. Since these costs are hidden—their existence is deduced, not observed or measured—no one can tell for certain how large they are.

In the end, therefore, the free market argument against DSM, and by extension against other public policy initiatives for resource conservation, is circular: it proves the market is superior only by assuming it to begin with. If everyone was already as happy as possible, change is bound to cause dissatisfaction. The magnitude of this dissatisfaction cannot be observed, but can be deduced from first principles, and referred to as "hidden costs." For anyone but a true believer, the resulting estimates of hidden costs appear implausibly high.[16]

While the analogy to utility DSM does not provide a ready-made formula for success in waste prevention, it does suggest the broader potential for resource conservation programs. The public utility framework is applicable to aspects of waste management, and, as Paul Hawken proposes, to other resource issues as well. That framework allows socially directed investments in resource conservation to be profitable, in a manner that cannot be matched by unregulated, competitive private firms.

The movement toward deregulation in the 1990s, which may undercut this potential for conservation, is in part due to technical and economic changes that allow greater scope for competition. In part, however, it simply reflects shifting political fashions; conservation is out of style, and reliance on the increasingly unfettered market is in. But beyond the changing environmental politics of America in the 1990s lie the questions of resource conservation and sustainability in the long run, the subject of the next and final chapter.

Notes

1. At the risk of sounding repetitive, this too is the subject of a study by Tellus Institute (the last one in this book!). See John Stutz and Paul Ligon, *Achieving Substantial, Measurable Results through Source Reduction* (Boston: Tellus Institute, 1994), and work in progress.

2. Eric Hirst and Joseph Ito, *Justification for Electric-Utility Energy-Efficiency Programs* (Oak Ridge National Laboratory Report ORNL/CON-419, August 1995); this is the source for the description of efficiency standards and DSM programs throughout this section.

3. A classic work on this subject is Karl Polanyi, *The Great Transformation* (New York: Farrar & Rinehart, 1944). For a more recent discussion, see Arthur Mac-Ewan, "The Construction of Markets," in his forthcoming *Economic Development Alternatives: Market Strategies versus Democratic Initiatives.*

4. Paul Hawken, *The Ecology of Commerce* (New York: HarperCollins, 1993), especially Chapter 11.

5. Frank Ackerman, "Solid Waste: The Hidden Utility," *BioCycle*, August 1990.

6. *WasteWi$e First-Year Progress Report* (EPA document EPA530-R-95-044, 1995). The figures for waste reduction are separate from the recycling efforts reported by WasteWi$e participants; cardboard was also the leading material in WasteWi$e recycling, accounting for 304,000 of a total of 956,000 tons.

7. For economic analysis of the potential for transport packaging reduction see

Diana Twede, *Less Waste on the Loading Dock,* Solid Waste Working Paper #2 (New Haven: Yale School of Forestry and Environmental Studies, 1995).

8. Box 130116, Ann Arbor, MI 48113. Or, its editors suggest, save paper by reading it on-line: send e-mail to subscribe-uls@cygnus-group.com, or browse at http://cygnus-group.com/ULS/About_ULS.html.

9. Bruce Nordman, "Paper Efficiency: Energy and Beyond" (Lawrence Berkeley National Laboratory, 1994; presented at the Electric Power Research Institute conference on "Energy Efficiency in Office Technology," New York, 1994) and other papers. In addition to two-sided copying and printing, Nordman advocates reduction from the current 20-lb standard office paper to thinner 18-lb, or even 16-lb paper (these weights, traditionally used to describe paper grades, are the weight of 2000 letter-sized sheets).

10. Hirst and Ito, *Justification for Energy-Efficiency Programs.*

11. *Demand-Side Report* (a McGraw-Hill publication, affiliated with *Electric Utility Week*), November 23, 1995. I thank Bruce Biewald for this reference.

12. Dexter Ewel, "Solid Waste Flow Control Statutes Are Unconstitutional," *BioCycle,* June 1994; and "Solid Waste Flow Control Update," *BioCycle,* May 1995.

13. Kay Martin, "Flow Control: The Wisdom of Doing Without," *MSW Management,* May/June 1995, excerpted from her forthcoming book, *Sustainable Recycling—Necessary Revolutions in Local Government Policy.* Martin refers frequently to the DSM analogy, although in a manner different from mine; for her, DSM refers to government policies that guide business use of and demand for secondary raw materials. While true to the literal meaning of the words "demand side management," her approach seems to me much less analogous to electric utility DSM programs.

14. Mark D. Levine and Richard Sonnenblick, "On the Assessment of Utility Demand-side Management Programs," (pro-DSM); and Albert L. Nichols, "Demand-side Management: Overcoming Market Barriers or Obscuring Real Costs?" (con); both in *Energy Policy,* Vol. 22, No. 10 (1994). See also the discussion in the same journal issue by Alan H. Sanstad and Richard B. Howarth, " 'Normal' Markets, Market Imperfections and Energy Efficiency."

15. In technical terms, economists argue that policies can be evaluated in terms of their impact on consumer surplus—and many initiatives that disturb the market equilibrium turn out to reduce consumer surplus. However, very strong *ceteris paribus* ("all else being equal") assumptions are required for the validity of the consumer surplus analysis. The opposing view, favoring interventions such as DSM, can be interpreted as an argument that the demand curve for energy, from which consumer surplus is calculated in this case, is not stable (or does not represent well-informed, utility-maximizing preferences). Programs promoting energy conservation are likely to shift the demand curves for energy and related goods, and change the patterns of consumption enough so that estimates of the change in consumer surplus on individual commodities based on pre-existing demand curves are no longer reasonable measures of the effect on consumer welfare.

16. The debate about the measurement of inferred, hidden costs of conservation has become technically complex; see Alan H. Sanstad, Carl Blumstein, and Steven E. Stoft, "How high are option values in energy-efficiency investments?," *Energy Policy,* Vol. 23, No. 9 (1995).

CHAPTER 10

Material Use and Sustainable Affluence

John Maynard Keynes, perhaps the most influential economist of the twentieth century, was famous for remarking that "in the long run, we are all dead." Much of his work was true to his witticism, focusing on short-run macroeconomics. However, he did turn his attention to the very long run in a fascinating speculative essay, "Economic Possibilities for Our Grandchildren."

The slow but steady growth of productivity, said Keynes, will make future generations much richer than the present. Annual productivity increases of just over 2%, consistent with long-term historical trends, result in an eight-fold rise in average incomes in a century. Writing in England in 1930, Keynes thought it was obvious that eight times the prevailing income levels would be more than enough to satisfy material wants. Thus he anticipated that people would increasingly choose leisure over additional income, working fewer hours and making more creative use of their free time. As the problem of scarcity receded in importance, the public celebration of competition, accumulation, and greed could be replaced by more religious or humanitarian morality. Economics would then become merely another narrowly defined professional specialty, Keynes hoped, of no more political and social importance than dentistry.[1]

Let us suppose that our society will survive; that is, leaving aside the annoying fact of personal mortality, assume that in the long run our descendants will not all be dead. What are the environmental possibilities for our grandchildren, and for the generations beyond them? For society to survive, it must become "sustainable": that is, the environmental impacts of production and consumption must be low enough to permit each successive generation to achieve the same level of well-being as its predecessor. There is ample evidence that the world economy today is far from sustainability. If it is possible to create an environmentally sustainable world, will it allow equitable enjoyment of the affluence that Keynes so optimistically predicted—or will scarcity, the celebration of greed, and the prominence of economics persist into the indefinite future?

This chapter imagines the patterns of material use in a sustainable future, and takes a last look at recycling in that context. There are three major parts to the story. First, an examination of the technical and economic requirements for sustainability reveals the need, in the long run, for increasing reliance on renewable materials, limits to population and consumption growth, continued technological progress—and waste prevention and recycling. Second, the arguments about sustainability and material use are then contrasted to the free-market critique, which claims that materials in general are becoming abundant; twentieth-century American affluence can be interpreted as an unprecedented relationship between high wages and low material prices, which undercuts the traditional economic motivation for recycling. Finally, however, even in an affluent society there are still reasons for reducing and recycling waste, both for its influence on the direction of technological change, and for its relationship to social values and economic behavior. The chapter concludes with my answer to the question posed in the title of the book: the fundamental reasons why we *do* recycle.

Play It Again, and Again

A sustainable economy must include levels of production and consumption which can be repeated, generation after generation, without cumulative or worsening environmental damage. Making the future equitable as well as sustainable will require substantial worldwide equalization of incomes and resources—hopefully, for the most part, in an upward direction.[2] The society we live in today is clearly neither equitable nor sustainable: developed-country consumption depends heavily on nonrenewable resources, particularly fossil fuels and metals; and economic development for the world's low-income majority will accelerate the exhaustion of these scarce commodities.

Shortages of nonrenewable resources are not imminent in the 1990s. Supplies of many metals and fuels would last from 20 years to well over 100 years at present rates of consumption (i.e., at present levels of economic development); coal, in particular, will last for several centuries.[3] For now, other environmental problems appear more urgent, including the threat of global climate change and the overexploitation of renewable resources such as forests and fisheries. The ways in which the world uses its temporarily abundant resources will create serious problems (such as air pollution from burning coal) long before the materials run out.

In the long run, however, the exhaustion of nonrenewable resources is sure to become critical. Steel, aluminum, oil, and even coal are available in only finite quantities, and will eventually be used up or dissipated (scattered) beyond recovery. Thus one great virtue of recycling, waste prevention, and energy conservation is that they postpone the exhaustion and dissipation of valuable scarce resources, gaining time to make the inevitable transition to substitute materials a smooth one. But no matter how careful we are, it is only a postponement that is available, not a permanent reprieve. No cycle of production, use, and recycling can recover 100 % of the material it began with; no nonrenewable resource can be used forever.

As we approach the post-oil, post-metal world of the future, the materials used in daily life will increasingly be made of renewable products of the land: wood, plant and animal fibers, paper—and plastics. Although mention of plastics today evokes the wasteful use of fossil fuels and the overpackaged effluvia of mass marketing, there is nothing in the technology of plastics production that requires either petrochemical feedstocks or tawdry outputs. Plastics began as plant-based materials; even the name of the first widely used plastic, celluloid, reflected its roots in the vegetable kingdom. It was made by chemical treatment of cellulose, usually derived from cotton. In its early days, celluloid was often used to make elaborate decorative objects.[4]

Plant-based plastics are just one example of a more general point about biomass resources. Useful hydrocarbon compounds, valuable both as fuels and as industrial materials, can be obtained from modern plants as well as from the fossils of ancient ones. Ethanol, derived from corn in the United States and on a much larger scale from sugar cane in Brazil, is a very close substitute for gasoline and can be used in motor vehicles with little or no modification of the engines. Ethanol production in both countries now looks like an expensive boondoggle, and incidentally uses substantial petroleum inputs in farming and processing—but this only reflects the fact that oil prices have remained so low. When oil prices rise, so will interest in ethanol.

A broad range of biomass-based plastics have been shown to be technically feasible, even though they look expensive when compared with petrochemical plastics at today's prices. If oil and gas rise in price, the plastics industry may first switch to using coal rather than biomass.[5] Yet this wide choice of raw materials confirms that plastics production can continue after the era of oil. Contrary to almost everyone's intuition, plastics are, along with paper, the common materials that could be produced on a sustainable basis.

To continue this celebration of plastics just a little longer, an astonishing range of material characteristics can be obtained in very lightweight objects made from different plastic polymers: flexibility or rigidity, heat and cold tolerance, transparency or opacity, etc. The ongoing advances in polymer chemistry, increasing the precision with which complex hydrocarbon materials can be manipulated, are actually hopeful signs for the technology of sustainability. It would of course be politically difficult to reorient the existing industry toward social and environmental goals. But in terms of technology, the same laboratories and research techniques that today turn out an ever-increasing variety of petroleum-based plastics could, in a different context, be used to help create a renewable, plant-based materials industry.

Let a Hundred Fibers Bloom

Although it is technologically possible to rebuild the material world with plant-based products, there is no guarantee that it is economically possible. One central problem of a sustainable economy will be the allocation of land. Production of plant-based materials will be only one among many land uses, in competition with production of food and fuel, expansion of urban and suburban settlement, and the desire for recreational and wilderness land. A biomass economy will undoubtedly experience a scarcity of arable land; in order to avoid unsustainable overexploitation of resources (such as present-day logging practices), there will be continuing pressure to reduce the resources needed for material production.

Will there be enough? That is, will the economy of the future be able to sustain a comfortable material existence for all? The answer depends on at least three factors: the level of total consumption; the productivity with which agriculture and industry supply consumption goods; and the rate of recycling of commodities, which affects the need for new raw material inputs.

The first factor, the level of total consumption, depends on both the number of people and their standards of living. Although gloom is traditional on this subject, some recent demographic forecasts are actually quite optimistic about an impending slowdown in population growth.[6] Even though there is no consensus on when and how growth will be stopped, it is difficult to imagine either population or per capita consumption increasing indefinitely. Thus in the long run, if there is to be a long run, both may be assumed to be constant.[7]

The second factor involves the technology of production, in both agriculture and industry. Innovations in agricultural technology may boost yields per acre, which will be crucial to biomass productivity. The plants that grow best in each area depend on the local climate, soils, and environment; an efficient biomass economy may be characterized by great local diversity. At present, China's paper industry (the world's third largest) obtains three-quarters of its virgin fiber from nonwood plant fibers such as straw, bagasse (sugar mill residue), reeds, and bamboo—materials that are almost never used in papermaking elsewhere.[8]

Innovations in industrial technology will likely continue to reduce the material required to make any given product. This tendency, sometimes awkwardly called "dematerialization," can be seen in the weight reductions in packaging discussed in earlier chapters, in the rapid shrinkage of computers and all things electronic, and in other examples as well. The earliest railroad locomotives weighed 1000 kg per horsepower; after more than a century and a half of steady improvement, European locomotives made in 1980 weighed only 14 kg per horsepower.[9] In a growing economy, lower material requirements per unit are often overshadowed by the increasing number of units: more packages, more computers, or more horsepower per locomotive can still mean more material use in the aggregate. But in a sustainable future economy with constant total consumption, the tendency toward dematerialization would no longer be hidden by growth in production.

The Role of Recycling

The third factor determining raw material requirements is the extent of reuse and recycling. The more uses that can be obtained from each unit of material, the smaller the original inputs that are needed to sustain a given level of consumption. Today's recycling efforts are a valuable step in this direction, but the sustainable economy of the future will need to go even further.

It will be important to conserve and recycle the remaining uses of metals and minerals, during the long transition into the age of renewables. Metal and glass recycling are well-established technologies, with consistently lower environmental impacts than virgin production.

Many developed countries have achieved high, and still rising, levels of recovery of these materials, as seen in earlier chapters.

But the growth industry will be the recycling of organic materials: wood, fiber, paper, and plastics. Here there is certainly room for improvement. Some types of paper, paperboard, and wood products are already recovered at fairly high rates, but others are not. Even for those paper products that are being recycled, better, less-polluting techniques could be developed. At present there are technical limitations to paper recycling: existing technology allows paper to make only a few trips through the recycling mill, since the fibers get shorter every time; and some paper recycling techniques generate large quantities of organic sludge, losing a significant fraction of the paper in the process of removing ink and debris.

Recovery and reuse of plastics are growing, but still quite limited. Only the two most common beverage container plastics, PET (soda bottles) and HDPE (milk and water bottles), are recycled in large quantities in the United States today. Recycling of other plastics was just beginning to spread in the 1995 price boom, and may not survive the next price slump or recession. Germany's more extensive efforts to recover and use waste plastics, described in Chapter 6, have not yet produced an economical approach to mixed plastics recycling; experiments in chemical recycling, however, may look more attractive when oil becomes scarce. The newest German strategy, use of waste plastics in the steel industry, is a problematical example of recycling: it does get two valuable uses from the material (first as plastics, and second as a reduction agent in steel mills), which is better than one—but sustainability may require learning to use everything much more than twice.

It is worth dwelling on the far-off prospects for a sustainable economy, because the current impetus for recycling can only be fully understood in relation to the long-run goal of material conservation. Whether or not recycling saves money on disposal costs, creates jobs, saves energy, reduces litter, or has other immediate benefits, many people participate because they believe that materials are scarce and that conserving them is the right thing to do. Only in the short run is this debatable.

Capitalism Unleashed

In the short run, however, the existence of scarcity and the importance of material conservation are often debated from a free-market perspective. This view is presented particularly passionately by Stephen Moore, an economist at the Cato Institute, who looks forward to "the coming age of abundance" with unbridled enthusiasm. "Every measurable trend of the past century suggests that humanity will soon be entering an age of increasing and unprecedented natural resources abundance," says Moore. "The very concept of 'finite natural resources' embraced by geologists is a flawed way of thinking about the earth and nature."[10]

Moore's argument, in more restrained terms, is that new resource discoveries and new technologies for extracting materials from the earth are increasing "proven reserves" (the reserves that can profitably be exploited) of many fuels and minerals, while the technology of the information age is reducing material requirements faster than the population is growing. The result is that raw material prices have been declining relative to hourly wages, or even relative to consumer prices. Low raw material prices, by definition, indicate a lack of scarcity, which Moore expects will continue worldwide throughout the next century.

This argument is not entirely wrong as a description of the recent past. The long-term trend in material prices has certainly been downward. The question is not whether new discoveries of oil and minerals have held down prices in the past, but whether the laws of geology have been amended to allow such discoveries to continue into the indefinite future. Likewise, the reduction in material requirements has been dramatic for some individual products, as in the story of locomotives. But in a growing economy, the increase in aggregate consumption can outweigh the per-unit savings. Computers today are much smaller than they were in the 1960s, but also more numerous; the result is that more, not fewer, resources are used by the computer industry as a whole.

On a worldwide basis, aggregate consumption and material requirements are clearly both growing. In the face of such growth, sustaining a hypothetical age of free-market abundance would require increasingly implausible good luck in oil and mineral discoveries to maintain resource supplies, and/or technological progress faster than in the past to slow the growth in resource demand.

The advocacy of free-market abundance is also free of any troubling thoughts about the environmental impacts of expanding energy and material consumption. If prices do not include the full social costs of resource use, then the market leads to too much consumption. At prices adjusted for environmental damage, natural resources would be less of a bargain.[11]

For the long run, the sustainable economy described above is a much better bet. It solves the problem of supply by "discovering" renewable materials; on the demand side it assumes an eventual limit to total consumption, something which the market is unlikely to achieve on its own. Shaped by environmental criteria and concerns, the sustainable society relies on a high level of recycling and reuse to minimize new resource needs.

Back to the Future

Yet, however unsustainable, the image of free-market abundance is an alluring one. It seems compatible with Keynes' vision of post-materialistic affluence—unlike some pictures of intensive recycling and reuse that are disturbingly all too real.

Landfill scavenging, described in Chapter 1 as a part of nineteenth-century urban America, continues today in many of the cities of the developing world. With enough scavengers, a high rate of material recovery can be achieved. Everything that is reusable or recyclable can be pulled out of urban garbage and sold to brokers, processors, or refurbishers of used materials. The recovered goods can go through the cycle again, and may be used repeatedly before their final disposal, gaining the maximum human use from a limited supply of material.

The picture of poverty sending us back to the dumps is not part of a credible plan for sustainable development. Landfill scavenging is a public health disaster and an affront to human dignity; countries that can afford to do so have moved to eliminate the practice. The reappearance in the United States of more modest forms of scavenging, for example involving the collection of deposit containers in bottle bill states, is evidence of our disgracefully unequal distribution of income in the midst of affluence.

Consider another image, less outrageous but still disquieting. Imagine a world of virtually perfect reuse and recycling. Clothes and linens are patched and resewn as long as possible, then made into rag rugs or homemade upholstery, and sold to a rag merchant only if they are beyond salvation. Furniture, containers, dishes, and tools are carefully repaired and used for years, even with visible imperfections of age and accident. Paper, largely made from the rags gathered by rag merchants, is treated with respect, and used primarily for books and periodicals. Food and other retail items are distributed in bulk, with no packaging except the wholesale shipping containers (themselves often reused many times), and the customer's own shopping bags and jars. Used wooden barrels and cartons are made into furniture. Kitchen waste is composted in the garden or fed to livestock, which provide an additional source of food for the household. Grease is saved for making candles or soap. Even ashes are used in soap or as fertilizer.

Such a world in fact existed in nineteenth-century America, according to historian Susan Strasser. Her forthcoming book documents the almost reverent attitude toward modest material possessions in that era, and the extraordinary effort that went into maintenance, repair, and reuse of goods that modern Americans would discard in a moment.[12] This household recycling of the past is an ambiguous image, at once conveying attractive qualities of thrift and self-sufficiency, and exhausting visions of endless domestic toil. The life of the nineteenth-century housewife, on balance, is not a future most of us would choose to go back to.

The economic foundation for both landfill scavenging and nineteenth-century household recycling is the combination of cheap labor and expensive materials. The relationship between wages and material prices is portrayed graphically in Figure 10-1. The materials shown, cotton sheeting and nails, were chosen because long data series were readily available.[13] The graph shows the ratio of the wholesale prices of these two materials to average wages, measured in minutes of labor required to buy the goods. It shows a precipitous drop from about 90 minutes of labor required to buy either a yard of cotton or a pound of nails around 1830, to well under 10 minutes for either commodity after World War II. Note that the graph is based on wholesale prices; the retail cost, which is not systematically recorded, was of course greater throughout the period. The cost of cotton went up during wars: the Civil War peak (not shown) was far off the chart, while World War I

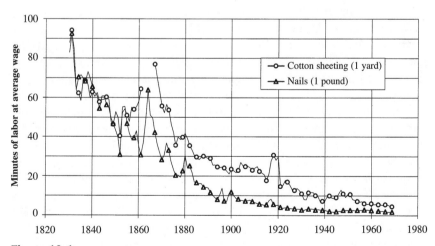

Figure 10-1
Labor time required to buy selected materials, 1830–1969. Wholesale prices divided by average manufacturing wage (1890–1969) or urban unskilled labor wage (1830–1889). Peak Civil War cotton prices (1862–1866) are omitted.

caused a good-sized blip. But wars aside, the downward trend is unmistakable.

Both past recycling and present abundance can be understood as positions on this graph. Landfill scavenging and intensive household recycling are practices that people engage in at the upper left-hand corner of the graph, when common materials cost many hours of paid labor. The affluence of modern developed countries is located at the lower right-hand corner of the graph, when the same materials can be bought for mere minutes of employment. Cast in these terms, economic history seems to support the free-market argument: surely there is no need to worry about expanding recycling now, while materials are so cheap. If and when we are forced back up the graph by future scarcity, greater levels of recycling and conservation will then become cost-effective, and will be implemented by market forces.

What's Wrong with This Picture?

From this perspective, contemporary recycling is the anomaly, located somewhere off the graph. Initiated when materials were cheap, it acts as if they were expensive. It is not simply a return to past practice; unlike nineteenth-century household recycling, modern recycling programs are designed for people in a hurry who believe their own time is scarce. Yet despite the hurry, they evidently believe that materials are scarce as well. Recycling today is industrialized: in terms of technology, the modern material recovery facility (MRF) is to traditional household recycling as the textile mill was to handloom weaving. But in terms of history, there is a break in the sequence. The household recycling of the past was not driven out of existence by dark satanic MRFs, but by urbanized affluence. Only much later did industrialized recycling arise.

Is there a role for this anomalous institution? Is modern recycling just a needlessly expensive detour from the least-cost path to economic growth, or can recycling "before we have to" play a role in reaching the long-term destination of sustainability? In the final analysis, there are two essential contributions that recycling today can make to our long-term future—two specifications of the vague intuition that it is important to start conserving material now despite low prices. One concerns the evolution of technology, and the other involves the nature of human values and behavior.

Conventional economic theory leaves little room for concern about or intervention in the choice of technology. Efficiency is presented as a purely technical matter, appropriately left to the market; competition will ensure the selection of the best available technology, given the existing prices and resources. But, as discussed in Chapter 3, the presumption that the market reaches a uniquely efficient outcome breaks down in cases like the QWERTY keyboard, where there are increasing returns to adoption of a technology (the more that others use a technology, the greater the benefits to you of doing the same). Although exiled from standard economics on grounds of mathematical inconvenience, increasing returns seem common in reality. Industry-wide learning curves, the existence of networks and standards for connection to them, and the advantages of hardware and software compatibility with others, all are evidence of increasing returns.

When there are rival technologies, each with increasing returns (think of MS-DOS/Windows versus Macintosh computers), then there is no longer a single efficient outcome. Rather, the choice of a dominant technology, which may depend on early chance events, determines which of two or more possible outcomes will eventually be reached by the market. In the discussion of beverage deposit laws in Europe and the United States (Chapters 6 and 7), we saw that refillable glass bottles could be either more or less energy-efficient than single-use containers, depending on the distance the containers were shipped and the reliability with which they were returned. Moreover, once the United States had largely switched to single-use containers, even a producer as powerful as Anheuser-Busch could not maintain its once-thriving distribution of refillable bottles in New England—an event that certainly suggests the presence of increasing returns.

The same forces are at work in many other choices about technology and resource use. Once any one approach becomes dominant, the snowballing advantages of accumulated engineering knowledge, production skills, and consumer acceptance makes it hard for alternatives to catch up. The basic decisions about resource use may therefore be made in the initial choice of the winning technology, not in the later details of its implementation. Recycling efforts are important in this respect; they can help determine which new technologies get a head start and become dominant in the future. By acting as if materials are more valuable than the market now thinks they are, and by creating legislative and grassroots pressure to make use of recovered wastes, recycling helps select which learning curves industry will slide down next.

In a world of increasing returns, there is no longer a theoretical argument in favor of leaving technology choice to the market. In fact, mathematical analysis shows that on average, public decisionmaking is more likely than private profit maximization to make the right choice. This provides a theoretical justification for government adoption of an active industrial policy, a frequently debated topic. However, if the future returns to rival techniques are uncertain, there is no decision process that is guaranteed to avoid errors.[14] Recycling now might be seen as social experimentation aimed at reducing uncertainty, by developing the technologies that will be needed to ease a future transition to a regime of resource scarcity.

The potential and the pitfalls for public intervention in technology choices are revealed in the contrasting fates of the computer and nuclear power industries. Each owes its existence to massive U.S. government spending in the years after World War II; they both began as spin-offs from the military and space programs. Today one industry soars higher and higher, often described (quite ahistorically) as a triumph of private enterprise; the other has long since made a crash landing. The goal of public influence on technology choice is of course to turn out more often like the computer industry than like nuclear power—and to recognize and promptly pull the plug on examples of the latter.

Public decisions that affect resource use and technology adoption are continually being made. To cite just one example, the paper industry gets one message about where to concentrate its research and development from low-cost opportunities for logging on public lands, and another from requirements for recycled content in government purchasing. The prevalence of recycling programs and public support for recycling exerts an indirect but powerful pressure on the choice of new technologies, favoring those that will conserve resources. With enough of such pressure, industry may develop along different, more sustainable lines. The interesting question is not whether the government should intervene, but how to do so skillfully enough to achieve the desired results.

Moderation, Ritual, and Final Answers

The behavioral meaning and implications of recycling also fit rather poorly into standard economic theory. The consumer found in the textbooks wants only to acquire the most stuff with the least effort, and would not comprehend Keynes' conclusion that there is such a thing as "obviously enough": eight times the present standard of living would be better than seven times, but not quite as good as nine times as much. Recycling, unless adopted as an idiosyncratic hobby, would be undertaken only in response to the kinds of economic incentives discussed in Chapter 2.

Fortunately, there is evidence that the world is not populated solely by such slothful gluttons. As argued in earlier parts of this book, the strength and breadth of support for recycling cannot be understood in terms of market incentives alone. Many environmental and other goals cannot be expressed within the market framework; as explained in Chapter 3, basic values and positions on public policy are not externalities waiting to be monetized. Much could be, and has been, said about alternative analyses of consumption.[15] For the story of sustainability and recycling, it will be sufficient to consider two major revisions to the textbook model of consumption, one negative and one positive.

First, the endless pursuit of more individual consumer goods and services is neither ecologically sustainable nor personally satisfying. While it is important to recognize that a majority of the world's population, and a sizable minority within the developed countries, suffer real material deprivation, it is equally important to see that the majority of us in the richer countries already have enough when it comes to private consumption.

This does not mean that we have solved all our economic problems. Almost all of us are to varying degrees "deprived" of economic security, meaningful work, creative leisure, public services, and a healthy environment—but to raise such issues is already to leave the paradigm of private consumption behind. Most of us are not deprived of food, shelter, fashionable clothing, or consumer electronics. Indeed, seeking to satisfy social deprivations through individual consumption keeps us on a treadmill of rising expenditure but stagnant satisfaction.

To create a sustainable future it will be necessary to act on the understanding that there is such a thing as enough, and that many of our remaining needs must be addressed through social change rather than private spending. Growth of incomes and consumption will remain desirable for those who are really poor; meanwhile, the increasing numbers who are not poor will need to develop an appreciation of sufficiency in private consumption. Although it is hard to see how to get there from here, arriving at stability in levels of consumption could be a liberating experience. A life of moderation, avoiding the extremes of either obsessive competition and accumulation on the one hand, or material deprivation on the other, could provide the freedom to pursue social goals and personal self-development. From the point of view of the economy as a whole, this path leads to a limit on total consumption, identified above as one of the requirements for sustainability.

Second, the textbook image of people as endlessly minimizing effort is also misleading. It is not only that effort minimizers would never recycle without monetary incentives; they would never develop social ties, participate in public life, or engage in countless other common activities. A positive conception of the fulfillment of human needs would have to include much more than material sufficiency; surely the good life entails the development of many other capabilities. Among these developmental goals are an awareness of and connection to our social and environmental context. The urge to recycle may be viewed as evidence of that broader connection, a statement of responsiveness and responsibility toward one's surroundings.

In this light it is interesting to consider an analysis of the psychological motivation of early participants in recycling. A survey of people in a college town just before the introduction of a curbside recycling program measured both recycling and reuse activity, and compared them to somewhat unconventional categories of personal desires. It found that both recycling and reuse were correlated with a desire for frugality; recycling was also correlated with the desire for public participation.[16] Although this is only one small survey of a single community, it is nonetheless suggestive of important possible meanings of recycling.

If our goals in life include a commitment to do the right thing for society and the environment, recycling is one of the most accessible, tangible symbols of that commitment. Participation in recycling is, in addition to its more literal purposes, a ritual of environmental belief. It is all the more valuable for being one of the few rituals that is shared widely throughout an increasingly fragmented society. Rituals at worst become empty forms, at best renew our dedication to a much greater common purpose; recycling as ritual of environmental commitment is no different in this regard. To return at last to the discussion that opened this book, perhaps recycling is a religion—and in a society that produces goods far more readily than satisfying beliefs, perhaps that is one of recycling's strengths.

We are at the end, at the point for final answers. Why do we recycle? In the short run, before we are all dead, we recycle (and reduce waste and reuse things) partly in order to avoid the need for new landfills and incinerators. But there is much more to it than dislike of disposal facilities. At times, recycling saves money; the struggle to make it cost-effective is a vital and ongoing one. But advocates push, very often successfully, to extend recycling beyond the point at which it pays for itself. Recycling lessens the need for virgin materials, and reduces pollution from material extraction and manufacturing. Some types of recycling prevent litter or reduce landfill emissions. Local recycling efforts may provide a basis for new businesses to use recovered materials, creating local jobs and incomes.

As important as all these benefits are, they are not the whole story. The well-defined short-run advantages cannot explain the passion or the extent of involvement in recycling. For that we must turn to the vague feelings about consumption and waste, the desires for frugality and public participation, the belief that materials are ultimately scarce and must be conserved. In the long run, the materials we use freely today will be scarce, and our descendants will have to create a strikingly different, renewable economy. Contemporary recycling points toward that far-off future.

The last dangling question, from the beginning of this chapter, remains unanswered. Will the sustainable economy of the future have the feel of late twentieth-century affluence, or the frugal, hard-working mood of nineteenth-century household recycling? There are too many uncertainties on the road to sustainability to offer a definite answer this early in the journey. But the practice of recycling pushes us in the right direction, toward the development of the technologies of sustainable material use, and toward the creation of less materialistic, more socially and environmentally engaged ways of living. There is no greater hope in any other direction. Indeed, in the long run there is nowhere else to go.

Notes

1. The essay can be found in John Maynard Keynes, *Essays in Persuasion* (New York: W.W. Norton, 1963), pp. 358–373.

2. From the point of view of energy and the associated emissions, worldwide attainment of 1990s American consumption levels would be disastrous, but a more modest developed-country standard, such as 1970s European consumption levels, might be globally sustainable. For a discussion of this and many related issues, see Alan Durning, *How Much Is Enough?* (New York: W.W. Norton, 1992).

3. World Resources Institute, *Natural Resources 1994–95* (Washington, D.C., 1995), Chapter 1.

4. Robert Friedel, "The First Plastic," in Penny Sparke, editor, *The Plastics Age* (Woodstock, New York: Overlook Press, 1993). Other contributors to the volume provide many striking illustrations of both artistic and functional uses of newer plastics.

5. T. Randall Curlee, "Biomass-derived Plastics: Viable Economic Alternatives to Petrochemical Plastics?," *Materials and Society,* Vol. 13 (1989), pp. 381–405.

6. Wolfgang Lutz, editor, *The Future Population of the World: What Can We Assume Today?,* revised edition (London: Earthscan Publications, 1996).

7. For analysis of and alternatives to endless growth in consumption, see Neva Goodwin, Frank Ackerman, and David Kiron, editors, *The Consumer Society* (Washington, D.C.: Island Press, 1997), and further discussion later in this chapter.

8. Peter Ince, *What Won't Get Harvested Where and When: The Effects of Increased*

Paper Recycling on Timber Harvest, Solid Waste Working Paper #3 (New Haven: Yale School of Forestry and Environmental Studies, 1995), p. 11.

9. Robert Williams, Eric Larson, and Marc Ross, "Materials, Affluence, and Industrial Energy Use," *Annual Review of Energy,* Vol. 12 (1987), pp. 112, 115.

10. Stephen Moore, "The Coming Age of Abundance," in Ronald Bailey, editor, *The True State of the Planet* (New York: The Free Press, 1995), pp. 109–140; quotes from pp. 110 and 134.

11. Although several much-discussed attempts to adjust prices to include externalities accomplish little or nothing in the field of solid waste, as seen in Chapter 2, there is some evidence that incorporation of externalities would have more of an effect on energy consumption. Price elasticities are greater for energy than for solid waste, and there is a wider range of technological options to choose from in many energy markets. However, as argued in Chapter 3, environmental problems cannot be completely reduced to externalities and adjustments in resource prices.

12. Susan Strasser, *Waste and Want: Disposal, Recycling, and American Consumer Culture* (New York: Metropolitan Books, 1998).

13. Price data are taken from the Census Bureau's *Historical Statistics of the United States, Colonial Times to 1970* (1975), Series E128 and E131. Wage data for 1890 to 1969 are from Historical Statistics, Series D802 and D848. Wage data for 1830 to 1889 are from Donald R. Adams, Jr., "Prices and Wages," in Glenn Porter, editor, *Encyclopedia of American Economic History* (New York: Charles Scribner's Sons, 1980), Table 4. Adams' urban wage index was set equal to manufacturing wages in the early 1890s, creating an hourly wage series for the entire period. The resulting hourly wages for the nineteenth century are in fairly close agreement with the reported wages for unskilled workers on the Erie Canal (*Historical Statistics Series* D718, assuming a ten-hour day).

14. Robin Cowan, "Tortoises and Hares: Choice among Technologies of Unknown Merit," *The Economic Journal,* Vol. 101 (1991), pp. 801–814.

15. See, for example, Goodwin, Ackerman, and Kiron, *The Consumer Society.*

16. Raymond DeYoung, "Some Psychological Aspects of Recycling: The Structure of Conservation Satisfactions," *Environment and Behavior,* Vol. 18 (1986), pp. 435–449.

BIBLIOGRAPHY

Ackerman, Frank, "Solid Waste: The Hidden Utility," *BioCycle,* August 1990.

———, "Waste Management—Taxing the Trash Away," *Environment,* June 1992.

———, "Analyzing the True Costs of Packaging," *BioCycle,* April 1993.

———, "Advance Disposal Fees and Incentives for Waste Reduction," *New Partnerships: Economic Incentives for Environmental Management* (Pittsburgh: Air & Waste Management Association, 1994).

———, "Trashing Recycling: The New Face of Anti-environmentalism," *Dollars & Sense,* November–December 1996.

Ackerman, Frank, and Monica Becker, "Economies of Scale in Landfill Costs," *Journal of Resource Management and Technology,* December 1990.

Adams, Donald R., Jr., "Prices and Wages," *in* Glenn Porter, editor, *Encyclopedia of American Economic History* (New York: Charles Scribner's Sons, 1980).

Alexander, Judd, *In Defense of Garbage* (Westport, Connecticut: Praeger, 1993).

Amato, Ivan, "The Crusade to Ban Chlorine," *Garbage,* Summer 1994.

Anderson, Peter, George Dreckmann, and John Reindl, "Debunking the Two Fleet Myth," *Waste Age,* October 1995.

Note: Reports available from Tellus Institute are listed separately at the end.

Arthur, W. Brian, "Competing Technologies, Increasing Returns, and Lock-in by Historical Events," *Economic Journal,* Vol. 99, No. 1 (1989).

Bailey, Jeff, "Curbside Recycling Comforts the Soul, But Benefits Are Scant," *Wall Street Journal,* January 19, 1995.

Baker, M. Douglas, Sally E. Moore, and Paul H. Wise, "The Impact of 'Bottle Bill' Legislation on the Incidence of Lacerations in Childhood," *American Journal of Public Health,* Vol. 76, October 1986.

R.W. Beck and Associates, *Review of the Waste Diversion Aspects of the California AB2020 Program* (National Soft Drink Association, 1994).

Becker, Gary S., Michael Grossman, and Kevin M. Murphy, "An Empirical Analysis of Cigarette Addiction," *American Economic Review,* Vol. 84, No. 3 (1994).

Blumberg, Louis, and Robert Gottlieb, *War on Waste: Can America Win Its Battle with Garbage?* (Washington, D.C.: Island Press, 1989).

Boerner, Christopher, and Kenneth Chilton, "False Economy: The Folly of Demand-Side Recycling," *Environment,* Vol. 36, No. 1, January/February 1994.

Bogner, Jean, and Kurt Spokas, "Landfill CH_4: Rates, Fates, and Role in the Global Carbon Cycle," *Chemosphere,* Vol. 26, Nos. 1–4 (1993), pp. 369–386.

Bohi, Douglas R., *Analyzing Demand Behavior: A Study of Energy Elasticities* (Baltimore: Johns Hopkins University Press, 1981).

Breslow, Marc, "Regulating Solid Waste Externalities Through Tax/Fee Systems," Ph.D. dissertation, Economics Department, University of Massachusetts—Amherst, 1993.

———, "Reducing Pollution and Disposal Costs by Taxing Materials," *Resource Recycling,* June 1993.

Brisson, Inger, "Packaging Waste and the Environment: Economics and Policy," *Resources, Conservation and Recycling,* Vol. 8 (1993), pp. 183–292.

Burt, Justine, *Green Light for the Green Dot?,* Masters thesis, Tufts University, 1994.

Cairncross, Frances, *Costing the Earth* (Boston: Harvard Business School Press, 1993).

———, *Green, Inc.: A Guide to Business and the Environment* (Washington, D.C.: Island Press, 1995).

Carless, Jennifer, *Taking Out the Trash: A No-Nonsense Guide to Recycling* (Washington, D.C.: Island Press, 1992).

Chang, Ni-Bin, and S. F. Wang, "The Development of Material Recovery Facilities in the United States: Status and Cost Structure Analysis," *Resources, Conservation and Recycling,* Vol. 13 (1995).

Chem Systems, Inc., *Vinyl Products Lifecycle Assessment* (Wayne, New Jersey: Vinyl Institute, 1992).

Container Recycling Institute, *Refillable Bottles: An Idea Whose Time Has Come, Again* (Washington, D.C., 1993).

Cowan, Robin, "Tortoises and Hares: Choice among Technologies of Unknown Merit," *The Economic Journal,* Vol. 101 (1991), pp. 801–814.

Curlee, T. Randall, "Biomass-Derived Plastics: Viable Economic Alternatives to Petrochemical Plastics?," *Materials and Society,* Vol. 13 (1989), pp. 381–405.

David, Paul A., "Clio and the Economics of QWERTY," *American Economic Review,* Vol. 75, No. 2 (1985).

DeYoung, Raymond, "Some Psychological Aspects of Recycling: The Structure of Conservation Satisfactions," *Environment and Behavior,* Vol. 18 (1986), pp. 435–449.

Dobbs, Ian M., "Litter and Waste Management: Disposal Taxes Versus User Charges," *Canadian Journal of Economics,* Vol. 24 (1991).

Duales System Deutschland, *Ecological Optimization of Packaging* (Köln, 1992).

———, *Packaging Recycling Worldwide* (Köln, 1995).

Dunlap, Riley E., and Rik Scarce, "Poll Trends: Environmental Problems and Protection," *Public Opinion Quarterly,* Vol. 55 (1991), pp. 651–672.

Durning, Alan, *How Much Is Enough?* (New York: W.W. Norton, 1992).

Energy Information Administration, *Federal Energy Subsidies: Direct and Indirect Intervention in Energy Markets* (Washington, D.C.: Government Printing Office, 1992).

Ewel, Dexter, "Solid Waste Flow Control Statutes Are Unconstitutional," *BioCycle,* June 1994.

———, "Solid Waste Flow Control Update," *BioCycle,* May 1995.

Fishbein, Bette K., *Germany, Garbage, and the Green Dot: Challenging the Throwaway Society* (New York: INFORM, 1994).

Frankland, E. Gene, and Donald Schoonmaker, *Between Protest and Power: The Green Party in Germany* (Boulder, Colorado: Westview Press, 1992).

Franklin Associates, *The Role of Recycling in Integrated Solid Waste Management to the Year 2000* (Stamford, Connecticut: Keep America Beautiful, Inc., 1994).

Friedel, Robert, "The First Plastic," *in* Penny Sparke, editor, *The Plastics Age* (Woodstock, New York: Overlook Press, 1993).

Fullerton, Don, and Thomas C. Kinnaman, "Household Demand for Garbage and Recycling Collection with the Start of a Price per Bag," National Bureau of Economic Research Working Paper 4670 (Cambridge: NBER, 1993).

———, "Garbage, Recycling, and Illicit Burning or Dumping," *Journal of Environmental Economics and Management,* Vol. 29 (1995), pp. 78–91.

Geller, Roger, *Wasted Forests: The Virgin U.S. Paper Industry and the Federal Policies That Support It,* Master's thesis, Tufts University, 1990.

Gieskes, Hanna, "Plastikgabeln unerwünscht: Immer mehr Kommunen erheben eigene Steuern auf Einweggeschirr," *Die Welt,* June 30, 1995.

Goodwin, Neva, Frank Ackerman, and David Kiron, editors, *The Consumer Society* (Washington, D.C.: Island Press, 1997).

Günther, A., and W. Holley, "Aggregierte Sachökobilanz-Ergebnisse für Frischmilch- und Bierverpackungen," *Verpackungs-Rundschau,* Vol. 46, No. 3 (1995), pp. 53–58.

Harvard Law Review editors, " 'Ask a Silly Question . . .': Contingent Valuation of Natural Resource Damages," *Harvard Law Review,* Vol. 105 (June 1992).

Hawken, Paul, *The Ecology of Commerce* (New York: HarperCollins, 1993).

Heller, Joseph, *Closing Time* (New York: Simon & Schuster, 1994).

Hernon, Peter, and Terry Ganey, *Under the Influence: The Unauthorized Story of the Anheuser-Busch Dynasty* (New York: Simon & Schuster, 1991).

Hirsch, Fred, *Social Limits to Growth* (Cambridge: Harvard University Press, 1976).

Hirst, Eric, and Joseph Ito, *Justification for Electric-Utility Energy-Efficiency Programs* (Oak Ridge National Laboratory Report ORNL/CON-419, August 1995).

Hosford, William F., and John L. Duncan, "The Aluminum Beverage Can," *Scientific American,* September 1994.

Howarth, Richard, and Richard Norgaard, "Intergenerational Transfers and the Social Discount Rate," *Journal of Environmental and Resource Economics,* Vol. 3 (1993), pp. 337–358.

Ince, Peter, *What Won't Get Harvested Where and When: The Effects of Increased Paper Recycling on Timber Harvest,* Solid Waste Working Paper #3 (New Haven: Yale School of Forestry and Environmental Studies, 1995).

Jenkins, Robin, *The Economics of Waste Reduction: The Impact of User Fees* (Brookfield, Vermont: Edward Elgar, 1993).

Jenkins, Virginia Scott, *The Lawn: A History of an American Obsession* (Washington, D.C.: Smithsonian Institution Press, 1994).

Kempton, Willett, James. S. Boster, and Jennifer A. Hartley, *Environmental Values in American Culture* (Cambridge: MIT Press, 1995).

Keynes, John Maynard, "Economic Possibilities for Our Grandchildren," *Essays in Persuasion* (New York: W.W. Norton, 1963), pp. 358–373.

Koplow, Douglas, *Federal Energy Subsidies: Energy, Environmental, and Fiscal Impacts* (Washington, D.C.: Alliance to Save Energy, 1993).

———, "Federal Energy Subsidies and Recycling: A Case Study," *Resource Recycling,* November 1994.

Koplow, Douglas, and Kevin Dietly, *Federal Disincentives: A Study of Federal Tax Subsidies and Other Programs Affecting Virgin Industries and Recycling* (Washington, D.C.: EPA Office of Policy, Planning, and Evaluation, 1994).

Levine, Mark D., and Richard Sonnenblick, "On the Assessment of Utility Demand-Side Management Programs" *Energy Policy,* Vol. 22, No. 10 (October 1994).

Lindemann, Michael, "Plastics Waste Strikes Oil," *Financial Times,* February 15, 1995.

Little Hoover Commission, *Beyond Bottles and Cans: Reorganizing California's Recycling Efforts* (Sacramento, 1994).

Lutz, Wolfgang, editor, *The Future Population of the World: What Can We Assume Today?,* revised edition (London: Earthscan Publications, 1996).

MacEwan, Arthur, "The Construction of Markets," in *Economic Development Alternatives: Market Strategies versus Democratic Initiatives* (forthcoming).

Martin, Kay, "Flow Control: The Wisdom of Doing Without," *MSW Management,* May/June 1995.

Martin, Russell, "Improving Recycling Through Market Forces," *BioCycle,* October 1994.

McGaw, Judith, *Most Wonderful Machine: Mechanization and Social Change in Berkshire Paper Making, 1801–1885* (Princeton: Princeton University Press, 1987).

Melosi, Martin, *Garbage in the Cities: Refuse, Reform, and the Environment, 1880–1980* (College Station, Texas: Texas A&M University Press, 1981).

———, "Down in the Dumps: Is There a Garbage Crisis in America?," *Journal of Policy History,* Vol. 5 (1993), pp. 100–127.

Miller, Benjamin, *The Fat of the Land: New York's Waste* (New York: W.W. Norton, 1996).

Miranda, Marie Lynn, Jess W. Everett, Daniel Blume, and Barbeau A. Roy, Jr., "Market-Based Incentives and Residential Municipal Solid Waste," *Journal of Policy Analysis and Management,* Vol. 13, No. 4 (1994).

Mirowski, Philip, *More Heat Than Light* (New York: Cambridge University Press, 1989).

Moore, Stephen, "The Coming Age of Abundance," in Ronald Bailey, editor, *The True State of the Planet* (New York: The Free Press, 1995), pp. 109–140.

Naughton, Michael, Frederick Sebold, and Thomas Mayer, "The Impacts of the California Beverage Container Recycling and Litter Reduction Act on Consumers," *Journal of Consumer Affairs,* Vol. 24 (1990), pp. 190–220.

Nichols, Albert L., "Demand-Side Management: Overcoming Market Barriers or Obscuring Real Costs?," *Energy Policy,* Vol. 22, No. 10 (October 1994).

Nordman, Bruce, "Paper Efficiency: Energy and Beyond" (Lawrence Berkeley National Laboratory, 1994; presented at the Electric Power Research Institute conference on "Energy Efficiency in Office Technology," New York, 1994).

Oliver, Thomas, *The Real Coke, The Real Story* (New York: Random House, 1986).

Pearce, D. W., and R. K. Turner, "Market-Based Approaches to Solid Waste Management," *Resources, Conservation and Recycling,* Vol. 8 (1993), pp. 63–90.

Peters, Irene, *A Study of the Impact of Material Charges on Packaging,* Ph.D. dissertation, Economics Department, Clark University, 1995.

Platt, Brenda, Christine Doherty, Anne Claire Broughton, and David Morris, *Beyond 40 Percent: Record-Setting Recycling and Composting Programs* (Washington, D.C.: Island Press, 1991).

Platt, Brenda, Henry Jeanes, and Anne Kaufmann, "Recycling Boosts the Local Economy," *BioCycle,* August 1995.

Polanyi, Karl, *The Great Transformation* (New York: Farrar & Rinehart, 1944).

Porter, Richard C., "A Social Benefit-Cost Analysis of Mandatory Deposits on Beverage Containers," *Journal of Environmental Economics and Management,* Vol. 5 (1978), pp. 351–375.

———, "Michigan's Experience with Mandatory Deposits on Beverage Containers," *Land Economics,* Vol. 59 (1983), pp. 177–194.

Powell, Jerry, "The Anti-recyclers: Who Are They?," and "The Anti-recyclers: What's Their Message?," *Resource Recycling,* September 1992.

———, "The PRFect Solution to Plastic Bottle Recycling," *Resource Recycling,* February 1995.

———, "Is Mixed Plastic Bottle Recycling Working?," *Resource Recycling,* September 1995.

Proctor & Redfern, *Estimation of the Effects of Various Municipal Waste Management Strategies on Greenhouse Gas Emissions* (Don Mills, Ontario, 1994).

Rathje, William, and Cullen Murphy, *Rubbish! The Archaeology of Garbage* (New York: HarperCollins, 1992).

Ready, Mark, and Richard Ready, "Optimal Pricing of Depletable, Replaceable Resources: The Case of Landfill Tipping Fees," *Journal of Environmental Economics and Management,* Vol. 28 (1995).

Repetto, Robert, Roger C. Dower, Robin Jenkins, and Jacqueline Geoghegan, *Green Fees: How a Tax Shift Can Work for the Environment and the Economy* (Washington, D.C.: World Resources Institute, 1992).

Reschovsky, James D., and Sarah E. Stone, "Market Incentives to Encourage Household Waste Recycling: Paying for What You Throw Away," *Journal of Policy Analysis and Management,* Vol. 13, No. 1 (1994).

Sagoff, Mark, *The Economy of the Earth* (Cambridge: Cambridge University Press, 1988).

Sanstad, Alan H., Carl Blumstein, and Steven E. Stoft, "How High Are Option Values in Energy-Efficiency Investments?," *Energy Policy*, Vol. 23, No. 9 (September 1995).

Sanstad, Alan H., and Richard B. Howarth, " 'Normal' Markets, Market Imperfections and Energy Efficiency," *Energy Policy*, Vol. 22, No. 10 (October 1994).

Saphire, David, *Case Reopened: Reassessing Refillable Bottles* (New York: IN-FORM, 1994).

Schall, John, *Does the Solid Waste Management Hierarchy Make Sense?*, Solid Waste Working Paper #1 (New Haven: Yale School of Forestry and Environmental Studies, 1992).

———, "Does the Hierarchy Make Sense?," *MSW Management*, January-February 1993.

Segall, Lori, "Source Separated Organics Programs in Europe," *Resource Recycling*, July 1993.

Sen, Amartya, "Behavior and the Concept of Preference," *Economica*, Vol. 40 (1973).

Sound Resource Management Group, *The Economics of Recycling and Recycled Materials* (Seattle: Clean Washington Center, 1993).

Staudt, Erich, "A Comparison of the Cost Structure and Fees for Domestic Waste Disposal and Recycling," (Ruhr-Universität-Bochum, abridged version, 1993).

Stavins, Robert, et al., *Project 88: Harnessing Market Forces to Protect Our Environment* (Washington, D.C., 1988).

Stavins, Robert, et al., *Project 88—Round II: Incentives for Action—Designing Market-Based Environmental Strategies* (Washington, D.C., 1992).

Steuteville, Robert, "Recycling Polycoated Packaging," *BioCycle*, March 1994.

———, "The State of Garbage in America: Part I," *BioCycle*, April 1995, and "Part II," May 1995.

Stevens, Barbara, "Scale, Market Structure, and the Cost of Refuse Collection," *Review of Economics and Statistics*, Vol. 60 (1978).

———, "Recycling Collection Costs by the Numbers: A National Survey," *Resource Recycling*, September 1994.

———, "What Does it Cost to Collect Yard Debris?," *Resource Recycling*, October 1994.

Strasser, Susan, *Waste and Want: Disposal, Recycling, and American Consumer Culture* (New York: Metropolitan Books, 1998).

Sullivan, John, "While Others Sell Recyclables, New York Pays to Get Rid of Them," *New York Times*, August 12, 1995, p. 23.

Tarres, Ralph, "Nachfrage übersteigt das Angebot—BASF verzichtet auf den Bau einer Recycling-Anlage," *Die Welt*, August 4, 1995.

Taylor, Daniel B., and John B. Hodges, "Impacts of Beverage Container Litter on Virginia Farms," *Virginia Agricultural Economics,* September-October 1985.

Thomas, Jo, "New York Starts Spinning Its Dross into Gold," *New York Times,* November 28, 1994.

Tierney, John, "Recycling is Garbage," *New York Times Magazine,* June 30, 1996.

Twede, Diana, *Less Waste on the Loading Dock,* Solid Waste Working Paper #2 (New Haven: Yale School of Forestry and Environmental Studies, 1995).

U. S. Census Bureau, *Historical Statistics of the United States, Colonial Times to 1970* (Washington, D.C.: Government Printing Office, 1975).

U.S. Department of Labor, Bureau of Labor Statistics, *BLS 790 Establishment Survey,* 1993.

U.S. Environmental Protection Agency, *The Solid Waste Dilemma: An Agenda for Action* (1989).

———, *Inventory of U.S. Greenhouse Gas Emissions and Sinks: 1990–1993* (1994).

———, *WasteWi$e First-Year Progress Report* (EPA530-R-95-044, 1995).

U.S. Senate Committee on Commerce, Science, and Transportation, hearing to consider *Beverage Container Reuse and Recycling Act,* 5 Nov. 1981 (Y4.C73/7.97-83).

Vatn, Arild, and Daniel W. Bromley, "Choices Without Prices Without Apologies," *Journal of Environmental Economics and Management,* Vol. 26, No. 1 (1994).

Vestal, Allan W., "Public Choice, Public Interest, and the Soft Drink Interbrand Competition Act: Time to Derail the 'Root Beer Express'?," *William and Mary Law Review,* Vol. 34 (1993), pp. 337–391.

Vining, Joanne, Nancy Linn, and Rabel J. Burdge, "Why Recycle? A Comparison of Recycling Motivations in Four Communities," *Environmental Management,* Vol. 16, No. 6 (1992).

Waldrop, M. Mitchell, *Complexity* (New York: Simon & Schuster, 1992).

Roy F. Weston, Inc., "Value Added to Recyclable Materials in the Northeast" (Brattleboro, Vermont: Northeast Recycling Council, Council of State Governments, 1994).

Williams, Robert, Eric Larson, and Marc Ross, "Materials, Affluence, and Industrial Energy Use," *Annual Review of Energy,* Vol. 12 (1987).

Woods, Randy, and Charles Peterson, "World War II and the Birth of Modern Recycling," *Recycling Times,* May 2, 1995.

Woodward, Donald, " 'Swords into Ploughshares': Recycling in Pre-Industrial England," *Economic History Review,* second series, Vol. 38 (1985), 175–191.

World Resources Institute, *Natural Resources 1994–95* (Washington, D.C., 1995).

Tellus Institute Reports Cited in the Text

All of the following are available from Tellus Institute, 11 Arlington St., Boston MA 02116; some are also available from the sponsoring agencies. It would be impossible to list everyone who participated in researching and writing these reports (see Acknowledgments); the Disposal Cost Fee Study and the Packaging Study each have more than a dozen authors, while the "California's Incentives" report drew on a lengthy list of California-based collaborators as well as Tellus staff.

Disposal Cost Fee Study: Final Report (1991).

Tellus Institute Packaging Study, 2 vols., 1992.

Ackerman, Frank, and Irene Peters, et al., *California's Incentives for Production of Virgin and Secondary Materials* (1993).

Ackerman, Frank, Paul Ligon, Lori Segall, and Brian Zuckerman, *Lifecycle Analysis and Legislation for Packaging Materials in Mexico* (1994).

Ackerman, Frank, Dmitri Cavander, John Stutz, and Brian Zuckerman, *Preliminary Analysis: The Costs and Benefits of Bottle Bills* (1995).

Ackerman, Frank, Deborah Salon, Lori Segall, and Brian Zuckerman, *Refillable Bottle Use in the Beer Industry* (1995).

Ligon, Paul, John Stutz, and Brian Zuckerman, *Increasing Participation Rates in Local Curbside Recycling Programs* (1995).

Segall, Lori, Frank Ackerman, Dmitri Cavander, Paul Ligon, John Stutz, and Brian Zuckerman, *Organic Materials Management Strategies* (1994).

Stutz, John, and Paul Ligon, *Achieving Substantial, Measurable Results through Source Reduction* (1994).

INDEX